Roland I

The Beatles

Roland Reiter (Dr. phil.) works at the Center for the Study of the Americas at the University of Graz, Austria. His research interests include various social and aesthetic aspects of popular culture.

ROLAND REITER
The Beatles on Film.
Analysis of Movies, Documentaries,
Spoofs and Cartoons

[transcript]

Gedruckt mit Unterstützung der Universität Graz,
des Landes Steiermark und des Zentrums für Amerikastudien.

Bibliographic information published by Die Deutsche Bibliothek
Die Deutsche Bibliothek lists this publication in the
Deutsche Nationalbibliografie; detailed bibliographic data
are available on the Internet at http://dnb.ddb.de

Layout by: Kordula Röckenhaus, Bielefeld
Edited by: Roland Reiter
Typeset by: Roland Reiter
Printed by: Majuskel Medienproduktion GmbH, Wetzlar
ISBN 978-3-89942-885-8

Contents

Introduction
7

Beatles History – Part One: 1956-1964
11

The Beatles on Film – Part One: 1964-1965
39

Beatles History – Part Two: 1964-1966.
A Contextual Interpretation of The Beatles' Image Change
in 1966
87

The Beatles on Film – Part Two: 1965-1970
93

Beatles History – Part Three: 1970-2008
137

Screening the Past: Film and History
145

Movies about The Beatles
151

Documentaries about The Beatles
181

Spoofs
191

Conclusion: Image, Myth, History, and The Beatles
195

Works Cited
203

The Author/Acknowledgments
211

INTRODUCTION

A star's image generally reflects the ideals of his or her average audience. It enables the fans to identify with their idol on an emotional and/or intellectual level. The potential of identification with a star can be an important factor for his or her commercial success. Today the music industry actually creates and designs the image of popular musicians according to contemporary fashion and ideology in order to appeal to a mass audience.

Every genre of popular music has its own paradigm of ideology connected with it, ranging from hedonism to aggression. Each of these genres has developed a set of specific dress codes and stereotypical behaviour the audience expects from a performer representing a certain genre. These dress codes and behaviour are often instantly recognizable to the audience and allow a quick categorization of the performer in a known genre. Rock manager Simon Napier-Bell (The Yardbirds, Wham!) points out the importance of a rock group's image and The Beatles' influence on image creation in popular music: "If you think of the Beatles, you think of four faces, because their imagery became so much stronger than their playing. This is rather an insult to the Beatles because they were such fantastic musicians and made amazing records, but you tend to think of the imagery dominating the music and I think that's what's happened ever since, that the imagery of a boy group has become more important than the music" (Geller 2002: 48).

While the contemporary music industry is able to supply custom-made idols to all kinds of audiences through a multitude of media channels, the development of such target-group oriented marketing of popular music was only made possible by the immense success of Elvis Presley in the 1950s and The Beatles in the 1960s. Both, Elvis as well as The Beatles, were supported and promoted by visionary managers who were aware of the importance of appearance and attitude expected by a large segment of a young mass audience.

In the sphere of popular music the visual media have always played a significant role in the creation and reinforcement of a star's image. Ever since Benny Goodman appeared in a number of movies in the 1940s, film has been used as a powerful medium to project certain images of popular musicians. By the mid-1950s television had become the most popular mass medium and an important platform for pop musicians, as they were able to present their songs to a large, nationwide audience. For instance, in 1956, Elvis Presley's appearance on *The Ed Sullivan Show* in front of a viewing audience of 52 million people contributed immensely to his popularity and his initial commercial success in the United States. In the 1960s The Beatles set out to overshadow Presley's popularity, and again it was Ed Sullivan who enabled them to sing their hits to a mass audience.

When 'Beatlemania' swept the United States in 1964, the band was promoted by an unprecedented marketing campaign which included the audiovisual media to a great extent. For example, The Beatles' first movie features *A Hard Day's Night* and *Help!* supported and promoted stereotypical images of each band member, which are still prevalent in the media perception of the group. Film critic and scholar Bob Neaverson is even convinced that "[p]erhaps more than any other broadcast media, their films were vital in communicating and showcasing the group's ever changing array of images, attitudes, ideas and musical styles. [...] *A Hard Day's Night* helped to disseminate their current visual 'look' to a global audience, and to develop their identities as four individuals [...]" (Neaverson 2000: 152). The semi-documentary style of The Beatles' first movie *A Hard Day's Night* and its intentional characteristic of establishing and distributing a credible image of the band and each individual member has contributed significantly to the confusion of facts and fiction in The Beatles' history and has shaped the way the public has perceived The Beatles ever since. The movie was the first major manifestation of Beatles myths, and its immense popularity and its status as a cult movie have led to a constant reinforcement of certain myths about the band.

In the course of only a few years The Beatles managed to convey their constantly evolving image through numerous different projects, reaching a wide-ranging and varied audience. They performed on numerous television shows all around the world, in order to promote their records and to reinforce their image. ABC-Television even broadcast a cartoon series featuring animated versions of the group members from 1965 to 1969. While this series mainly reached a juvenile target group, The Beatles' self-produced promotional films as well as their experimental television special *Magical Mystery Tour* were deliberately created for a more intellectual, adult audience. These works as well as the group's animated feature *Yellow Submarine* and their documentary *Let It Be* supported The Beatles' reputation as pop artistes and documented the band's break with their self-created 'happy Mop-Top' image.

Whereas The Beatles' influence on popular music is universally recognized, their promotional films and feature movies are often regarded only as commercial by-products, created to cash in on the Beatles craze at the height of their success. In fact, however, The Beatles and their creative partners were pioneers in the development of the music video, establishing its function as well as its aesthetics. Bob Neaverson's *The Beatles Movies* has been the only notable academic book about The Beatles' cinematic output, while Roy Carr's *The Beatles at the Movies* and Bill Harry's *Beatlemania* offer casual facts and recollections from the people involved in the production of the group's movies. All three works were very helpful for my own analysis, and they are certainly the pioneering books in the field of Beatles film books. However, it was my aim to provide a more thoroughly researched historical background, as well as a contextual interpretation of the movies and their function as projectors of The Beatles' image at different stages in their career. In addition, this project also includes an analysis of all of The Beatles' promotional films and videos, as well as their television cartoon series and their self-produced television special *Magical Mystery Tour*.

Besides The Beatles' feature movies and promotional films, my analysis also contains documentaries, such as *Anthology* and *The Compleat Beatles*, as well as dramatizations of the band's history, such as *Backbeat*, *The Hours and Times*, and *Two of Us*. It is my aim to identify the projection of certain images and to contextualize their historic meaning and significance. In addition, this analysis examines the authenticity of such portrayals and describes their contribution to the evolution of popular cultural legends and myths.

The system of reference consists of an extensive bulk of autobiographies, biographies, interviews and documents, with the help of which I attempt to reconstruct The Beatles' history in a comprehensive and, hopefully, fairly objective way. To clarify conflicting information and to advance the specific aim of this project I have had the great pleasure to meet and interview many contributors to The Beatles' history. In addition, the academic writings of Roland Barthes, Seymour Chatman, Simon Frith, Dick Hebdige, Tony Barta, John E. O'Connor, Silke Riemann, and Peter Wicke provided the framework for the contextualization of my own ideas and insights.

BEATLES HISTORY - PART ONE: 1956-1964

January 1956-June 1957:
The 'Skiffle Craze'

In January 1956, Lonnie Donegan's recording of "Rock Island Line" stormed into the British hit parade and started what would become known as the 'skiffle craze' in Great Britain (vgl. McDevitt 1997: 3). Skiffle was originally an amateur jazz style comprising elements of blues, gospel, and work songs. The instrumentation resembled New Orleans street bands called 'spasms,' which relied on home-made instruments. Before skiffle was first professionally recorded by American jazz musicians in the 1920s and 1930s, it had been performed at 'rent parties' in North American cities like Chicago and Kansas City. Many African-American migrant workers organized rent parties in order to raise money for their monthly payments (vgl. Garry 1997: 87). Skiffle provided the musical entertainment at these parties, as everybody was able to participate in the band, which usually consisted of home-made acoustic guitars or a piano backed by a rhythm section of household instruments, such as a washboard, a washtub bass, and a jug (vgl. McDevitt 1997:16).

Jazz trumpeter and guitarist Ken Colyer pioneered the skiffle scene in Great Britain. In 1949, he formed the Crane River Jazz Band in Cranford, Middlesex, together with Ben Marshall (guitar), Pat Hawes (washboard), and Julian Davies (bass). Their repertoire included skiffle songs "to illustrate aspects of the roots of jazz and to add variety to a programme" (Dewe 1998: 4). After leaving the group in 1951, Colyer migrated to the United States to work with jazz musicians in New Orleans. When he returned to Great Britain in 1953, he joined a band featuring Chris Barber (trombone), Monty Sunshine (clarinet), Lonnie Donegan (banjo), Jim Bray (bass), and Ron Bowden (drums) (vgl. Dewe 1998: 6). Tensions within the group caused Colyer to leave the group in May 1954, while his former band colleagues Lonnie Donegan, Chris Barber, and Monty Sunshine formed Chris Barber's Jazz Band (vgl. McDevitt 1997: 5). In July 1954, Chris Barber's Jazz Band released an album called *New Orleans Joys*, featuring two skiffle songs, "Rock Island Line" and "John Henry," credited to The Lonnie Donegan Skiffle Group (vgl. Dewe 1998: 16). When Decca Records released "Rock Island Line" as a 78-rpm single in late 1955, it became an unexpected chart success for Lonnie Donegan and his band (vgl. Davis 2003). Donegan's recording brought skiffle to the fore in Great Britain and spawned a series of skiffle hits by professional musicians like The Chas McDevitt Group, Nancy Whisky, The Vipers, and many others (vgl. McDevitt 1997: 9). What is more, the simple musical structure and instrumentation inspired literally thousands of young people all over Britain to form their own skiffle bands (vgl. Dewe 1998: 134).

By mid-1956, 15-year-old John Lennon had become fascinated with American rock and roll music. He particularly favored the music and appearance of Elvis Presley, whose "Heartbreak Hotel" had been a great success in Great Britain in early 1956: "Nothing really affected me until I heard Elvis. If there hadn't been Elvis, there would not have been the Beatles" (Harry 2000: 881). Since Elvis and many other American rock and roll stars were usually backed by professionally trained musicians whose skills could not easily be imitated, teenagers would not naturally conceive of the idea of forming a rock and roll band themselves. However, when Lonnie Donegan introduced skiffle to a large audience, young people realized the possibility of performing music with a set of cheap and home-made instruments.

John Lennon's friend Len Garry points out that "[s]kiffle and the ability for people to access such music easily acted only as a catalyst and precursor to [John Lennon's] continuing obsession for Rock 'n' Roll music" (Garry 1997: 95). The music of Lonnie Donegan and his followers inspired John Lennon to learn to play the guitar, and he borrowed one from a schoolmate (vgl. Davies 2001: 38). Later, Lennon's mother Julia paid for his own guitar, an inexpensive instrument he had ordered from a mail order advertisement in the Daily Mail (vgl. Coleman 1992: 137). A hobby banjoist herself, Julia taught her son a few banjo chords which he applied on his guitar, simply ignoring the guitar's two bottom strings (vgl. Beatles 2000: 11).

In the fall of 1956, George Lee, one of Lennon's friends from Quarry Bank High School, suggested to John Lennon that he form a skiffle band (vgl. Garry 1997: 109). Lennon approached his best friend Pete Shotton with this idea, and within a few weeks, the boys had recruited mates from Quarry Bank High School and the Liverpool Institute to form their own band. Dismissing their initial name The Black Jacks, John Lennon, the bandleader, decided to call the group The Quarry Men, as a reference to a line from the school song: "Quarry Men, strong before our birth" (Harry 2000: 896). Although the line-up went through several minor changes at the very beginning, a quite firm constellation had evolved by the end of 1956. For approximately eight months The Quarry Men consisted of

John Lennon (guitar), Pete Shotton (washboard), Eric Griffiths (guitar), Rod Davis (banjo), and Colin Hanton (drums).

Rod Davis recalls the band's equipment: "We just had two cheap guitars and a very old banjo, a tea chest bass made from a box bought from the grocer's for a few shillings, a washboard found in Pete Shotton's mother's shed and Colin's drum kit, which was the cheapest in the shop, but nevertheless it put us in a different category of skiffle group, bec[au]se very few of them could afford drums" (Davis 2003). As the band's initial tea chest bass player Bill Smith turned out to be rather unreliable, Len Garry and, occasionally, Ivan Vaughan were asked to master this typical skiffle instrument. John Lennon was the group's lead vocalist, supported by the other members on the choruses. George Lee, the boy who had suggested forming a skiffle band, never joined The Quarry Men.

According to Eric Griffiths, he and John Lennon initially took guitar lessons from a classical guitarist in Hunt's Cross, Liverpool (vgl. Davies 2001: 40). The boys, however, soon realized that they would not need a theoretical background to play the music they liked and gave up the lessons. The Quarry Men, like several hundred other skiffle groups in Great Britain at the time, learned and rehearsed a number of traditional American songs that had been popularized by Lonnie Donegan and other prominent skiffle musicians. Their early repertoire included songs such as "Rock Island Line," "Cumberland Gap," "Freight Train" and "Midnight Special," which were all based on three guitar chords.

As bands conventionally had a uniform stage outfit, The Quarry Men usually wore black jeans and white shirts at their performances. Rod Davis points out that "this was because we all had white shirts and therefore did not need to go and buy a special shirt" (Davis 2003).

The band's rehearsals took place in an old air-raid shelter in Pete Shotton's garden, at Colin Hanton's home and, without drums, in Julia Lennon's bathroom (vgl. Davies 2001: 42). At first, they only publicly performed at their friends' parties. As soon as they considered themselves good enough to perform for money, Nigel Whalley, one of John Lennon's friends who had also played the tea chest bass in The Quarry Men for a short while, appointed himself The Quarry Men's manager and tried to secure bookings for the band. Whalley had at least three different kinds of visiting cards printed and put notices in shop windows announcing "Country – Western – Rock 'n' Roll – Skiffle. The Quarry Men. Open for Engagements" (vgl. Coleman 1992: 140) In 1957, he actually organized performances at St. Peter's Youth Club, at Lee Park Golf Park, and at the Cavern Club in Liverpool (vgl. Davies 2001: 48-49). In June 1957, The Quarry Men even entered a skiffle contest for Carroll Levis's television show *Discoveries*, but they failed to pass the initial audition (vgl. Lewisohn 2000: 14).

July 1957-October 1961:
From The Quarry Men to The Beatles

On July 6, 1957, The Quarry Men Skiffle Group performed three sets at the 'Garden Fête' of St Peter's Parish Church in Woolton, a village bordering Liverpool city center. After the evening performance, the band's occasional tea-chest bass player Ivan Vaughan introduced to John Lennon and the other band members his classmate Paul McCartney, a 15-year-old rock and roll fan from Allerton, Liverpool (vgl. Lewisohn 2000: 12).

Paul McCartney had grown up in a musical family, his father being the pianist in a traditional jazz band. When his mother unexpectedly died in 1956, he developed an almost obsessive interest in music. After dismissing his first instrument, a trumpet, because he wanted to be able to sing and play at the same time, McCartney acquired a £15 acoustic Zenith guitar (vgl. Miles 1997: 21). Even though he was fond of various kinds of music, he became especially attracted to skiffle, rock 'n' roll, as well as American rhythm and blues, which he used to listen to on Radio Luxembourg, as these genres of popular music were virtually ignored by the BBC (vgl. Miles 1997: 24-25). Paul McCartney's friend George Harrison, who was nine months younger and a class below McCartney's at the Liverpool Institute, showed a similar enthusiasm for skiffle and rock and roll music. Moreover, he was also an aspiring guitarist and owned a £30 Höfner President (vgl. Beatles: 2000: 28). Together they tried to figure out guitar chords from a guitar manual and learned to play songs such as "Don't You Rock Me Daddy-O" and "Besame Mucho" (vgl. Giuliano 1991: 17). Paul McCartney was soon able to play a number of contemporary hit songs. What is more, at the age of fourteen, just having mastered three chords on the guitar, McCartney composed his first song called "I Lost My Little Girl" (vgl. Beatles: 2000: 20).

When The Quarry Men first met Paul McCartney, his knowledge of rock and roll songs as well as his ability of playing and tuning a guitar particularly impressed John Lennon: "He could obviously play the guitar. I half thought he's as good as me. [...] Now, I thought, if I take him on, what will happen? It went through my head that I'd have to keep him in line, if I let him join. But he was good, so he was worth having. He also looked like Elvis" (Davies 1969: 42). Days later Lennon actually had Pete Shotton ask him to join the group. After some time of consideration and a two-month break at a scout camp, Paul McCartney finally became a member of The Quarry Men in the fall of 1957 (vgl. Coleman 1992: 147).

According to Colin Hanton, The Quarry Men's drummer, Paul McCartney influenced the band's stage appearance from the very beginning: "Once Paul joined The Quarry Men – that's when things started to change [...]. White jackets for him and John as the lead singers, the rest of us in white shirts and black ties. That all came from Paul" (*A Long and Winding Road* 2003: DVD 1). Apparently, Paul McCartney had already developed a sense of promotion and public image in entertainment, which he admits in his official biography: "I have a reputation now of being a PR man, which has grown over the years, because anything you promote, there's a game that you either play or you don't play. I decided very early on that I was very ambitious and I wanted to play" (Miles 1997: 34). While The Quarry Men had previously been a rather unconcerned group of amateur musicians, Paul McCartney and John Lennon now developed a more professional attitude toward their performances. By wearing suits, shirts and ties instead of casual outfits at several performances, The Quarry Men became more acceptable for an adult audience. Although these early attempts at displaying a homogeneous stage image were inspired by conventional outfits worn by traditional jazz bands and skiffle groups, The Quarry Men's repertoire was becoming more oriented toward rock and roll music than skiffle. Shortly before McCartney joined the band, Rod Davis had quit The Quarry Men because of this development:

"[Skiffle] came out of New Orleans jazz bands in the UK, but jazz fans hated rock 'n' roll, which they thought was trashy manufactured music, exploiting teenagers, and was not 'traditional'. Equally the rock 'n' roll fans, who were more likely to be teddy boys – there was an element of class distinction there – hated the university intellectual types who liked jazz. [...] I have to confess that I did not like Elvis Presley and rock 'n' roll [...]" (Davis 2003).

Consequently, banjoist Rod Davis left The Quarry Men to form a jazz trio, while Pete Shotton, the group's washboard player, had already quit months before. The Quarry Men now featured three guitarists, John Lennon, Eric Griffiths and Paul McCartney. Tea chest player Len Garry's association with The Quarry Men ended when serious health problems forced him to leave the band in August 1958.

By mid-1958 Paul McCartney's friend George Harrison had replaced Eric Griffiths as the third guitarist in the band. When The Quarry Men recorded their first demonstration disc in mid-1958, they had already developed into a pure rock 'n' roll band. This is confirmed by John Lowe, an occasional pianist with The Quarry Men, who also participated in the band's first recording session at Percy Phillips' home recording studio in Liverpool: "When I was in the band we never played any skiffle. [...] We played covers of 57/58 rock/ballad music normally from USA – Buddy Holly, Everly Bros, Elvis, Chuck Berry etc." (Lowe 2003). While the band members had occasionally worn suits and ties on stage during the band's skiffle period, they now returned to more casual outfits. John Lowe remembers The Quarry Men's appearance on stage in 1958: "We all wore jeans (I had to borrow a pair off John) and black/white country & western shirts with tass[el]s going across the chest" (Lowe 2003). This kind of outfit, combined with a certain hairstyle, is usually associated with the image of a 'Teddy Boy'.

When drummer Colin Hanton left The Quarry Men after a disagreement in early 1959, the group basically ceased to exist (vgl. Davies 2001: 79). George Harrison became a member of The Les Stewart Quartet, while John Lennon rather carelessly pursued his studies at the Liverpool College of Art, where he had started his first term in September 1957. At the art college, John Lennon met Stuart Sutcliffe, Bill Harry and Rod Murray, with whom he developed a close friendship (vgl. Harry 2000: 669). He also met his future wife Cynthia Powell around that time.

George Harrison initiated a reunion of The Quarry Men in August 1959, when he and guitarist Ken Brown quit The Les Stewart Quartet. Their bandleader had not wanted the group to perform at the opening night of a new youth club, the Casbah Club, in West Derby, Liverpool. Brown and Harrison, who were eager to perform at the new venue, asked John Lennon and Paul McCartney to join them. They decided to use the name Quarry Men for this new line-up, which now consisted of four guitarists (vgl. Harry 2000: 211). Ken Brown points out that the group members did not wear a particular stage uniform at these performances: "[W]e just wore casual wear – jeans – jumpers – sweatshirts – or sometimes slacks with a shirt and loosely tied tie" (Brown 2003). The Quarry Men regularly performed at the Casbah Club until October 1959, when John Lennon, Paul McCartney and George Harrison walked out on Ken Brown and club owner Mona Best after a dispute concerning their payment.

Lennon, McCartney, and Harrison stayed together as a group and again joined a sequence of preliminary talent contests for Carroll Levis' popular ABC television show *Discoveries*. For these performances, they renamed their band Johnny and The Moondogs, a name inspired by American performers Buddy Holly and The Crickets, whose "Think It Over" they performed at the contest (vgl. Beatles 2000: 23). This time they reached the local finals and performed in Manchester, where the strength of audience applause was supposed to determine the winner at the end of the show. Johnny and The Moondogs, however, had to leave early in order to catch the train back to Liverpool. Therefore, they were not able to participate in the final voting (vgl. Beatles 2000: 31).

In January 1960, John Lennon persuaded Stuart Sutcliffe, his friend and colleague at the Liverpool College of Art, to buy a bass guitar and join the band. Sutcliffe had sold one of his paintings to John Moore who organized prominent exhibitions at the Walker Art Gallery in Liverpool. The money Sutcliffe obtained for his painting was invested in a Höfner President bass guitar. David May, a Liverpool bass guitarist, and George Harrison initially taught him basic bass patterns, as Sutcliffe had never played guitar before (vgl. Harry 2000: 1048).

Even though Stuart Sutcliffe's abilities as a musician reportedly were quite modest (vgl. Beatles 2000: 44), he contributed significantly to the band's progress by organizing performances and equipment. For instance, through Sutcliffe and his friend Bill Harry the group was hired to play at Saturday dances at the Liverpool College of Art (vgl. Harry 2003). As the band members did not have any money for proper stage equipment, Sutcliffe and Harry, who were both members of the Students' Union Committee, suggested that the Students' Union finance a proper amplifier system for the 'college band' Johnny and The Moondogs (vgl. Harry 2000: 1048).

Although the group's name seemed to be acceptable at the time, Sutcliffe and Lennon were trying to find a more appropriate band name that would reflect their interest in beatnik lifestyle and emphasize their basic idea of not featuring only one particular singer. In the course of 1960 the name developed from Sutcliffe's original idea 'Beatals' to 'Silver Beats' and 'Silver Beetles,' until the band finally decided to call themselves The Beatles (vgl. Lewisohn 2000: 18).[1]

Stuart Sutcliffe became a key influence on the group's stage image, as his appearance as well as his manners on stage contributed an air of mystery to the Beatles' stage act (vgl. Harry 2000: 1049). According to his sister Pauline, he modelled his outer appearance on Polish actor Zbygniew Cybulski: "[...] Stuart [was] taken by the style of Cybulski, the

---

1   John Lennon insists that the name Beatles with its reference to beat music and beetles was inspired by the double meaning of "Crickets," the name of Buddy Holly's backing band (vgl. Davies 1969: 73). Recent band histories suggest that Sutcliffe and Lennon were inspired by the movie *The Wild One*, which features a motorcycle gang called Beetles (vgl. Beatles 2000: 41). Bill Harry points out that this is impossible, as *The Wild One* was not shown in cinemas around Britain until the late sixties (vgl. Harry 2000: 104).

lookalike of a young Jean-Paul Belmondo, with wavy, swept-back black hair, and cool sunglasses and manner" (Sutcliffe/Thompson 2002: 100). Sutcliffe adapted Cybulski's look and even wore sunglasses on stage. He did this also for practical reasons, as he had rather weak eyesight, just like his friend John Lennon. While Lennon found his glasses incompatible with his image as would-be Teddy Boy, Sutcliffe managed to look 'cool' and be able to see by wearing self-made clip-on shades (vgl. Kirchherr 2003). On stage, he would often play with his back to the audience, in order to hide his poor musical abilities.

It was also through Stuart Sutcliffe that the newly named Silver Beetles got involved with Liverpool concert promoter and coffee bar owner Allan Williams. After Sutcliffe and his friend Rod Murray had decorated the walls of Williams' coffee bar, the Jacaranda, he asked Allan Williams for his assistance in finding bookings for the band. Williams, who had been asked to organize auditions of Liverpool bands to back singer Billy Fury on a tour, arranged for the Beatles to appear at these auditions. As the group did not have a drummer, Williams hired Tommy Moore to play with The Silver Beetles. However, when it was their turn to play, their new drummer had not yet arrived. Therefore, Johnny Hutchinson, the drummer with Liverpool group Cass & The Cassanovas sat in for the audition.

Even though Fury's manager Larry Parnes did not consider The Silver Beetles fit to accompany his most popular singer, he wanted them to join his most recent discovery, Liverpool singer Johnny Gentle, on a tour of Scotland. In May 1960, John Lennon, Paul McCartney, George Harrison, Stuart Sutcliffe and drummer Tommy Moore set out to back Johnny Gentle on his seven-date tour of Scotland (vgl. Gentle/Forsyth 1998: 31).

In June and July 1960, The Silver Beetles were quite busy performing at different venues in and around Liverpool. Tommy Moore, who was seven years older than John Lennon, quit The Silver Beetles in June 1960, and Paul McCartney temporarily took over the role as the group's drummer. Another short-term drummer was Norman Chapman who quit the band after only three concerts, as he was called up for National Service (vgl. Harry 2000: 255).

Band promoter Allan Williams had secured bookings for Liverpool band Derry & The Seniors in Hamburg, Germany, where they played at a club called Kaiserkeller in the city's red-light district St. Pauli. Because of the group's great success, club owner Bruno Koschmider asked Williams to send more bands to Hamburg. Since Liverpool's top group Rory Storm & The Hurricanes had accepted another engagement, Williams offered the job to the re-named Beatles, who were eager to go abroad. The Beatles, however, did not have a drummer at that point. Williams arranged an audition with Pete Best, the son of Mona Best, who had hired The Quarry Men to play at her coffee club, the Casbah, the year before. Best easily passed the audition and became The Beatles' drummer (Best/Doncaster 2001: 29).

In August 1960, Allan Williams drove The Beatles to Hamburg, where they were expected to play at a former strip club called Indra. Horst Fascher, who became The Beatles' friend and bodyguard in Hamburg, remembers their stage outfit at the beginning of their engagement: "[A]n dem Abend, an dem sie das erste Mal auftraten, [trugen sie] Teddyboy-Kleidung, die damals getragen wurde in England. Mit spitzen Schuhen [...], engen Jeans und einfachen Hemden mit etwas längeren Kragen" (Fascher 2003). They performed forty-eight nights at the Indra and subsequently played fifty-eight nights at the Kaiserkeller (vgl. Lewisohn 2000: 28). Until the end of November, The Beatles performed seven nights a week, between four and five hours a night at these bars (vgl. Miles 1997: 58), which were both owned by Bruno Koschmider. These extensive performances vastly improved the band's musicianship, and The Beatles became one of the most popular acts at the Reeperbahn, attracting a varied audience. While The Beatles were very popular with regular visitors, such as seamen, workers, and prostitutes, they also became close friends with a small circle of local art students who called themselves 'the existentialists'. In particular, Astrid Kirchherr, Jürgen Vollmer, and Klaus Voormann had a lasting impact on the group's image and history.

Astrid Kirchherr was the first person to take professional photographs of the band. The first photo session took place at the fairgrounds in Hamburg. The Beatles, still wearing their Teddy Boy outfits, posed at the Dom, on a carousel and a Ferris wheel at the city funfair, on an old lorry, and outside a market tent. Although the band had become well known for their lively and wild performances at the Kaiserkeller by then, they appear calm and thoughtful in Kirchherr's black and white photographs. According to Astrid Kirchherr, it was her intention to reveal a warm, human, but also a gloomier facet of The Beatles (vgl. Kirchherr 2003).

Astrid Kirchherr and Stuart Sutcliffe fell in love with each other and became an inseparable couple, which led to a strong connection between the 'Exis' and The Beatles. They influenced each other's conceptions of philosophy, lifestyle and art. While Klaus Voormann points out that he and his friends had a profound influence on The Beatles' general conception of art and literature (vgl. Voormann 2003), Astrid Kirchherr remembers a mutual fascination with each other, which also included outer appearance and image (vgl. Kirchherr 2003). For instance, the Exis inspired

The Beatles to gradually drop their Teddy Boy outfits in favor of black leather clothes which were popular among the existentialists. Pete Best recalls The Beatles' initial fascination with leather: "We all fell in love with Astrid's black leather outfits. Influenced by her, Stu was the first to appear in a black leather jacket. George soon followed suit in a jacket bought off a waiter for £5. Then the rest of us got into line; buying cheap bomber-style models which we wore with the tightest of jeans and cowboy boots" (Best/Doncaster 2001: 66). In Hamburg, leather was worn by art students as well as by working class 'rock 'n' rollers.' Kirchherr and her friends were fascinated by the appearance of Gene Vincent and Marlon Brando, both of whom were also idolized by the rock and roll fans. However, the two youth groups could easily be distinguished by their outfit and hairstyle, as the existentialists were more obviously influenced by French movie stars and philosophers (vgl. Kirchherr 2003). Horst Fascher points out the differences between 'Exis' and 'Rockers' in terms of fashion: "Die Rock 'n' Roller trugen Leder; und auch die Exis trugen Leder, wobei die Exis eher schwarze Kleidung dazu trugen. Schwarze Hose oder vielleicht schwarzes Sakko, und die Rock 'n' Roller trugen eine schwarze Hose und ein weißes Hemd" (Fascher 2003). Fascher explains that rockers liked to wear white shirts in order to be well visible in bars where ultra-light made the shirts appear to be 'double-white,' while the exis originally preferred 'to vanish in darker jazz cellars' (vgl. Fascher 2003).

On October 15, 1960, John Lennon, Paul McCartney and George Harrison joined members of the Liverpool band Rory Storm & The Hurricanes for a recording of the songs "Fever" and "Summertime" at the small Akustik Studios in Hamburg (vgl. Harry 2000: 18). This recording session, which had been organized by Allan Williams, was the first time Lennon, McCartney and Harrison performed together with Ringo Starr, who was the drummer with Rory Storm's group.

At the end of October, a new music club, the Top Ten, opened at 136 Reeperbahn in Hamburg (vgl. Harry 2000: 363). The venue was owned by Peter Eckhorn, who hired The Beatles' friends Tony Sheridan and The Jets for the opening night. In 1960, Sheridan was probably the most successful British performer in Hamburg, having gained the reputation of being "the best rock guitarist in Britain" (Clayson 1997: 52). While Tony Sheridan taught guitar chords to George Harrison, John Lennon was soon to copy Sheridan's high-chested guitar stance (vgl. Clayson 1997: 70), which would become Lennon's trademark at stage performances throughout the 1960s.

Although The Beatles' contract forbade the group to play in any other club but the Kaiserkeller, Horst Fascher, who now worked for Eckhorn, persuaded the group to perform at the Top Ten, where they would receive higher payment and a nicer accommodation (vgl. Norman 1981: 100-101). Soon after The Beatles had deserted Bruno Koschmider, police authorities deported George Harrison because he was under 18 years old, and therefore he was not allowed to be in a nightclub after midnight. What is more, none of The Beatles had official work permits allowing them to perform in Germany. Within a few days, Koschmider also informed the police that Paul McCartney and Pete Best had tried to set fire to their former accommodation, the Bambi Kino. They were arrested on a charge of suspected arson and had to leave Germany on 30 November 1960 (vgl. Lewisohn 2000: 24-25). John Lennon also returned to Liverpool in December, while Stuart Sutcliffe stayed in Hamburg with his fiancée Astrid Kirchherr.

In December 1960, The Beatles performed four concerts in Liverpool. As Stuart Sutcliffe had remained in Hamburg, Pete Best's friend Chas Newby was asked to play bass guitar at these performances. On 27 December, when they performed at the Town Hall Ballroom in Litherland, Liverpool, local promoters as well as the audience realized that The Beatles had developed into Liverpool's top rock and roll group during their stay in Hamburg, where they had spent more than 500 hours on stage. Pauline Sutcliffe, who was in the audience in Litherland, remembers The Beatles' unexpected effect on the audience: "The audience screamed and danced, danced, and danced, crowding the stage for a closer look at these fabulous rock and rollers. They were wild for the Beatles. The reaction was so dramatic it could have been operatic […]. Beatlemania? Well, most certainly the start of it" (Sutcliffe/Thompson 2002: 114).

The Beatles' success in Litherland caused many promoters to book them for 'jive dances' and other events in Liverpool. Between January and March 1961, The Beatles performed at more than 80 concerts in the Liverpool area. They regularly played at the Casbah Coffee Club as well as the Cavern, a former jazz cellar (vgl. Lewisohn 2000: 38-42).

After Allan Williams, Pete Best and Stuart Sutcliffe had organized visas and work permits for The Beatles, John Lennon, Paul McCartney, George Harrison, and Pete Best returned to the Top Ten Club in Hamburg, where they performed five hours a day for thirteen weeks. Again, their friends from the Hamburg art scene inspired an image change. As recalled by Pete Best, the group especially liked the leather trousers worn by Astrid Kirchherr: "Predictably, Stu was the first Beatle into leather trousers […]. It wasn't all that long – as soon as we could afford it, in fact – before the rest of the Beatles were draping their legs in black leather and looking for longer jackets to replace the bomber-style models now showing signs of wear" (Best/Doncaster 2001: 94). Furthermore, Stuart Sutcliffe also had his hair styled by Astrid Kirchherr, who recalls the creation of the famous 'mop-top':

"Das kam durch meinen Freund Klaus Voormann, der das hatte. [...] Die ganze Kunstschule war von französischen Schauspielern beeinflusst. Wenn Sie sich alte Photos ankucken, zum Beispiel von Gérard Philippes und Jean Marais – die hatten schon diese Frisuren, nur eben kürzer. Und mein Freund Klaus Voormann hatte – und hat immer noch – ganz doll abstehende Ohren. Ich habe mir überlegt, was man machen kann, damit man die Ohren nicht sieht; und dann kam ich auf die Idee, dass er einfach die Haare länger wachsen lassen muss. Und daraus ist dann dieser Beatles-Haarschnitt entstanden (Kirchherr 2003)"

Kirchherr's fiancé Stuart Sutcliffe was the first Beatle to adopt this particular hairstyle. While John Lennon and Paul McCartney initially expressed their amusement with Sutcliffe's new hairstyle, George Harrison soon wore his hair the same way.

In June 1961, The Beatles were hired to support British singer and guitarist Tony Sheridan on a recording produced by German record producer Bert Kaempfert. After having recorded two demonstration discs in 1958 and 1960, this was The Beatles' first professional recording, although on the record sleeve the group was credited as The Beat Brothers. Besides recording a rock and roll version of "My Bonnie Lies Over The Ocean" and some other songs for Sheridan's 1962 record release *My Bonnie*, The Beatles were also offered the chance to record the classic "Ain't She Sweet" featuring John Lennon as lead vocalist, as well as "Cry For A Shadow," an instrumental pastiche of The Shadows' "Frightened City" (vgl. Harry 2000: 315) credited to George Harrison and John Lennon.

As The Beatles felt that they had organized their engagement at the Top Ten themselves, John Lennon refused to pay manager Allan Williams his commission. In fact, however, they were only allowed to perform in Germany through Williams' agency Jacaranda Enterprises. When Williams sent The Beatles a letter to remind them of his contributions, they simply ignored him (vgl. Williams 2003).

The Beatles returned to Liverpool on 3 July 1961. Two days later, Stuart Sutcliffe's friend Bill Harry published the first issue of *Mersey Beat*, a music magazine containing reports on the Liverpool music scene. *Mersey Beat*, which Harry had been planning since 1960, pioneered British pop and rock music magazines with its innovative approach, as it contained, for instance, the first weekly listing of record releases and the first British Top 100 charts. Many of these ideas were later adopted by the traditional music press: "My aim in *Mersey Beat* was to give the musicians a voice and I tried to draw out their talent. I did this with the photographers, getting them to photograph groups on stage and on location, rather than the stereotyped photos in the standard music press" (Harry 2003).

Mersey Beat was distributed through three main wholesalers and was also sold by several local venues, musical instruments and record stores. The first issue, written and published by Bill Harry and his girlfriend Virginia, sold 5,000 copies in Liverpool (vgl. Harry 2003b). The magazine's increasing popularity also proved to be very positive for The Beatles, whom Harry promoted extensively in his magazine. The Beatles were also personally involved with the magazine from its very beginning. John Lennon contributed a short absurd biography of The Beatles to Issue No.1, which Bill Harry called "Being A Short Diversion On The Dubious Origin Of Beatles. Translated From The John Lennon." Issue No. 2 devoted the entire front cover to The Beatles, featuring a report on the group's recording sessions with Tony Sheridan. A photograph taken by Astrid Kirchherr in Hamburg supplemented the report, which was headlined "Beatles Sign Record Contract!" (vgl. Harry 2003b). *Mersey Beat* became The Beatles' main instrument for publicity in 1961, as it included reports covering the group's progress, as well as a regular column by John Lennon and a series of letters written by Paul McCartney. As pointed out by Bill Harry, the magazine made The Beatles known to a large young local audience: "When *Mersey Beat* came out [...], selling 5,000 of the very first issue and increasing every issue after that, virtually all the kids in Liverpool began to read about them – there was no other publicity but that in *Mersey Beat* throughout 1961" (Harry 2003).

Brian Epstein, the manager of North End Music Stores in Whitechapel, Liverpool, became interested in the local music scene when he realized the great success of *Mersey Beat*, which sold in large quantities at his record store. He contacted Bill Harry in order to learn more about The Beatles, whom he had apparently read about in Harry's magazine: "Brian asked me to describe the local scene and was particularly interested in the Beatles cover story and the fact that a local group had made a record. He immediately booked advertising space and asked if he could review records. I appointed him record reviewer, beginning with issue No. 3 [...]" (vgl. Harry 2003b).

From July to September, The Beatles performed almost daily at various venues in Liverpool. They regularly played at The Cavern Club, a popular youth club located at 10 Mathew Street.

In October, John Lennon and Paul McCartney went on a two-week holiday to Paris, where they met up with their German friend Jürgen Vollmer. While they had previously resisted their friends' attempts to re-style their hair, they now asked Vollmer to cut their hair: "John and Paul visited me and decided to have their hair like mine. A lot of French youth wore it that way. I gave both of them their first Beatles haircut in my hotel room on the Left Bank" (Miles 1997: 77).

November 1961-September 1963: On the Way to Fame

On November 9, 1961, 27-year-old Brian Epstein and his personal assistant Alistair Taylor attended a lunchtime performance by The Beatles at The Cavern Club. At that time The Beatles consisted of John Lennon and George Harrison on guitars, Paul McCartney on bass guitar and Pete Best on drums.

Even though neither Epstein nor Taylor particularly liked rock and roll music, they were impressed by the band's energy as well as by their charisma and humor (vgl. Epstein 1998: 98). However, Epstein noticed that the band's presentation on stage lacked discipline and professionalism: "They were rather scruffily dressed – in the nicest possible way or, I should say, in the most attractive way: black leather jackets and jeans, long hair of course. And they had a rather untidy stage presentation, not terribly aware, and not caring very much, what they looked like" (Lewisohn 2000: 34-35).

Epstein, who had grown weary of managing his father's record store, recognized the band's commercial potential and realized their need of a professional management. Although he had never before considered managing an artist, let alone a rock group (vgl. Epstein 1998: 99), he arranged two meetings with the band to discuss a possible business relationship. At the second meeting, on December 6, 1961, he suggested becoming The Beatles' manager. The group almost immediately accepted Epstein's offer, and a contract was finally signed on Wednesday, January 24, 1962 (vgl. Lewisohn 2000: 36).

As soon as Brian Epstein had taken on the responsibility of managing the Beatles, he introduced substantial changes concerning the group's stage image. Epstein, who had studied at the Royal Academy of Dramatic Arts from 1956 to 1957, was very well aware of principal rules of presentation in show business. He advised the band to change their stage outfits and helped them develop a distinct style of presenting themselves on stage. Pete Best remembers Epstein's initial influence on the group: "He claimed that no one in the world of entertainment outside our present environment would tolerate our slovenly look, our chatting to the birds near the stage, our eating and drinking on the stand, our playful butting and jostling and generally enjoying ourselves" (Best/Doncaster 2001: 123). While The Beatles' previous performances had been characterized by spontaneity and improvisation, Epstein insisted on carefully planned stage shows and advised the group to select their songs and the running order before the actual performance (vgl. Brown/Gaines: 2002: 64).

Epstein's assistant Alistair Taylor points out that the manager wrote down a set of rules The Beatles had to follow on stage: "They were told in writing that they must stop swearing onstage, they must stop joking with the girls, they must stop smoking onstage or carrying cans of Coke onstage" (Geller 2002: 43). While it is generally agreed that Epstein never tried to interfere with the group's music (vgl. Taylor 2003: 32), he entirely modified the Beatles' appearance on stage.

In order to make the band more acceptable to the large target audience envisioned by Epstein, The Beatles were persuaded to abandon the leather clothes they had acquired in Hamburg in favour of more respectable and more fashionable tweed suits. Hence, they were taken to tailor Beno Dorn in Birkenhead where Epstein bought them a set of identical dark blue mohair suits with matching ties (vgl. Harry 2000: 352). Paul McCartney points out that their image change actually did have an influence on their initial commercial success: "We picked out some very groovy mohair suits, which were OK. [...] It was a good thing. It did open doors for us. He was right. It meant that people who wouldn't accept the leather look could have us looking a bit more seemly" (Geller 2002: 43).

Brian Epstein personally attended most of The Beatles' performances and supervised the group's choreography. Paul McCartney explains the way Epstein advised the Beatles: "If you're in a theatrical endeavour the only way you can tell if you're doing good is if you have someone out there who says, 'That was really good. When you moved over, they lost you. Don't do that next time.' He was a director" (Geller 2002: 49).

Even though it has been suggested that Brian Epstein actually invented The Beatles' outfit and their stage choreography (vgl. Geller 2002: 48), both were initially inspired by the stage image projected by Cliff Richard's former backing group The Shadows. As recalled by *Mersey Beat* editor Bill Harry, "[Epstein] took them to the Empire Theatre to watch the Shadows, pointing out how they were dressed in mohair suits and dickie bows and how they bowed to the audience at the end of the show" (Harry 2003). Epstein realized that it was necessary to create a unique visual image of the group on stage, in order to distinguish The Beatles from other pop groups at the time. While the suits and an organized stage show were necessities in show business, The Beatles' haircut and their rather static and detached attitude on stage distinguished them from other pop artists at the time. Performers such as Elvis Presley and Gene Vincent were famous for their lively performances and their provocative movements on stage. On the other hand, guitar groups such as The Shadows moved their guitars simultaneously. The Beatles, however, deliberately dropped such show elements and remained rather motionless on stage. In 1970, John Lennon explained how The Beatles created their stage image to distinguish themselves from conventional pop groups.

"In the early days in England all the groups were like Elvis and a backing group. And the Beatles deliberately didn't move like Elvis. That was our policy because we found it stupid and bullshit. And then Mick Jagger came out and resurrected bullshit movement, wiggling his ass and that. So then people began to say, 'The Beatles are passé because they don't move.' But we did it as an intellectual [sic] – when we were younger, we used to move, we used to jump around, do all the things they're doing now [...]" (Wenner 2000: 13).

The Beatles' other distinctive feature was their unique haircut which was basically a tidier version of the hairstyle originally designed by Astrid Kirchherr and Jürgen Vollmer. Alistair Taylor remembers taking John Lennon, Paul McCartney and George Harrison to Horne Brothers in Liverpool, "who then had a reputation as very classy hairdressers. Their long hair was trimmed and styled into a much more clean-cut image. [...] Much to their relief, the hair was still left reasonably long but the greasy untamed look was definitely a thing of the past" (Taylor 2003: 33).

Epstein immediately fixed higher rates for The Beatles' performances and put great effort into promoting the group. Besides the local promotion in *Mersey Beat*, Epstein tried to organize performances in radio and television shows. On 8 March 1962, The Beatles made their radio debut on the BBC program *Teenager's Turn – Here We Go*. Despite this initial success, Epstein found it difficult to find promotional support by the music press. Tony Barrow, the record reviewer for the *Liverpool Echo*, pointed out to Brian Epstein that The Beatles would need to release a record to raise media interest. Even though Epstein made use of his connections to the recording industry in order to find the group a recording contract, The Beatles were rejected by all major record labels, including Columbia and HMV. With Tony Barrow's help, Epstein was able to arrange a recording audition for the band at Decca Records, one of the leading British record companies at the time (vgl. Lewisohn 2000: 37). On 1 January 1962, The Beatles auditioned in London, where Decca's A & R assistant Mike Smith recorded fifteen songs from the group's stage repertoire on tape. Although The Beatles were quite convinced to have secured a recording contract, the company turned them down in favour of Brian Poole and The Tremeloes, who auditioned on the same day (vgl. Harry 2000: 938). When Brian Epstein had their audition tape transferred to a 78-rpm demonstration disc, the engineer Jim Foy referred him to a publishing company, Ardmore & Beechwood, whose general manager Sid Coleman put Epstein into touch with George Martin, the head of A & R at Parlophone, a label owned by EMI (vgl. Lewisohn 2000: 53). George Martin listened to the demonstration disc and arranged an audition with The Beatles at Abbey Road Studios in London on 6 June 1962 (vgl. Martin/Hornsby: 1994: 122).

From January to June, The Beatles headlined various concerts in the Merseyside area. On 11 April 1962, they left Liverpool for another engagement in Hamburg. Astrid Kirchherr awaited them at the Hamburg airport with the devastating news that her fiancé, The Beatles' friend and former bass player Stuart Sutcliffe, had died of a brain haemorrhage the day before.

Despite the tragic death of Stuart Sutcliffe, the group stayed in Hamburg to perform 48 nights at the Star Club, a new rock and roll club owned by Manfred Weissleder. Horst Fascher, the former 'bouncer' at the Kaiserkeller and the Top Ten, had become Weissleder's assistant and had negotiated The Beatles' contract with Brian Epstein. Fascher points out that the new, clean image did not diminish The Beatles' popularity in Hamburg. In fact, suits, shirts and ties had become fashionable at that time.

"Auch das hat man akzeptiert – auf einmal liefen die Beatles mit Schlips und Kragen rum und mit Anzügen, die ein bisschen anders geschnitten waren als unsere. Aber wir trugen auch Anzüge [zu der Zeit]. Das Erste, was man sich von seinem Geld, das man sich erarbeitet hatte, gekauft hat, war ein Hemd und einen Schlips. Und einen Anzug. [...] Das wurde auf einmal Mode. Das ging ein bisschen weg vom Saloppen. Man wollte elegant sein" (Fascher 2003).

During their third engagement in Hamburg, The Beatles participated in another recording session with Tony Sheridan, and after The Beatles had returned from their seven-week long engagement at the Star Club in Hamburg, they attended their first recording session at Abbey Road Studios in London. They presented several of their own compositions as well as some favorites from their stage act to A & R and record producer George Martin. Martin, who had a reputation of producing comedy records with Peter Sellers and Spike Milligan, was not enormously impressed by The Beatles' own material and did not offer The Beatles a recording contract right away. When George Martin finally decided to sign the group in July, he was still not sure who was going to be made the 'star' of the group, as pop groups usually featured only one lead singer, such as Cliff Richard and The Shadows and Brian Poole and The Tremeloes.

"I put them all on test individually, getting them to sing numbers in turn, and my original feeling was [that] Paul had a sweeter voice, John's had more character, and George was generally not so good. I was thinking, on balance, that I should make Paul the leader. Then, after some thought, I realised that if I did so I would be changing the nature of the group. Why do that? Why not keep them as they were? It hadn't been done before – but then, I'd made a lot of records that hadn't been 'done before'. Why not experiment in pop as I had in comedy?" (Martin/Hornsby 1994: 124).

Although he liked The Beatles' personalities, George Martin was least impressed with Pete Best's drumming. He suggested to Brian Epstein that Pete Best stay the group's drummer at live performances, while a professional studio musician should replace him at recording sessions. (vgl. Martin/Hornsby 1994: 123). He did not know that John Lennon, Paul McCartney and George Harrison had actually been thinking about replacing Pete Best with Ringo Starr, a Liverpool drummer who had become their friend in Hamburg. When Brian Epstein told Pete Best about the other Beatles' decision, he was shattered. Sam Leach, a concert promoter from Liverpool, who had been supporting The Beatles' career from a very early stage, explains why Ringo Starr was the perfect drummer for The Beatles: "For me, Ringo was the original Beatle. Prior to his joining The Beatles, his image was that of an immaculately-dressed, talented and dedicated performer with a sharp, somewhat off-beat sense of humour. That is exactly what The Beatles became known for around the world" (Leach 1999: 175).

On 4 September 1962, The Beatles with their new drummer Ringo Starr traveled to London to record their debut single. George Martin wanted the group to record a song called "How Do You Do It," written by Lionel Michael Stitcher under the pseudonym Mitch Murray. The Beatles, however, detested the song and persuaded George Martin to let them record "Love Me Do," a song Paul McCartney and John Lennon had written in Germany the year before. Although George Martin had considered Murray's song to be more commercial, it was decided that "Love Me Do" would be released as The Beatles' first single.[2] Its release

---

2   The Beatles' recording of "How Do You Do It" served as a demonstration tape for Gerry and The Pacemakers who topped the British charts with their version of the song in 1963. The Beatles' version of "How Do You Do It" was finally included in the group's first *Anthology* compilation in 1995.

date being set on 5 October 1962, Brian Epstein organized a promotion campaign for his protégés. Again, Epstein consulted Tony Barrow from the *Liverpool Echo*, this time asking him to become The Beatles' official press agent. Barrow, who was working for Decca Records, initially declined the offer and referred Epstein to his former colleague Tony Calder, who had set up an independent PR firm with Andrew Loog Oldham (vgl. Harry 2000: 96). Subsequently, Calder was hired to send out press releases and to arrange press interviews: "The week before ["Love Me Do"] came out Brian Epstein asked if I could drum up some press on them. They meant nothing in London, but I talked everybody into it and trotted them down to *Melody Maker*, *NME* and *Disc* – and they all did these little 15-minute interviews, which was all you got in those days" ("Unsung": 67). In order to reach their target audience, The Beatles gave live concerts, signed copies of their single at record stores, and performed and gave interviews for radio shows, such as *The Friday Spectacular* on Radio Luxembourg and *Here We Go* on the BBC Light Programme (vgl. Miles 2001: 72-73). On 17 October 1962, they made their first appearance on television. Granada TV's *People and Places* showed The Beatles as they performed two songs live at the Cavern Club in Liverpool (vgl. Miles 2001: 72-73). Epstein asked Bill Harry, still one of The Beatles' personal friends, to 'plug' the group's first single release in his magazine *Mersey Beat*. According to Epstein's autobiography, Harry's work contributed significantly to the local success of the single, and "the kids of Liverpool bought it in the thousands" (Epstein 1998: 121). The week after their first television appearance, "Love Me Do" entered the *Record Retailer* charts at position 49. It was the first time The Beatles experienced the commercial power of audiovisual media. Until the end of the year, The Beatles toured the Merseyside area and fulfilled two concert bookings at the Star Club in Hamburg, which had been arranged prior to their record release in Britain. On 27 December, "Love Me Do" peaked at position 17 in the *Record Retailer* singles charts.

In January 1963, The Beatles went on a tour leading them through Scotland and England. On January 11, their second single "Please Please Me" was released in Great Britain. Backed by an extensive publicity campaign "Please Please Me" became The Beatles' first hit record in Great Britain, reaching the No. 2 spot in the *Record Retailer* charts and the No. 1 position in the *New Musical Express* and *Disc*. On February 11, 1963, The Beatles recorded the remaining ten tracks to complete their first album *Please Please Me*, which was released on March 22.

During the following months, the group engaged in several tours through Great Britain, causing mass excitement at many concerts. The British media realized The Beatles' overwhelming effect on teenage audiences and began to take more interest in the group. In addition to their live performances, The Beatles appeared in various radio and television programs.

In the summer of 1963, George 'Bud' Ornstein, the head of United Artists' branch in London, conceived of the idea of making a movie with The Beatles (vgl. Carr 1996: 11). At the time it was very common for pop stars to appear in movies where they would lip-sync several of their songs. Most of these movies were low-budget productions, designed to cash in on the short-lived fame of teenage idols and pop stars such as Tommy Steele and Helen Shapiro. Often a movie like this would only serve as a vehicle for an accompanying soundtrack album, which generated high profits for the film production company that licensed or distributed the album. As The Beatles had become such tremendously popular entertainers in Great Britain, Ornstein's idea to produce a movie with them was based on the assumption that it would be another inexpensive exploitation picture, aimed at a youth audience which had become fascinated with a pop group that was expected to be only a passing phenomenon (vgl. Murray/Rolston 2001: 6).

Ornstein contacted independent film producer Walter Shenson, who had produced several rather successful low-budget comedies. Shenson agreed to produce the Beatles' first movie. The budget for the film was set at only £200,000, as the production company did not have great confidence in the commercial durability of The Beatles (vgl. Neaverson 1997: 12).

October 1963-July 1964:
The Beatles Conquer the World

While their first movie was being prepared in London, The Beatles continued their series of successes in the sphere of popular music. From October 1963 to January 1964, The Beatles went on a concert tour leading them through Great Britain, Sweden, Ireland and France. In November 1963, they released their second album, *With The Beatles*, as well as a new single, "I Want To Hold Your Hand," both of which reached the top of the charts in Great Britain. Again, they made numerous appearances on television as well as on radio to promote their recent releases.

Although The Beatles had become one of the most successful pop groups in Europe, they had not yet been able to establish their records in the American market. As Capitol Records, EMI's branch in the United States, had not been interested in The Beatles' first singles, Parlophone had offered the singles to small independent labels, Vee Jay Records and

Swan Records, which, however, did not have the financial means to introduce a new act to a large audience.[3] When press reports of the group's tremendous success in Britain reached the United States, Capitol Records began to show more interest in The Beatles (vgl. Epstein 1998: 55). In addition, Ed Sullivan, the most popular television host in the United States at the time, and Sid Bernstein, an independent promoter in New York, had contacted Brian Epstein. Bernstein had become aware of The Beatles through English newspapers. As soon as February 1963, he called Brian Epstein, offering The Beatles an appearance at the Carnegie Hall in New York. As The Beatles had not had any charts successes in the United States, Epstein suggested that Bernstein give The Beatles a year to become known in America. Consequently, Bernstein booked the Carnegie Hall for a show in February 1964.

Sullivan had witnessed the effects of Beatlemania at Heathrow Airport in London in October 1963: "There was the biggest crowd I've ever seen in my life! I asked someone what was going on, and he said, 'The Beatles!' 'Who the hell are the Beatles?' I asked. But I went back to my hotel, got the name of their manager, and arranged for them to do three shows" (Harry 2000: 1043). In order to guarantee The Beatles a maximum of publicity, Brian Epstein made an efficient arrangement with the show's producer Bob Precht. While performers usually received a payment of $7,500 for one appearance in *The Ed Sullivan Show*, Epstein accepted a total of $10,000 for The Beatles' appearance in three shows, provided that they were presented as the main attraction. Having already arranged concerts in New York, The Beatles now were also to perform in Sullivan's show on three dates in February 1964.

Backed by The Beatles' tremendous commercial success in Europe as well as by Sullivan's and Bernstein's bookings, EMI and Brian Epstein now pressed Capitol Records to release The Beatles' new single "I Want To Hold Your Hand." Epstein personally called Alan Livingstone, the president of Capitol Records, and persuaded him to release the single on the Capitol label: "He was a gentleman and he was persuasive. I called him back and said, 'OK, we'll put them out.' Brian said, 'Wait a minute. I'm not going to give them to you unless you spend $40,000 to promote their first single" (Geller 2002: 71). Realizing the commercial

---

3   Vee Jay Records issued the singles "Please Please Me" and "From Me To You" in 1963. Swan Records released "She Loves You" in 1963. None of these releases initially charted, except for "From Me To You," which peaked at number 116 in *Billboard* magazine. After The Beatles had reached the top of the charts with "I Wanna Hold Your Hand," the two independent labels re-released these recordings, each selling several millions copies (vgl. Harry 2000: 1118).

potential of The Beatles in the United States, Livingstone agreed to Epstein's conditions, even though Capitol Records had previously never spent more than $5,000 on promoting a single record (vgl. Harry 2000: 226). The single was released on 26 December 1963, accompanied by an extensive publicity programme including posters, stickers, T-shirts and close cooperation with radio stations to ensure air play. Livingstone remembers that "[i]t was very easy at that time to get air play. Particularly for Capitol, who had a good following. So that was the promotion. As far as the press was concerned it was almost automatic. [...] It was the easiest promotion I've ever seen" (Geller 2002: 72). American teenagers were enthused by The Beatles' music, and "I Want To Hold Your Hand" became the most successful single record in the United States to date, selling in excess of five millions copies. Although the music itself was the biggest selling point, such a tremendous success could only be achieved by the support of a company that had the capacity of providing the necessary means to distribute and promote the product.

The publicity campaign for "I Want To Hold Your Hand" went hand in hand with an announcement of The Beatles' first visit of the United States in February. Powered by Capitol Records, the media created an unprecedented hype surrounding the group's arrival in New York, which introduced the phenomenon of 'Beatlemania' in the United States. Prior to the arrival, Capitol Records had produced five million badges announcing "The Beatles Are Coming!" and distributed free buttons and T-shirts in New York. A December 23, 1963, memo from Paul Russell, National Album Merchandiser Manager, explained the extensive Beatles publicity campaign to Capitol Records employees. The information contained in this memo makes it quite clear that Capitol Records played an enormous role in launching The Beatles in the United States.

"On Monday, December 30, a two-page spread will appear in *Billboard* (it may be in *Cash Box*, too, on that day, or it will run a week later. [...]
Shortly after the first of the year, you'll have bulk quantities of a unique see-through plastic pin-on button. Inserted in each button is a shot of the Beatles, with each boy identified. What to do with the buttons? First, have all of your sales staff wear one. Second, offer them to clerks and jocks. Third, arrange for radio station give-aways of the buttons. [...]
Again shortly after the First, you'll have bulk quantities of a Beatle hair do wig. As soon as they arrive – and until further notice – you and each of your sales and promotion staff are to wear the wig during the business day! Next, see how many of the retail clerks in your area have a sense of humor. [...] Get these Beatle wigs around properly, and you'll find you're helping to start the Beatle Hair-Do Craze that should be sweeping the country soon. [...]

As soon as possible after the First, you'll have fantastic quantities of these two-inch by three-inch teaser stickers. [...] Put them up anywhere and everywhere they can be seen [...]. It may sound funny, but we literally want your salesman to be plastering these stickers on any friendly surface as they walk down the street or as they call on radio or retail accounts. [...] Make arrangements with some local high school students to spread the stickers around town. [...]
On or before the release date [...] you'll have exceptionally large quantities of both promo albums and jackets" (Spizer 2003: 73)

Radio stations were constantly playing Beatles records, and the disc jockeys informed the public of details concerning The Beatles' arrival. On 7 February 1964, when their Boeing 707 landed at John F Kennedy International Airport in New York, between 3,000 and 5,000 teenage fans and approximately 200 reporters enthusiastically welcomed The Beatles. Comments by The Beatles at the time as well as more recent interviews suggest that they were unaware of the great effort Epstein and Capitol Records had put into the publicity campaign. They seemed genuinely surprised by their apparently instant popularity and the almost frantic reception in New York City. While their music and the media hype surrounding their arrival in the States had built up local hysteria in New York City, it was the media coverage of The Beatles' press conference at the airport, which endeared them to the American public and finally resulted in a national interest in The Beatles. Having learned how to deal with the media in Great Britain, The Beatles managed to impress the press representatives with a witty press conference that set the tone for all subsequent press conferences in the United States.

"[Reporter:] Would you please sing something?
[Lennon:] No, we need money first. [Laughter]
[Reporter:] How many are bald if you have to wear those wigs?
[Starr:] All of us!
[McCartney]: I'm bald.
[Lennon:] Oh, we're all bald, yeah.
[McCartney:] Don't tell anyone, please. [Laughter]
[...]
[Reporter:] Do you hope to get a haircut?
[All:] No!
[Harrison:] I had one yesterday. [Laughter]
[...]
[Reporter:] Why does [your music] excite them so much?
[McCartney:] We don't know really.
[Lennon:] If we knew, we'd form another group and be managers. [Laughter]"
(*The First U.S. Visit* 2000).

The Beatles' humor, which had contributed significantly to their popularity in Great Britain, became elementary in the press coverage of The Beatles' visit of the United States. In 1970, John Lennon explained that the British media had served as a training ground for the group: "[W]e really were professional by the time we got here. We learned the whole game. When we arrived here, we knew how to handle press. The British press are the toughest in the world – we could handle anything" (Wenner 2000: 108). In the course of the two weeks The Beatles remained in the United States, they were virtually omnipresent in the American media. While newspapers featured the group in the headlines every day, The Beatles also gave interviews to numerous radio stations. New York disc jockey Murray the K, one of the most popular radio stars at the time, was instrumental in promoting the group and accompanied them on their trip from New York City to Washington DC. As it would have been impossible to grant exclusive interviews to all radio shows, and in order not to miss the opportunity of reaching the group's target audience, Capitol Records distributed a promotional 7-inch EP to all the relevant stations. This EP contained an 'open-end' interview with The Beatles, featuring pre-recorded answers to a set of questions printed on the record sleeve. Radio disc jockeys could now create the illusion of The Beatles being in the studio, answering questions he or she read off the record sleeve.

"[Reporter:] Welcome to the show, fellas!
[All:] Thank you!
[McCartney:] Thank you very much.
[Starr:] Pleasure to be here!
[Reporter:] Say, John, how did you ever decide on a name like The Beatles?
[Lennon:] Well, I had a vision when I was twelve, and I saw a man on a flaming pie. And he said, 'You're Beetles with an A!' And we are!
[…]
[Reporter:] Ladies and gentlemen, The Beatles have now taken over the world!
[Harrison:] That's a nice thing to say, isn't it?"
(Beatles 1964a)

In order to provide disc jockeys with more 'exclusive' material, Capitol Records as well as Vee Jay Records issued several additional promotional records to American radio stations in 1964. In September, Vee Jay distributed the promotional album *Hear The Beatles Tell All* to 7,000 radio stations (Miles 2001: 169), while *The Beatles Introduce New Songs* was distributed by Capitol Records in order to promote several Lennon/McCartney compositions recorded by other artists. Finally, Capitol Records released a double LP called *The Beatles' Story* in November. The records contained a "narrative and musical biography of Beatlemania", providing biographies of each group member as well as excerpts from interviews and The Beatles' hit records. In addition, the album also contained information on Brian Epstein and George Martin, whose importance to the group had been publicized from the very beginning of The Beatles' career. However, the concept of The Beatles' Story was not new, as similar releases had been on the market since reporter Ed Rudy had issued an interview album called *The American Tour with Ed Rudy*, which had reached No. 20 in the *Billboard* charts in June 1964. Realizing the commercial potential of interview releases, The Beatles' record company Capitol Records promoted *The Beatles' Story* along with the group's most recent single "I Feel Fine". The album proved to be a considerable success, reaching No.7 in the *Billboard* Album Charts in November.

In order to capture the event of The Beatles' first U.S. visit on film, Granada Television in association with Brian Epstein's NEMS company had contacted Albert and David Maysles, two pioneers in the field of cinéma vérité documentary films. The Maysles brothers filmed the group's arrival and stayed with the group during their entire stay in America. While part of the film was shown in Great Britain as early as 12 February 1964[4], the Maysles' documentary *The Beatles in America* premiered in the United States on CBS on 13 November 1964 (vgl. Lewisohn 2000: 144).

The Beatles' omni-presence in radio and newspapers caused a nationwide interest in the group, peaking on 9 February 1964, when The Beatles performed live on *The Ed Sullivan Show*, one of the most popular television shows in the United States at the time. Their first live television performance in the States reached an estimated number of 73 million viewers, the highest rating in the history of American television to that date. They performed "All My Loving," "Till There Was You," and "She Loves You" in the first half of the show, and "I Saw Her Standing There" and "I Want To Hold Your Hand" at the end.

While the day after The Beatles' first appearance on *The Ed Sullivan Show* was entirely dedicated to press interviews and presentations, the group travelled to Washington DC to perform in front of more than 8,000 fans on 11 February 1964. CBS filmed The Beatles' first concert in the United States, which characteristically only lasted half an hour. The concert footage was shown as a closed-circuit telecast in cinemas across the United States in March 1964 (vgl. Lewisohn 2000: 146). The day after their concert in Washington, The Beatles headlined two shows at the

---

4　Granada Television showed 36 minutes of the Maysles brothers' film footage titled *Yeah, Yeah, Yeah! – The Beatles In New York* on 12 February 1964 and repeated the documentary the following day.

Carnegie Hall in New York, which had been booked by Sid Bernstein the year before. On 13 February, The Beatles flew to Miami, Florida, where they attempted to relax while continuing their publicity campaign. Besides a photo session for *Life* magazine, The Beatles also granted a telephone interview to ABC TV's *Dick Clark's American Bandstand*. Their second appearance on *The Ed Sullivan Show* was broadcast live from Florida, and it proved to be another triumph for Ed Sullivan and The Beatles, as approximately 70 million viewers tuned in to see the group perform (vgl. Miles 2001: 134).

When The Beatles arrived back in London on 22 February, they were enthusiastically welcomed by a crowd of several thousand fans. The group's triumphant arrival was covered by various television and radio shows.

Only three days after The Beatles had returned to Great Britain, they began recording the songs Lennon and McCartney had written for the forthcoming movie soundtrack. A week later, on March 2, 1964, filming of The Beatles' first movie started at Paddington Station, London (vgl. Miles 2001: 135). The movie was shot within eight weeks, during which The Beatles not only attended the filming schedule but also managed to finish the recording of the soundtrack album and to appear in British and American television shows. In addition, John Lennon engaged in promotional activities for his first book *In His Own Write*, which was published by Jonathan Cape on 23 March 1964. The book's instant commercial and critical success supported Lennon's public image as 'the intellectual Beatle.'

Filming for *A Hard Day's Night* ended on 24 April 1964. Until the movie's world premiere in July, The Beatles engaged in various promotional activities for their recent record releases.[5] Besides radio interviews and live performances for BBC radio shows, The Beatles starred in a British television special called *Around The Beatles*, which was aired on 6 May, 1964.

5　In March, the single "Can't Buy Me Love" was released by EMI and Capitol Records in Britain and the United States. Vee Jay Records released "Do You Want To Know A Secret" and Tollie Records released "Love Me Do" as singles in the U.S. in April. On 4 April 1964, The Beatles occupied twelve positions in the *Billboard* Singles Charts, including the top five positions ("Can't Buy Me Love," "Twist And Shout," "She Loves You," "I Want To Hold Your Hand" and "Please Please Me"). On 10 April, Capitol released an album titled *The Beatles' Second Album*, containing "You Can't Do That," a song written for *A Hard Day's Night*, as well as songs from the European release *With The Beatles* and other recordings previously available on singles.

In June, The Beatles went on a world tour leading them through Denmark, The Netherlands, Hong Kong, Australia and New Zealand. As Ringo Starr had previously collapsed suffering from acute tonsillitis and pharyngitis, he was temporarily replaced by session drummer Jimmy Nichols.

On 6 July 1964, The Beatles' movie *A Hard Day's Night* premiered at the London Pavilion.

THE BEATLES ON FILM - PART ONE: 1964-1965

A Hard Day's Night

Production History

Following the success of American pop musicals starring Bill Haley, Eddie Cochran and Elvis Presley, similar exploitation films had also become commonplace in British cinema by the mid-sixties. British film producers churned out numerous vehicles for British pop stars, such as Tommy Steele and Cliff Richard, to capitalize on the emerging teenage market. Most of these movies were low-budget productions, designed to exploit the market by generating maximum profits for the lowest possible investment (vgl. Neaverson 1997: 11). As The Beatles had never liked any of the movies featuring their musical heroes, they wanted their film to be different from the formulaic contemporary pop movies. John Lennon points out that The Beatles did not want to participate in a stereotypical exploitation picture: "We'd made it clear to Brian [Epstein] that we weren't interested in one of those typical nobody-understands-our-music plots where the local dignitaries are trying to ban something as terrible as the Saturday Night Hop" (Carr 1996: 30). In fact, The Beatles had already turned down a movie offer before meeting Walter Shenson, who was reportedly the first producer to show genuine interest in The Beatles as performers.[1]

Producer Walter Shenson consulted director Richard Lester, who he had previously worked with on a movie called *Mouse on the Moon* in 1963. To The Beatles, however, Lester was known as the director of *The Running, Jumping and Standing Still Film*, which he had created with British comedy stars Peter Sellers and Spike Milligan in 1959. Paul McCartney says that "[w]hen Walter Shenson came up with the idea of Dick Lester to direct what became *A Hard Day's Night*, we were excited, for as far as we were concerned anyone connected with *The Goon Show*

---

1   According to Paul McCartney, The Beatles had been offered a film called *The Yellow Teddy Bears* (vgl. Yule 1994: xi).

and *The Running, Jumping and Standing Still Film* had to be the goods" (Yule 1994: xi).

Richard Lester had worked as a director of live television shows in the 1950s. Since the mid-fifties he had directed several shows featuring Peter Sellers and Spike Milligan, such as *Idiot Weekly* and *A Show Called Fred* (vgl. Yule 1994: 31). After his Academy Award nomination for *The Running, Jumping and Standing Still Film*, Lester had directed *It's Trad, Dad!*, a pop musical starring teenage idol Helen Shapiro, and *Mouse on the Moon* featuring Margaret Rutherford. His work with Sellers and Milligan is often considered to be the direct precursor to Monty Python's television series *Monty Python's Flying Circus* in the 1960s, since *Idiot Weekly*, *A Show Called Fred*, and *Son of Fred*, as well as *The Running, Jumping and Standing Still Film* shared a similar mode of presentation and the same surreal sense of humor that is now typically associated with Monty Python.

In 1955, Richard Lester had worked with Liverpool actor Alun Owen, when both appeared on *The Dick Lester Show* (vgl. Yule 1994: 37). Since then Owen had become a successful writer of plays and television productions. One of his most noted works was *No Trams on Lime Street*, a television play set in Liverpool. Lester contacted Owen when he learned that his first choice, Johnny Speight, was not available.[2] Owen turned out to be the perfect choice for this project, as he was familiar with the Liverpool area and understood the group's mentality and humor. He agreed to write the script for the movie, and on 30 October 1963, The Beatles' press agent Tony Barrow announced to the press that Alun Owen was going to work on a story for The Beatles' first feature film. Producer Walter Shenson explained the way Owen was to collaborate with the band: "Alun Owen is going to spend a lot of time with the boys and create characters for them that reflect their own. We want to put over their non-conformist, slightly anarchist characters. We want to present their almost Goon-like quality" (vgl. Carr 1996: 25).

While it was quite common in the genre of pop musicals for musicians like Elvis Presley and Cliff Richard to impersonate fictional characters, Richard Lester points out that it was clear from the beginning that The Beatles would play characters based upon their own public personae

---

2   Richard Lester had wanted Johnny Speight (*Til Death Do Us Part*) to write the screenplay for The Beatles' movie debut. As Speight was not available, he and Shenson suggested Alun Owen to Brian Epstein and The Beatles (vgl. Carr 1996: 30). Paul McCartney's official biographer claims, however, that, according to Walter Shenson, "it was Paul [McCartney] who suggested Alun Owen as the scriptwriter for The Beatles' first film" (Miles 1997: 158).

in their first movie: "I don't think it ever occurred to us to ask The Beatles to play the Musketeers, to be anything but themselves" (*A Hard Day's Night* 2002: DVD 2). In another interview Lester explains the reasons why this decision was made.

"It was the most logical thing to have four people who were not actors to play themselves in situations and conditions that were normal to them. They were used to doing press conferences, they were used to running from their fans, they were used to getting in and out of cars, they were used to being shouted at and pushed around. All we were asking them to do was to do what they normally did" (Soderbergh 2005).

Owen actually spent three days with The Beatles on tour in Dublin and in London in order to gain basic information for a script which was to portray an exaggerated day in the life of The Beatles. Paul McCartney remembers the way Owen worked with The Beatles:

"The journalist Michael Braun wrote a book, *Love Me Do*: The Beatles' Progress, after he'd hung out with us, so this became the way to do it. When it came time to do *Hard Day's Night*, we just applied the same idea. They'd hang with you and pick up the feel then they'd go away and write the story and they always wrote something cool because they'd got our sense of humour or they saw we were tongue in cheek. [...] So Alun came around with us and picked up all the little things like 'He's very clean, isn't he?' [...] And it eventually found its way into the film" (Miles 1997: 159).

After the basic idea of creating some sort of fictional documentary had been agreed upon, Alun Owen had complete freedom with the script (vgl. Harry 1985: 16). On November 1, 1963, the British music magazine *New Musical Express* already ran an article about The Beatles' movie plans. At that point Owen had made up his mind about the way he wanted to present The Beatles in the movie: "I aim to create the story around 90 minutes of their own fantastic lives at the top of the pop music profession. But it will be fictional, despite the fact that the things which happen to them in the film are probably the sort of things that happen to them in reality. I aim to utilise their fantastic personalities and sense of humour" (Sutherland 21).

It has become part of official Beatles history that Ringo Starr suggested the title for the group's first movie. Although it is quite possible that Starr had originally invented the phrase, it first appeared in John Lennon's surreal short story "Sad Michael" (vgl. Lennon 1997: 29),[3]

---

3 It should be noted that The Beatles' official biographer Hunter Davies was the first to have pointed out the connection between John Lennon's writing

which was published before the movie title was agreed upon. Probably Starr came up with the phrase "a hard day's night" when Lennon was writing the story, and Lennon, who admitted that he was sometimes inspired by Ringo Starr's absurd word creations and phrases, used it in the story.[4]

The Beatles began filming their first feature movie on March 2, 1964. Since the day their movie had been announced, the group had conquered the American market with their single "I Want to Hold Your Hand", which had reached the number one spot in the *Billboard* charts in January 1964. Their visit to the United States in February 1964 had generated a mass hysteria that seemed to top even Elvis Presley's effect on teenage crowds in the late 1950s. Within weeks The Beatles had managed to become the most popular entertainers in the western hemisphere.

While the movie had initially been designed for the British market, it now became an important property for the American market as well. It was thought to be the perfect vehicle to define and project each Beatle's role within the group and to promote and distribute The Beatles' collective image. With *A Hard Day's Night*, The Beatles were able to establish and introduce their image to a worldwide audience. Consequently, the way the band was to be portrayed in the film was being considered very carefully by the producers as well as by The Beatles and their management.

A Hard Day's Night and The Beatles' Image

Since The Beatles and their manager Brian Epstein had previously tried to project an image of a homogeneous band without an actual leader, this kind of group image had been the main reason why "the British and American publics had only the vaguest notion of individual Beatles. Their defining qualities, to most adult minds, were the identikit Mop-tops and peculiar accent" (Du Noyer 2002: 74). At that point it became important to the group as well as the management to introduce each individual Beatle to the public. Consequently, newspapers and magazines began publishing articles and features such as "Close-Up on a Beatle," a series of four articles in the *New Musical Express*, each concentrating on a particular Beatle. Also, solo activities by the group members were promoted

---

and the movie's title, although he falsely refers to "Sad Michael" as poem (vgl. Davies 1969: 219).

4   Some of the rejected titles reportedly were *Beatlemania, Moving On, Travelling On, Let's Go* and *Who Was That Little Old Man?* (vgl. Miles 2001: 137).

extensively for the first time while the movie was being filmed in March and April 1964. For instance, when John Lennon's first book *In His Own Write* was published in March, the event was covered by the mass media, and John Lennon became known and accepted as an artist in his own right. Richard Lester confirms that the creative team around The Beatles did indeed intend to create a certain kind of image for each Beatle: "When we started on *A Hard Day's Night* the importance of separating out The Beatles' individual personalities was something which we deliberately concentrated on [...]" (Carr 1996: 44).

Even though it has been stated that financial reasons forced the production team to film *A Hard Day's Night* in black-and-white (vgl. Du Noyer 2002: 76), the decision to make a black-and-white movie seems also logical from an artistic point of view. First of all, Richard Lester and Gilbert Taylor, the director of photography, had previously only made black-and-white films. Second, The Beatles themselves had established a black-and-white image of themselves in the media since the release of their second LP *With The Beatles*. According to George Harrison, The Beatles had remembered the artistic look of the black-and-white photographs Astrid Kirchherr and Jürgen Vollmer had taken of the group in Hamburg and consequently had asked cover photographer Robert Freeman to try to create a similar artistic look for their second album cover (Beatles 2000: 107). The result was one of the iconic album covers of the time. Initially, EMI, The Beatles' record company, and Brian Epstein did not want to use the photograph, because they thought it was too radical. However, The Beatles and George Martin managed to convince the record company to use the photo (Du Noyer 2002: 66).

The cool, serious look The Beatles displayed at the time actually played a quite important role in the way the public and the media perceived the group. It contributed significantly to the group's credibility as artists and serious musicians. While similar album covers had previously only been used for jazz releases, it was probably the first time a pop group deliberately tried to establish a link between pop music and highbrow culture.[5] Their new image had quite some impact on the way they were perceived by the media and by the public, which is evidenced by the great interest serious music critics and artists suddenly took in the work of The Beatles. For instance, the classical music critic of *The Times* drew a now legendary comparison between John Lennon, Paul McCartney and Gustav Mahler (Du Noyer 2002: 66). Ray Coleman, the

---

5   Photographer Robert Freeman had actually taken some impressive black-and-white pictures of John Coltrane. With these pictures he applied for a job at The Beatles' management. Brian Epstein and The Beatles liked his work and commissioned him to photograph their second album cover.

former assistant editor at the *Melody Maker*, remembers how The Beatles broke with the conventions of traditional music journalism in Britain.

"Started in 1928, the paper had a tradition for upholding 'good musicianship'. Pop singers who 'sang in tune', like Frank Sinatra, were often allowed to cross the line into the paper, but teenage pop had been treated with contempt, as if it had nothing to do with music, [...] The events of that year, and the infectious change in emphasis of the bestselling record charts towards new 'beat music', forced the paper to switch its policy and report the new sounds. [...] The worlds of jazz and adult music, which had grown too holy and insular, found themselves threatened not merely by great, energetic, self-made music led by the Beatles; in Lennon, above all, they faced an articulacy unheard of in popular music" (Coleman 1992: 291-293).

Photographer Robert Freeman, who had designed the innovative album cover for *With the Beatles*, was also consulted for *A Hard Day's Night*. He designed the album cover for the soundtrack LP as well as the movie's closing credits, where his 'polyphoto' images of the individual Beatles are fast-dissolved so that each Beatle morphs into one of his colleagues (vgl. Murray 2002: 116). The fact that he was asked to take photographs of The Beatles for *A Hard Day's Night* suggests that the group was indeed striving for a continuity of the black-and-white image they had established the year before.

Storyline and Aesthetics

Although many indoor-scenes for *A Hard Day's Night* were filmed at Twickenham Film Studios, London, the production team decided to shoot several scenes on authentic locations in order to achieve a sense of realism. Denis O'Dell, the movie's associate producer, points out that real locations were needed to convey the impression of a documentary: "Because we wanted the film to be made in a loose cinéma vérité style, it was vital to incorporate as many real locations as possible [...]" (Neaverson/O'Dell 2002: 33). To achieve the desired effect of authenticity, whole sequences were shot at Paddington Station, on a train constantly going from London to Minehead, at the Les Ambassadeurs Club, at the Scala Theatre, at Marylebone Station, in Notting Hill Gate, at Thornbury Playing Fields, Isleworth, and in West Ealing.

Since The Beatles had not had experience in the field of acting, Alun Owen constructed their dialogues in a way that restricted their individual contributions to one-liners. Actually, this closely reflected The Beatles' natural talk at press conferences. As pointed out by Paul McCartney, "[t]he more we told [Alun Owen], the more of us he'd get in it, which is always a good thing, it would just reflect back. We could play it easier, we could identify with it all easier, and this was our first film" (Miles 1997: 160). The fact that The Beatles were only asked to deliver short sentences was a crucial factor in enabling them to feature in a full-length film. It was probably the first time that a feature film starred four non-actors. In order to preserve the spontaneity of the dialogue, director Richard Lester often made use of two or three cameras at a time, a technique he had developed the year before.

"On every film I've made since *It's Trad, Dad,* I've always used at least two cameras simultaneously. I have never understood why it was not the way that films were made. I see no disadvantages, only phenomenal advantages both artistically and emotionally in terms of the relationship between the film company and its actors. To keep them fresh, to keep them from becoming bored with the actual process of shooting any movie which can often be very slow" (Carr 1996: 23).

In addition to the artistic advantages gained by this technique, using up to three cameras at a time enabled Richard Lester to shoot *A Hard Day's Night* in only eight weeks and to stick to the tight budget United Artists had provided for the movie. The whole production was achieved in a very short period of time. May and June were spent editing the movie and recording the soundtrack. When *A Hard Day's Night* premiered on 6 July, 1964, it had only taken four months from the first day of shooting the movie to presenting it in the theatre.

The movie's plot is rather simple; it basically revolves around The Beatles' adventures on the way to a television performance. In order to create conflict, Alun Owen invented the character of 'Paul's Grandfather,' a mean old man causing chaos. At the time of the movie's release United Artists published the following synopsis:

"Once upon a time there were four happy Liverpool lads called Paul, John, George and Ringo and they played their music all over the country. Now, when they'd finished playing in one place they'd run to the nearest railway station and go on to a new place to play some more of their music, usually pursued by hundreds of young ladies.
On the day of our story, John, George and Ringo get to the station and fight their way into the railway compartment where they meet up with Paul, who has a little old man with him, a very dear little old man. Anyway, who is he? The little old man is 'mixing' John McCartney, Paul's Grandfather [Wilfrid Brambell]. Grandfather is dedicated to the principle of divide and conquer. The mere sight of a nice friendly group of clean-cut lads like the Beatles brings him out in a rash of counterpoints.

Norm [Norman Rossington], the boys' road manager, who is conducting a war of nerves with John, the group's happy anarchist, collects Grandfather and together with Shake [John Junkin], the general dogsbody[, h]e retreats to the restaurant car for coffee, leaving the boys to settle in for their journey to London and a live television show. However, a well-established first-class ticket holder [Richard Vernon] drives the boys out of their carriage by being pompously officious, so they go and join Norm, Shake and Grandfather in the restaurant car.

By this time Grandfather has managed to get Norm and Shake at each other's throats and Paul warns the others that this could be only the beginning. Sure enough, Grandfather has started a campaign of dissension that leads to frightening schoolgirls, a proposal of marriage to a chance acquaintance and general chaos culminating with Grandfather being locked in the luggage van where he and the boys complete their journey making music.

When the group arrives in London, they go to their hotel where Norm leaves them to sort out their fan mail. However, Grandfather has noticed that a certain amount of good-humoured banter is directed at Ringo. Here, thinks Grandfather, is the weak link in the chain. Instead of staying in the hotel the four boys sneak out to enjoy themselves at a twist club and Grandfather, trading his clothes for a waiter's suit, heads straight for a gambling club, passing himself off as Lord John McCartney. Again the boys have to rescue him, much to the old man's indignation.

The following day sees the boys plunged into the bustle of the television world. Press conferences, rehearsals, make-up, running from place to place, being shepherded by the harassed Norm and got at by the television show's neurotic director [Victor Spinetti], and always in the background is Grandfather, interfering, disrupting and needling Ringo.

Only for a moment are the boys free. They can enjoy themselves playing in a large, open field, but even that doesn't last. John, however, does make the most of every second, he is always for the here and now. Paul tries keeping things on an even keel and George has a blind doggedness that sees him through. But the strain begins to tell on Ringo.

Grandfather, of course, plays on this, pointing out the barrenness of Ringo's life and finally goading him into walking out into the world outside of the group.

The other three boys go out searching for Ringo, leaving Norm to fume and the director to worry himself to near collapse at the possibility of no show.

Meanwhile, Ringo has found the world outside not too friendly, and through a series of encounters and misunderstandings, gets himself arrested. He is taken to the station, where he meets up with Grandfather who has been taken into protective custody. Grandfather storms at the Police Sergeant [Deryck Guyler] and manages to escape, leaving Ringo behind in the police station.

He gets back to the television theatre and tells the boys who, pursued again, but this time by the police – go and rescue Ringo.

Finally they are able to do their show in front of a live audience.

The show does well but as soon as it is finished, again it is the mad dash on to the next plane for the next show. The past thirty-six hours have been a hard day's night. The next thirty-six will be the same" (Gross 1990: 18-19).

The plot contains several themes that are developed as the movie progresses. One of the most dominant themes is the theme of escape. On the one hand, The Beatles are constantly trying to escape the hordes of screaming fans pursuing them throughout the movie. On the other hand, the theme is a direct part of the storyline, as Ringo Starr escapes from the band in order to reflect on his own identity. The theme of escape is combined with a sense of permanent movement, around which the narrative in *A Hard Day's Night* is tightly structured (vgl. Murray/Rolston 2001: 14). As pointed out by Alun Owen, "[t]hey are always on the move, usually from one box to another, hotels, cars, dressing rooms, but they know what they want [and] where they are going" (Harry 1985: 16).

Themes and Styles

The first sequence already establishes the predominant sense of movement and escape. To the sound of the title song "A Hard Day's Night" The Beatles (without Paul) are shown as they are running from a mob of fans. John, George and Ringo are running along a pedestrian way, while a mass of people is chasing them. Ringo and George stumble and fall but get up again just in time not to be run over by their fans. They manage to get on a train that leaves the station as soon as The Beatles are aboard. The following scenes take place on the train, where The Beatles move from their compartment to the restaurant car and finally finish their journey performing their song "I Should Have Known Better" in the luggage car. In order to convey an air of authenticity, Richard Lester shot the train sequences on a real train constantly going from London to Minehead and back. Associate Producer Denis O'Dell confirms that it was important to Richard Lester to use a real train instead of back-projected images in a studio in order to evoke the flair of documentary: "I wanted to shoot these sequences on a genuine moving train, which pleased Richard who was glad to be working closely with someone who shared his vision and who was prepared to go to the extra distance to achieve the necessary effect. [...] We had makeshift camera dollies specially built to fit the walkways and aisles of the train's interior and a carriage fitted out with a power generator" (Neaverson/O'Dell 2002: 34).

In *A Hard Day's Night*, The Beatles always seem to be on the run, or at least on the move. The theme of escape is, however, one of the dominant themes in all of The Beatles' movies, except *Let It Be*. While the need to escape from their fans was certainly a phenomenon based on The Beatles' real experiences, the focus on escape in The Beatles' movies in the context of the times they were produced, also allows a more general interpretation of The Beatles as representatives of a new generation escaping from the restraints of the traditional social system in Great Britain.

"Die Flucht ist nicht nur Bewegung im Raum der Stadt bzw. der Genre-Topik, sondern bringt darüber hinaus einen schöpferischen élan vital jenseits stabiler Organismen, Identitäten und Bedeutungen zur Wirkung. Dieses – sagen wir es ruhig – revolutionäre Moment der Flucht tritt in *A Hard Day's Night* nicht viel weniger deutlich zutage als in späteren Beatles-Filmen (im TV-Special *Magical Mystery Tour*, 1967 und in *Yellow Submarine*, 1968), in denen die Flucht zum psychedelischen Trip, zur Drogen-, Bus- und U-Boot-Reise in neue Empfindungswelten wird. Der Film verbindet die euphorische Gewissheit, dass die neue Jugendkultur alle Körper und Beziehungen in Leichtigkeit und Bewegung versetzen werde, mit Momenten des spielerischen Verteilungskampfes um sozialen Raum (Beatles vs. Polizei, Parkwächter, Spießer im Zugabteil)" (Robnik 2000: 188).

The way The Beatles deal with authority in *A Hard Day's Night* illustrates the change of social paradigms in Great Britain and introduces the theme of generation gap in a light-hearted manner. The character of Paul's Grandfather is an important factor in developing this theme throughout the movie. By contrasting Grandfather's mean ways with The Beatles' humorous and good-natured attitude, The Beatles become representatives of a new generation of humorous and decent young men, who have little in common with the war generation. Although this theme is often used in the genre of pop musicals, it is developed in a rather innovative way in *A Hard Day's Night*, as The Beatles counter the insults targeted at them by characters representing their parents' generation with their characteristic surreal sense of humor and sarcasm. In addition, with Paul's Grandfather being the interfering troublemaker, Owen achieves a reversal of the usual generation gap argument. While The Beatles are portrayed as rather decent and well meaning young men, "the representative of the older generation in their midst is far less law abiding" (Murray/Rolston 2001: 35). While this approach would probably appeal to a large segment of The Beatles' young target audience, it also showed older viewers that The Beatles are funny and decent people. In 1964, this way of portraying the pop group caused a greater acceptance of The Beatles among viewers belonging to different generations (vgl. Murray/Rolston 2001: 35). As pointed out by Bob Neaverson, *A Hard Day's Night* "helped to consolidate their appeal to a teenage audience.

Conversely, however, it also helped to develop and expand their appeal beyond that of contemporary youth [...]" (Neaverson 1997: 27). While The Beatles' music and the portrayal of their screen personae mainly attracted their younger fans, "the form and ideology of the film appealed more to the aesthetic tastes of an adult audience than any previous pop movie" (Neaverson 1997: 27).

Another main theme consists of the relations between image, identity, and reality. Basically, this theme mirrors The Beatles' playful attitude toward their own representation in the media, which they had developed at an early stage in their career. Lester and Owen engage in a subtle game concerning reality and fabricated image. Although Lester uses the formal characteristics typical of documentaries to establish a sense of reality and immediacy, the viewer is constantly reminded that *A Hard Day's Night* is actually a fictional movie, as The Beatles are repeatedly shown in short surreal sequences. Film scholar Bob Neaverson identifies the most dominant aesthetic influences coming from "a number of different genres, most notably drama-documentary and 'direct-cinema' documentary" (Neaverson 1997: 16). The use of real locations, hand-held cameras, and naturalistic lighting contribute to a sense of actuality which resembles the newsreel documentary material about the Beatles filmed at the time.

For a long time scholars and critics have neglected Albert and David Maysles' documentary *What's Happening! The Beatles in the USA*, which the two filmmakers produced during The Beatles' first U.S. visit. Although Richard Lester has apparently never commented on it, The Maysles brothers' film seems to have been a quite substantial influence in the way *A Hard Day's Night* was realized.

Albert and David Maysles had established a reputation as two of America's most adventurous direct cinema documentary film-makers when they received a call from Brian Epstein's management agency, asking them to capture The Beatles' arrival in the United States on film and to produce a behind-the-scenes documentary about the group's first trip to the United States (vgl. Geller 2002: 73). The Maysles had the opportunity to accompany and film The Beatles for the whole duration of their stay. In a 2003 interview, Albert Maysles explained that it was only possible to follow The Beatles' every move because he and his brother David owned modern equipment that allowed them to move easily: "That was at a time, fortunately, when my brother and I had already perfected the kind of instruments we needed. The camera that I could hold on my shoulder would be very quiet and the tape recorder [...] was so technically advanced that we could shoot without being connected with one another" (*The First U.S. Visit* 2003). The Maysles' direct cinema approach with hand-held camera and natural lighting allows a credible and apparently authentic look at The Beatles as they prepare their performance at the *Ed Sullivan Show* and as they travel from New York to Washington. The camera follows The Beatles to their hotel rooms and even films them at a late-night party at a nightclub in New York. The way The Beatles are portrayed backstage, in a car, in their hotel rooms, on the train, at press receptions, and at the airport strikingly resembles several scenes in *A Hard Day's Night*. This is hardly surprising, however, as it was indeed Lester and Shenson's intention to create a fictional documentary based upon The Beatles' actual public lives.

The British television channel Granada Television already broadcast a hastily edited version of The Maysles brothers' film on February 12, 1964. The short documentary was called *Yeah! Yeah! Yeah! – The Beatles in New York*, and it was repeated the next day, when fans inundated Granada Television with requests (vgl. Miles 2001: 133). Although it was only a rough cut of the filmed material, its immediacy and the excitement it conveys probably inspired Lester to make some aesthetic decisions concerning his own portrayal of The Beatles.

In 2002, Albert Maysles explained how his film was kept from being released for decades: "The Granada deal was that we'd have the complete rights for the US and they'd have the complete rights for England. However, because of the English laws The Beatles never signed release forms. Our film was finished, Richard Lester went and saw our film and … that's all I'm prepared to say" (Male 2002: 80). For years, the Maysles brothers' film was lost in The Beatles' archives. Finally, in 1994, Apple decided to release an edited version of the movie on DVD in the United States. Another ten years later, the film was repackaged again and saw its first worldwide release on DVD to commemorate the 40th anniversary of The Beatles' invasion of the United States. The anniversary received national attention in the U.S. and led to another revival of public interest in The Beatles, and the DVD release *The First U.S. Visit* even topped the *Billboard* DVD charts in February 2004.

Although it is quite certain that Lester and his team saw the Maysles' documentary on television, it must be noted that there were several other important reasons for the aesthetic decisions made by the producers of *A Hard Day's Night*. First of all, the basic idea of making a fake documentary about The Beatles already dictates certain aesthetic devices in order to make the movie credible. For instance, The Beatles always being on the move means that a hand-held camera is likely to be used to convey the immediacy of movement and a sense of realism. Second, Richard Lester has repeatedly stated that he has always admired the French New Wave cinema. The genre's most prominent exponents, Jean-Luc Godard and François Truffaut, wanted to achieve a realistic portrayal of life using black-and-white film stock, hand-held cameras, and naturalistic lighting (vgl. Murray/Rolston 2001: 49). In addition, the genre of 'kitchen sink films' had been popularized in Great Britain. This was another genre concerned with the portrayal of realistic situations and everyday life. Prominent examples of kitchen sink dramas are the movies *A Kind of Loving* (1962) and *This Sporting Life* (1963). Considering the contemporary trend of realism in movies and Richard Lester's own background in making films, the cinematic means and devices for creating such immediate, realistic films were certainly well known to Lester at the time *A Hard Day's Night* was made, and he became the first auteur to apply the aesthetic and techniques common to realist genres to the genre of musicals. Inspired by the realism of the 'nouvelle vague', Lester and his production team made use of real locations, such as the train, the train station and the theatre. Not only does this aesthetic decision work well in the tradition of direct cinema and nouvelle vague, but it also reflects a realistic situation in The Beatles' every day life as touring entertainers. While Albert Maysles likes to point out the fact that *A Hard Day's Night* includes a train ride similar to the one in his own documentary, it must be mentioned that The Beatles often travelled by train when they were on tour, especially in Europe. Therefore it is not necessarily true that Alun Owen and Richard Lester were inspired by the Maysles' portrayal of The Beatles' train ride from New York to Washington.

The influence of nouvelle vague films on *A Hard Day's Night* is, however, by no means restricted to the aesthetic dimension of the movie. It is also apparent in the development of plot and storyline as well as in the depiction of the individual characters. Although the movie does not completely lack conventional cause-effect chains, the narrative contains a number of sequences that do not contribute to the advancement of the plot. This kind of storytelling is very much in the tradition of the nouvelle vague, where characters are not depicted as goal-oriented but merely 'exist' in rather independent sequences (vgl. Neaverson 1997: 17). Unlike most of the contemporary British pop musicals, *A Hard Day's Night* did not merely imitate conventional narrative structure and film style of the Hollywood musical (vgl. Neaverson 1997: 15). In *A Hard Day's Night*, the group members are actually portrayed very much in the fashionable and contemporary way of the nouvelle vague, where characters often "drift aimlessly" and "engage in actions on the spur of the moment" (Bordwell/Thompson 1979). For instance, Ringo Starr's solo sequence is a perfect example of such New Wave aesthetic. In this famous sequence, Starr is shown as he walks wistfully along a river bank. He has escaped the television studio and has disguised himself in order not to be recognized by hysterical fans. However, being by himself he appears to feel lonely and melancholic. When he encounters a young boy at the river bank, the two strike up a short conversation. As the boy leaves to play with three of his friends waiting for him by the river, Ringo realizes that he also needs to be with his three friends, the other Beatles, in order to be happy (vgl. Murray/Rolston 2001: 44). The constellation of the boys clearly parallels The Beatles' group structure, and the scene of the boys playing and running around the river bank echoes the "Can't Buy Me Love" scene which allows The Beatles to break free on a soccer field. In his solo sequence, Starr resembles the protagonists of Truffaut's and Godard's early movies. The way Starr walks down the streets of London and along the river bank is quite similar to the way François Truffaut's most famous character, Antoine Doinel, wanders through the streets of Paris in the films *The 400 Blows* (1959) and *Bed & Board* (1970).

Image and Identity

Ringo is the best-developed character in *A Hard Day's Night*, as his solo sequence provides a more detailed depiction of his inner feelings and thoughts than the solo sequences of John and George. In addition, Ringo is also the central character of the movie, as the movie's denouement depends on his return to the band at the end of *A Hard Day's Night*. By providing this central role for Ringo Starr and allowing their drummer to become the key figure in their first feature film, The Beatles' management compensated for the lack of attention given to Starr in the media at the time. It was important to The Beatles to be seen as a unit consisting of four equally important band members. While the group's singers Lennon, McCartney, and Harrison usually had a more obvious presence on The Beatles' records than Ringo Starr, Starr's natural talent for acting allowed him to play the group's main character in *A Hard Day's Night*, *Help!*, *Yellow Submarine* and in *The Beatles* television series. In *A Hard Day's Night*, Ringo is portrayed as a thoughtful and slightly melancholic character that feels neglected and is worried that nobody really loves him. Owen, who tried to use the real Beatles as basis for the characters, was apparently aware of the fact that The Beatles' drummer had always enjoyed slightly less public attention than the others and, having joined the band last, he was still trying hard to be accepted as an equal band member, although The Beatles' management intended to represent them as democratic and equal in public. In his autobiography, published already in 1964, manager Brian Epstein hints at the fact that it had actually taken a while for Starr to be fully accepted by The Beatles and their staff.

"Ringo Starr, last to become a Beatle, came into the group not because I wanted him but because the boys did. To be completely honest, I was not at all keen to have him. I thought his drumming rather loud and his appearance unimpressive and I could not see why he was important to the Beatles. But again I trusted their instincts and I am grateful now. He has become an excellent Beatle and a devoted friend. He is warm and wry-witted, a good drummer, and I like him enormously. He is a very uncomplicated, very nice young man" (Epstein 1998: 164-165).

Some facts in the Beatles' history suggest that Starr's alter ego in the movie was certainly based upon his own characteristics: At Starr's first recording session with The Beatles, George Martin replaced him with a session drummer because he had been disappointed by Starr's predecessor Pete Best (vgl. Martin/Hornsby 1994: 123). Starr felt very insulted and reportedly never forgave George Martin. According to Martin, Starr still brings up the topic every time they meet (vgl. *Beatles Anthology* 2003: DVD 1). In 1968, Ringo Starr was the first Beatle to temporarily leave the band during The Beatles' recording sessions for their double album *The Beatles*. In the band's official autobiography, *The Beatles Anthology*, he explains that he felt unloved and did not think he was a good drummer anymore. Only after the other Beatles had assured him that he was 'the best drummer in the world' he returned to the group (vgl. *Anthology* 2003: DVD 4). It seems as though Starr did actually feel neglected by his band-mates at times, and that he was treated like an outsider by some members of The Beatles' staff. Apparently, Owen realized Starr's unique position in the band and designed the character traits of Starr's movie persona by exaggerating some of Ringo Starr's actual characteristics.

Throughout the film, the theme of image and identity is explored in various ways. Each individual Beatle features in a solo-sequence, in which his screen personae finds or defines his own image and identity, except for Paul McCartney, whose solo sequence was cut from the film. By providing a starring scene to John, George, and Ringo, it was possible to introduce them as individuals. What is more, by highlighting each Beatle's individuality, "the film offers its audience a range of personalities with which to empathise" (Murray/Rolston 2001: 31).

While Ringo Starr's key role in the film projected a rather many-sided image of the drummer, the characterizations of his band-mates are considerably more stereotyped. John Lennon is portrayed as a sharp-witted cynic and rebel, continuously provoking Norm, The Beatles' manager in the film. As described by Rolston and Murray, the character of John would "rather be cracking dirty jokes or chatting up school girls than discussing anything serious with the management. [...] His comic antics and surreal behaviour usually have an undermining effect on the older characters and authority figures in the film" (Murray/Rolston 2001: 32). Besides the manager Norm, also the gentleman on the train and the television director are on the receiving end of John's relentless sarcasm. His solo sequence features a dialogue with an actress called Millie who is not sure whether John is who she thinks he is. The sequence quite cleverly reflects the movie's theme of real identity and public image, as John and the actress engage in a short conversation about John's identity.

"[Millie:] Hello.
[John:] Hello!
[Millie:] Wait a minute – don't tell me...
[John:] No, I'm not.
[Millie:] Oh, you are.
[John:] I'm not.
[Millie:] Oh, you are. I know you are.
[John:] I'm not. No.
[Millie:] You look just like him.
John:] Do I? You're the first one that's said that ever.
[Millie:] Yes, you do. Look.
[John (looking in a mirror):] No, my eyes are lighter.
[...]
[Millie:] Oh, yes. Your nose is, very.
[John:] Me nose. Is it?
[Millie:] Well, I would have said so.
[John:] Oh, you know him better, though.
[Millie:] I do not. He's only a casual acquaintance.
[John:] That's what you say.
[Millie:] What have you heard?
[John:] It's all over the place
[Millie:] Is it? Is it really?
[John:] Mmm, but I wouldn't have it. I stuck up for you.
[Millie:] I knew I could rely on you.
[John:] Thanks.
[Millie (putting on glasses):] You don't look like him at all.
[John (turning away, off):] She looks more like him than I do."
(*A Hard Day's Night* 2002)

When Owen was writing the screenplay, he was certainly aware that the movie would serve as a vehicle to convey The Beatles' individual images. Having witnessed The Beatles' rather playful attitude toward their public image, Owen included Lennon's solo sequence as some sort of reflection on the movie's theme of image and identity on a slightly surreal level. Out of nowhere the character of Millie appears backstage at The Beatles' rehearsal for a television show. She stops John, convinced she knows his identity. When John denies being 'him,' the woman is struck by 'their' resemblance. Millie and John even examine John's reflection – his image – in the mirror. Finally, when Millie ends the dialogue by pointing out that John does not "look like him at all," John appears to be very insulted and turns away. The dialogue works as a direct reference to the relationship between public image and real identity. Millie cannot see a difference between John and his image at first. When John insists that he is not 'him', she believes that they are at least quite similar. Only when she puts on her glasses to take a very close look at John, she realizes that there is no resemblance between John and his image. While the dialogue is taking place, actors in full costume rush about in the background, supporting the movie's game with masked identities.

Throughout *A Hard Day's Night* John is repeatedly provoking Norm, The Beatles' manager in the movie. Consequently, Norm, who is played by actor Norman Rossington, threatens to tell the 'truth' about John. Interestingly, The Beatles' real manager Brian Epstein had actually experienced similar harassments from John Lennon, as depicted in his autobiography.

"None of the Beatles suffer fools gladly. John suffers them not at all and can be very acid, even cruel, if he is goaded. [...] Sometimes he has been abominably rude to me. I remember once attending a recording session at EMI Studios in St. John's Wood. The Beatles were on the studio floor and I was with their recording manager, George Martin, in the control room. The intercom was on and I remarked that there was some sort of flaw in Paul's voice in the number "Till There Was You." John heard it and bellowed back: "We'll make the records. You just go on counting your percentages." And he meant it. I was terribly annoyed and hurt because it was in front of the recording staff and the rest of the Beatles" (Epstein 1998: 164).

Owen was apparently aware of Lennon's tendency to provoke Brian Epstein and bases the conflicting relationship between John and Norm upon the actual situation between Lennon and Epstein.

Rolsten and Murray insist that "[t]he film subtly highlights the fact that the Beatles' public personae are a creation, quite detached from their actual personalities. The film, too, is at heart a piece of Beatles merchandising, rather than 'the truth'" (Murray/Rolston 2001: 41). Although there can be no doubt as to the artificiality of The Beatles' public personae in general, the distinction between reality and image is quite blurred in *A Hard Day's Night*. On the one hand, the movie is realized in a way to evoke the sense of realism because of its documentary-like aesthetics. What is more, not only do The Beatles play a band called The Beatles, but also the names of the other characters partially resemble the actors' real names. All of these facts support the notion of *A Hard Day's Night* being a mere merchandising vehicle designed to deceive a juvenile audience into believing the artificial public image projected by the movie. On the other hand, the surreal moments as well as the meta-textual reflections on image and identity are used in a way to suggest that what is presented in the movie is certainly not the truth. The last sequence shows The Beatles ascending to the sky by helicopter, and they cast to the ground the publicity photographs Paul's Grandfather had wanted to sell to the fans. It indeed seems as though The Beatles symbolically discard their public personae by throwing away the publicity images featuring the group members posing happily and in a perfectly acceptable way, as well as the fake-autographs designed by Paul's Grandfather (vgl. Murray/Rolston 2001: 41).

This rejection of public images is also the main focus in George Harrison's solo sequence, which takes place in a fashion editor's office. When George walks into the office, he is mistaken for "a good type, a real one," that is, someone in the style of The Beatles. As they directly confront him, the fashion professionals cannot tell George from his image. "To the characters in the film, The Beatles' fabricated images are more real than the actual Beatles" (Murray/Rolston 2001: 40). Actually, the fashion editor in the office wants to transform George into a role model for 'teenage consumers.' George shocks the editor when he expresses his contempt for other teenage idols that have been 'created' by the editor's agency. George discards these idols' artificiality and emphasizes the fact how terribly ridiculous he and his friends find such role models, because they are often completely out of touch with reality. The way George Harrison confronts the fashion designer with his honest opinion supports The Beatles' image of credible young men who break showbusiness-conventions insofar as they are apparently 'authentic' instead of glamorous and superficial.

Again, Brian Epstein's description of George Harrison supports the public image projected by *A Hard Day's Night*.

"George is remarkably easy to be with. [...]
George is the business Beatle. He is curious about money and wants to know how much is coming in and how and what best to do with it to make it work. [...] Strangers find him an easy conversationalist because he is a good listener and shows a genuine interest in the outside world.

Virtually, if Paul has the glamour, John the command, Ringo the little man's quaintness, George with his slow, wide, crooked smile is the boy next door" (Epstein 1998: 166-167).

The description of George Harrison provided by Epstein in his autobiography is quite adequate in relation to *A Hard Day's Night*. In his solo scene, George Harrison is actually portrayed as very aware of business decisions and mechanisms, while he also appears to be the most easygoing of the four throughout the movie.

Considering contemporary press reports, television appearances, radio shows, and press conferences, the individual Beatles' public image, which was based upon some of their actual character traits, is presented consistently in a variety of media. The only exception is the portrayal of Paul McCartney in *A Hard Day's Night*, which did quite awkwardly not support the high profile he generally had in the media at the time. In *A Hard Day's Night*, Paul McCartney comes across as the least 'natural' Beatle. According to Richard Lester, this is probably because McCartney was very much interested in theatre at the time and constantly went to performances with his girlfriend, actress Jane Asher. Therefore, he might have been trying to act more theatrically than the other Beatles (vgl. Murray 2002: 116). It is quite possible that McCartney's theatrical approach to acting resulted in his solo sequence being cut from the film. In interviews Lester usually claims that the scene simply did not work very well in the finished film. However, leaving it out inevitably led to a rather flat portrayal of Paul McCartney's screen ego. While he was regarded as the 'cute one' among The Beatles, *A Hard Day's Night* did nothing to expand or improve McCartney's public image. John Lennon, George Harrison, and especially Ringo Starr's screen egos were much more developed than Paul McCartney's character. As they were also portrayed in a rather stereotyped way, certain qualities could now easily be attributed to them, while McCartney's most important characteristic in *A Hard Day's Night* apparently was to look good. However, while Paul McCartney's performance in *A Hard Day's Night* did not prove adequate to his actual role in The Beatles, he developed a more multi-faceted image in subsequent years. McCartney has since designed one of the most complex public images in the music business. His varied activities – ranging from experimental music to children's cartoons – have led to conflicting portrayals in the mass media, which sometimes give the impression that Paul McCartney is actually several different artists.

In 1964, Epstein already hinted at Paul McCartney's multi-faceted character:

"Paul is temperamental and moody and difficult to deal with, but I know him very well and he me. [...] But he has enormous talent and inside he has a great tenderness and great feeling which are sometimes concealed by an angry exterior. I believe that he is the most obviously charming Beatle with strangers, autograph hunters, fans, and other artists. He has a magnificent smile and an eagerness both of which he uses, not for effect, but because he knows they are assets which will bring happiness to those around him. Paul is very much a world star, very musical, with a voice more melodic than John's and therefore more commercially acceptable" (Epstein 1998: 160-161).

The portrayal of The Beatles in *A Hard Day's Night* is designed to evoke an authentic and realistic impression. This is achieved by aesthetic devices typical of realist genres such as the documentary or cinéma vérité. On the level of storyline, however, reality is left behind as soon as the fictional character of Paul's Grandfather appears. First of all, Wilfrid Brambell, the actor portraying Paul's Grandfather, was a prolific actor widely known by British television audiences for his role as Albert Steptoe in the television show *Steptoe and Son*. In the series, Albert Steptoe's son often calls his father a 'dirty old man,' which resulted in a running joke in *A Hard Day's Night*, where The Beatles repeatedly point out that Paul's Grandfather is a 'very clean old man.' While this remark works quite well on the level of surrealism projected by the film, it is also a clever in-joke to British audiences familiar with Brambell's popular television series. Although The Beatles declare Paul's Grandfather to be a clean old man, he is the character causing most of the unpleasant situations for the group. Grandfather is introduced by Paul as a 'king mixer' and stirs up dissent and anxiety within the ranks of the band, and hence instigates the dramatic situations in the film. For instance, he uses Ringo's invitation to enter a casino, where the band finally finds him and drags him away; he creates a running feud between the TV director and the band; he persuades Ringo to go 'parading' on the streets of London rather than sitting in a TV studio (vgl. Murray/Rolston 2001: 35). Therefore, Paul's Grandfather fulfils the dramatic need to instigate conflicts to advance the movie's plot.

Performance Scenes

As pointed out above, *A Hard Day's Night* features performances of songs The Beatles wrote and recorded specifically for their first movie. Bob Neaverson correctly states that "prior to *A Hard Day's Night*, the majority of British and US pop musicals had relied upon the long-established tradition of song performance derived from the classical Hollywood musical" (Neaverson 2000: 154). Therefore, musical sequences in pop movies were generally based around the presentation of lip-synched performances of songs by the star, which essentially attempted to create and convey the illusion of actual diegetic performance. Previous stars such as Elvis Presley and Cliff Richard would perform their songs to a musical backing which was usually provided by a band seen on the screen. Sometimes these songs would serve some narrative purpose, expressing the performer's inner feelings or emphasizing a certain situation in the narrative (vgl. Murray/Rolston 2001: 39). In *A Hard Day's Night*, The Beatles' performances are not used to merely illustrate the narrative. Instead, Lester introduces a variety of innovations to highlight The Beatles' performance and to visualize the songs. For instance, thirteen minutes into the film, The Beatles, who are still on the train to London, suddenly break into a performance of their song "I Should Have Known Better." In this sequence, scenes of The Beatles performing "I Should Have Known Better" are inter-cut with scenes showing them playing cards in the same setting. In this sequence, Lester broke with the conventions of traditional musicals and pop musicals, as it was the first instance of a song performance in a musical that is not tied to the narrative in any way. What is more, by juxtaposing clips of a performance with seemingly arbitrary footage of the performers, Lester pioneered the field of modern music video, the main task of which is to illustrate popular music in a way to promote the musician or the musical product. While it had been common to have bands mime to their music, pop songs did not have to be tied to performance in movies anymore after *A Hard Day's Night*.

"I Should Have Known Better" is also another example of the director's intention of creating something more than a fictional documentary, as it contains elements pioneering the non-diegetic level of modern music videos. It is not the only sequence in *A Hard Day's Night* where the film takes a non-conformist attitude to both time and space. Richard Lester explains that he intended to introduce the audience to the surrealistic dimension of *A Hard Day's Night* by careful preparation of the scenes.

"[I]t was always clear that if you're going to play games with time and space for music, you need to warm the audience of its coming. A perfect example is the performance, on the train, in the baggage cage when The Beatles suddenly switch from playing cards to singing "I Should Have Known Better." Three or four minutes before that sequence, there's this scene where, first, The Beatles are in the carriage and then suddenly there's this quick shot of them outside the carriage, running and cycling and banging on the window to be let in. It's just a little thing to let the audience know that all is not just documentary" (Carr 1996: 31).

Following their disagreement with a conservative gentleman in the train compartment, The Beatles suddenly appear outside the moving train, pulling faces and taunting him with the schoolboy cliché, "Hey, Mister, can we have our ball back?" (Neaverson 1997: 18). After this surreal interlude, The Beatles perform "I Should Have Known Better," and the audience is now prepared for the unconventional way this scene is edited.

The sequence featuring "I Should Have Known Better" was groundbreaking, as it introduced a new way of presenting popular music on the movie screen. However, the way Richard Lester illustrated The Beatles' song "Can't Buy Me Love" was even more revolutionary in mainstream cinema. In the narrative, "Can't Buy Me Love" marks the point when The Beatles manage to break free from the confinements of their celebrity, if only for a short while. They are portrayed running and jumping around in a playing field, accompanied by their own hit single "Can't Buy Me Love". Some of the footage was shot from a helicopter, and the shaky pictures filmed by Gilbert Taylor using a hand-held camera show The Beatles from above as they enjoy their escape from stardom on a soccer field. In his autobiography, associate producer Denis O'Dell explains how Richard Lester managed to turn financial restrictions into stylistic innovations in this particular sequence.

"When we were doing the aerial shots from the helicopter, we realized that there would be a problem with camera shake, but we didn't have the time or the money to obtain gyroscopic stabilization equipment to overcome this. Rather than abandon the shooting, Richard told Gil Taylor to shoot on regardless. In the final edited version the camera shake works beautifully to echo the excitement of the soundtrack song and adds a new and experimental dimension to the movie as a whole" (Neaverson/O'Dell 2002: 32-33).

With the sequences featuring "I Should Have Known Better" and "Can't Buy Me Love," *A Hard Day's Night* was arguably the first film of its genre to fully realize the illustrative potential of pop music. As explained by Neaverson, "the 'Can't Buy Me Love' sequence [...] broke entirely with conventional approaches and in the process freed the musical from its traditional generic slavery" (Neaverson 2000: 154). The pop song works in a similar manner to conventional incidental music, "as an abstract entity capable of punctuating action which is not performance-oriented" (Neaverson 1997: 19). Therefore, the sequence conveyed and supported the emotion inherent in The Beatles' song more adequately than a mere performance segment would probably have done.

While the footage supporting The Beatles' songs "I Should Have Known Better", "Can't Buy Me Love," and the opening sequence featuring "A Hard Day's Night" could be regarded as precursors of contemporary music videos,[6] Lester's direction of The Beatles' concert at the end of the movie set standards concerning the way concert performances have been filmed ever since. For this particular film shoot, the La Scala Theater in Soho was converted to a television rehearsal studio. Lester used six cameras to film this performance sequence to shoot seventeen minutes of footage on only one day (vgl. Yule 1994: 14). The use of six cameras allowed Lester and Gilbert Taylor, the director of photography, to capture the interaction between The Beatles and their audience in an authentic way, as it was possible to juxtapose footage of The Beatles' performance with footage showing the fans' immediate, hysterical reactions in close-ups. This way of filming enabled Lester to edit the film in a dynamic way which reflected the excitement and hysteria surrounding The Beatles' performance and conveyed The Beatles' live impact to the movie screen.

Lester's portrayal of The Beatles on stage differed greatly to the way performance clips had previously been produced. On TV as well as in movies, performances had usually been filmed statically from front and side, with most emphasis upon vocal performance rather than instrumentation, as the main diegetic source (vgl. Neaverson 1997: 19). The performances filmed at the Scala Theatre are fundamentally different from this conventional approach, as The Beatles are filmed from a multiplicity of angles – from above and behind. What makes the performance footage in *A Hard Day's Night* special is the fact that Lester also provides a detailed view of the instrumentation, i.e. close-ups of George Harrison's guitar and Ringo Starr's drums. By focusing on the instruments, Lester contributed significantly to popularizing The Beatles' gear, which became an important factor in the visual representation of the band until they stopped touring 1966. After seeing *A Hard Day's Night*, The Beatles' fans were definitely aware of Starr's Ludwig drum kit, McCartney's particular Höfner bass guitar, and Lennon and Harrison's Rickenbacker guitars. In addition, Richard Lester also managed to convey the group's typical stage attitude of playing their instruments and singing their songs without any apparent effort. This seemingly careless way of performing had become an important part of their stage show, and it distinguished them from other contemporary groups, such as The Who or The Rolling Stones, whose members seemed to be entirely engaged in the performance. The Beatles' performances seemed rather detached in comparison – the band members evoked the impression as though they were actually thinking about something else than performing in front of an audience. Drehli Robnik provides an accurate description of how Les-

---

6   When MTV was launched in the mid-eighties, Richard Lester was actually awarded a birth certificate by MTV America.

ter visualized The Beatles' live performance, and how it supported their apparently careless attitude toward performance.

"Was, so frage ich (mich), gibt es für Ringo in praktisch jeder Playback-Szene von *A Hard Day's Night* und *Help!* zu grinsen? Wohin schaut er da immer, während er so tut, als würde er trommeln, was sieht er da im Off der Szenerie [...]? [...] Abseits von Kausalität und Intentionalität ist die hartnäckig wiederkehrende Abgelenktheit nichtsdestotrotz bezeichnend und sinnwirksam im Rahmen einer Inszenierung, die das Musikmachen mit Nachdruck als etwas zeigt, das keiner sonderlichen Konzentration bedarf. Der Akt des Musizierens kommt bei Lester gänzlich dezentriert und anti-expressiv ins Bild, als eine beiläufig und im Halbschlaf ausgeführte Tätigkeit [...]. Diese entspannte Distanz zum Einsatz von Stimmen und Instrumenten, aus der heraus nicht nur Ringo, sondern alle Fab Four mehr oder weniger zerstreut und zumeist in verschiedene Richtungen ins Off grinsen, unterscheidet sich wesentlich von jener existenziellen Phänomenologie des Musikmachens, welche die Visualisierung populärer Musik dominiert. Üblicherweise sieht man PopmusikerInnen (sofern sie singen oder Instrumente bedienen) in pathetischer Anspannung und Konzentration von Körper und Bewusstsein, und ihre Musik erscheint als kreativer Ausdruck, der sich in klarer Ausrichtung an ein anvisiertes Gegenüber (Sexualpartner, Rivale, Publikum...) wendet. Das gilt sowohl für Musikfilme, TV-Auftritte und Clips im Gefolge der Beatles-Filme als auch für die ihnen vorangehenden Filme mit Rock 'n' Rollern wie Elvis, Johnny Halliday oder Peter Kraus" (Robnik 2000: 187-188).

The Impact of *A Hard Day's Night*

According to journalist Roy Carr, United Artists executives from the United States tried to persuade Richard Lester "into wiping The Beatles' voices from off the soundtrack and re-dubbing it with mid-Atlantic voices supplied by professional actors" (Carr 1996: 46). The American company apparently feared that the American public would not be able to understand The Beatles' Liverpool 'Scouse' accent and would consequently not want to see the movie. Lester was reportedly furious about this suggestion and did not replace The Beatles' voices. In Great Britain, The Beatles' way of speaking had been an important factor in the Beatlemania phenomenon. The British public had become used to The Beatles' particular way of talking and regarded it as an entertaining feature that was also exploited in the press. With their Liverpool accent, they were regarded as 'four ordinary boys next door.' As pointed out by Bob Neaverson, "[t]he group's unselfconscious projection of themselves as 'ordinary' and largely 'unaffected' working-class boys further endeared them to the grassroots 'underdog' sympathies of the British public and popular press, who, in their patriotic stories of the group's fame, wealth and international 'conquests', upheld them as symbols of the new social mobility and 'classlessness' of sixties Britain" (Neaverson 1997: 22). The way The Beatles' artificially stuck to their Liverpool accents was actually a quite considerable factor in the way they contributed to undermining the British class system. Before The Beatles, artists had usually tried to avoid local dialects, because dialects had diminished their chances to succeed nationwide. Peter Brown, one of Brian Epstein's personal assistants, explains that "[i]n London, the Liverpool accent was a sign that you were poor and badly educated. It was important if you were going to be successful that you get rid of it" (Wiener 1993: 148). As unusual as The Beatles' vernacular initially was in British public life, it was considered to be even more peculiar in the United States and almost led to *A Hard Day's Night* being re-dubbed. The following year, The Beatles actually had to comply with King Features' proviso that they use an American actor for the voices of John Lennon and George Harrison in The Beatles cartoon series.

A Hard Day's Night was the first production in film history already making profits before the actual movie was being distributed to the cinemas. This unique situation unfolded because of the high advance orders for The Beatles' soundtrack LP of the same title. With orders of more than 2 million, The Beatles were already topping the charts before the album was actually released. Since United Artists had acquired the license to release the movie soundtrack, they had already earned back the £200,000 budget and gone into profit by the time the film prints were finally distributed to the theatres. If United Artists had not earned anything with the soundtrack album, they would still have been very pleased with the commercial success of the movie itself as, according to Roy Carr, "demand for *A Hard Day's Night* resulted in the unprecedented world wide order of between 1,500 and 1,800 prints of the movie. The United States alone accounted for 700 prints while the UK took a minimum of 110" (Carr 1996: 47). The movie simultaneously opened in 500 cinemas and earned $1.3 million in rentals during its first week. The movie brought in approximately $14 million on its initial release (vgl. Harry 1985: 27). Considering the low production costs, the movie became one of the most profitable films of all time. In addition to the movie's commercial success, it also received two Academy Award nominations. Alun Owen was nominated for an Oscar for his script, while George Martin was nominated for best musical direction.

The world premiere of *A Hard Day's Night* was celebrated at the London Pavilion on July 6, 1964. Princess Margaret and Lord Snowdon were also in attendance and posed with The Beatles for the press. The presence of royalty added another touch of acceptance by the establishment to The Beatles' reputation, making The Beatles the first pop group to be officially approved by establishment figures.

A Hard Day's Night was first shown on American television in 1968 and has received repeated screenings in the United States and in Great Britain. In Britain the film was broadcast over the Christmas period in 1970, 1971 and 1973. The first-ever television screening of *A Hard Day's Night* generated quite some public interest and was even responsible for the re-entry of the soundtrack album into the charts, where it peaked at number 30.

The Beatles' image from 1964 was still projected to the world at a time when they had already completely changed their appearance and attitudes, i.e. when they had dissolved as a working unit. As The Beatles themselves had reduced their television appearances since the height of Beatlemania in 1964, the effect of reinforcing their anachronistic image in 1968 should not be underestimated. While they were still highly successful recording artists, they had estranged themselves to a considerable part of their target audience, as many of their fans did not share The Beatles' views on drugs, culture and politics. Showing *A Hard Day's Night* on television in 1968 thus reminded the public of The Beatles and their image at the time they had reached the pinnacle of their popularity. Producer Walter Shenson, however, was not very pleased with the fact that The Beatles' movies were shown on television: "I'm angry with United Artists. I don't think they ever had the respect for the Beatles' films that they deserve. They considered them exploitation films and let them go for stupid hundred dollar bookings and TV. They should have held them back" (Harry 1985: 27). In 1979, Walter Shenson regained control of the film. He re-released it in the theaters for a limited time in 1981 and licensed the release as a video cassette in 1984. In 2001, Miramax released *A Hard Day's Night* on DVD in the United States and in Great Britain. The Beatles themselves did not promote any of the re-releases. For instance, none of The Beatles took part in the 1994 television special *You Can't Do That: The Making of A Hard Day's Night*, hosted by Phil Collins, nor in the production of an extensive bonus DVD released in a package with the original film in 2001. Finally, in July 2004, Paul McCartney attended a private screening of *A Hard Day's Night*, in order to commemorate its 40th anniversary and to promote the movie's worldwide release on DVD.

HELP!

'Another Exploitation Picture': The Story of The Beatles' Second Movie

The worldwide success of *A Hard Day's Night* and The Beatles' continuing success as the world's most popular band encouraged United Artists to produce a second movie starring the Fab Four. The Beatles had actually signed a contract for three movies with United Artists, which suggests that they were indeed looking for a way to establish themselves as actors.

The Beatles' second movie was budgeted at £400,000, which, according to producer Walter Shenson, "still wasn't a lot of money in those days" (Gross 1990: 25), although it was twice the budget provided for The Beatles' first movie. As with *A Hard Day's Night*, the production company treated the movie as another exploitation picture. Screenwriter Marc Behm had handed in a script called *Eight Arms to Hold You* to Richard Lester via actor Peter Sellers. Lester asked Charles Wood, who had written the screenplay for Lester's movie *The Knack...and How to Get It*, to revise the screenplay. In only ten days Wood redrafted the script and returned it to Lester (vgl. Yule 1994: 95).[7] However, *Eight Arms to Hold You* proved to be an impossible song title for John Lennon and Paul McCartney, who had been asked to compose the movie's theme song. Consequently, Lester was asked to come up with a new title for the second Beatles movie. He initially changed the name to *Help, Help*, but was informed that such a title had already been registered with the Writers' Guild of America (vgl. Carr 1996: 68). To avoid legal confrontation, Lester decided to just place an exclamation mark at the end of the title. Thus it was decided to call the movie *Help!*, and John Lennon and Paul McCartney composed the title song for it.

On October 30, 1964, the press was informed that The Beatles' second movie would be a comedy-thriller. As pointed out by Walter Shenson, *Help!* was "an attempt not to do another day in the life of the Beatles" (Gross 1990: 25). Richard Lester confirms that while he and the production team "had to make certain that they still played themselves" it was important not to do what had been done with *A Hard Days Night* – "show [The Beatles] at work" (Carr 1996: 61). Consequently, a spectacular fantasy story was dreamed up and The Beatles were shown on the run

---

7   Bob Neaverson's account of how the screenplay came into existence slightly differs. He claims that Richard Lester and Joe McGrath wrote the original treatment for the movie and that Marc Behm was asked to write the screenplay by Lester (vgl. Neaverson 1997: 32-33).

from religious fanatics and a mad scientist determined to obtain one of Ringo's rings. While the movie still retains the notion of The Beatles being themselves, the makers of *Help!* had no intention of attempting to construct an illusion of reality (vgl. Neaverson 1997: 32). United Artists' press release provides a summary of the movie's storyline:

"In the Eastern Temple of the Goddess Kaili a human sacrifice is about to be made. But the executioner, the High Priest Clang, is stopped by the beautiful Ahme, priestess of the cult who has discovered that the victim is not wearing the sacrificial ring essential for the ritual.

On the other side of the world the Beatles are performing. Ringo sits on the stage playing the drums and amongst his many rings is – the ring – a present from an unknown fan of another continent.

In the days that follow a series of mysterious events make no sense to the Beatles. At home, on the street, a strange force seems to be directed by Ringo. A gang of thugs descend upon the boys and attempt to amputate Ringo's entire hand – and the Beatles realise that it is Ringo's new ring they must have.

After several more attempts, Clang and his gang nearly succeed in stealing Ringo's whole person, but just in time they are saved by Ahme.

A few days later, while the boys are waiting for a meal in an Indian restaurant, the dreaded Clang and his henchman Bhuta appear disguised as waiters. They tell Ringo that since they cannot remove the ring from his finger he is to be sacrificed to the Goddess. The boys flee to the nearest jewellers and ask the man to cut off the offending ring. But the metal breaks the files and the cutting wheel.

The boys call next at a science laboratory run by Professor Foot and his assistant Algernon who put Ringo and his ring through every machine they have – to no avail; the ring resists all the assaults known to science. Foot decides that the ring has properties which could give the owner the power to rule the world and he confides to Algernon that he must get the ring. So the Beatles have two more enemies who will stop at nothing to retrieve the ring. Ahme once again comes to the rescue and they all flee from the laboratory – to the Alps!

In no time the Beatles' winter sport activities are interrupted by the arrival of Foot and Algernon intent on mayhem to be joined almost at once by Clang and his gang. After a frantic chase through snow and ice up mountains and down ski-lifts the boys scramble to the nearest railway station and gasp to the ticket man, 'London!'

Back home they confide their troubles to a Superintendent of Scotland Yard and tell him they must have protection in order to record in peace.

The next day the boys record two songs on Salisbury Plain, under the protection of the British Army, but Clang and his murderous thugs arrive and put the Beatles to flight. Ahme, in a tank, rescues them in the nick of time.

Back in London the murder attempts increase and the Beatles decide to leave the country until the heat is off. Heavily disguised they fly off to the Bahamas. But, alas, the world is too small a place for the Beatles, Clang and his gang and the two power-drunk scientists. Soon, the whole fray is resumed. But Ringo

learns the formula which releases him from the ring. The ring slips off and he hands it to Clang who hastily hands it on to Foot who tries to pass it on to Algernon and so on down the line.
Ahme and the Beatles at last find peace and the dreaded Kaili will have no more victims" (Harry 1985: 30-32).

Richard Lester failed to re-enlist cameraman Gilbert Taylor, who had been Lester's innovative collaborator on *A Hard Day's Night*. Instead, the assignment was handed to David Watkin, who had already worked on Lester's previous film *The Knack...and How to Get It*. Lester and Watkin set out to create their first color film in a way that emphasized the very fact that it was in color.

In 1962, Sean Connery had debuted in his first James Bond film *Dr No*. Since then, the James Bond movies had become the most popular British film productions. It seemed quite natural to Lester to incorporate some of the clichés from the Bond cycle in The Beatles' second movie. On the one hand, this attracted a contemporary, young audience that loved the Bond movies, and it proved that The Beatles were always up-to-date with the latest trends. On the other hand, this also provided an opportunity to make fun of the genre, which supported The Beatles' and Lester's reputation of being masters at playing and re-interpreting the products of contemporary popular culture. As observed by Bob Neaverson, "[a]lthough clearly not conceived from the outset as a Bond parody or pastiche, *Help!*'s finished screenplay manages to mine the popularity of the Bond films in a number of ways. First, the subject matter and narrative construction of the film seem highly reminiscent of the Bond cycle [...]" (Neaverson 1997: 27). One of the most obvious parallels to the Bond movies was the multitude of exotic settings featured in *Help!*. While Paul McCartney claims that these locations were chosen just because The Beatles had never been to the Bahamas or Austria (vgl. Carr 1996: 65), the selection of these particular locations also makes sense in reference to the James Bond cycle, which traditionally took place in unusual and remote settings, in order to add to the visual power of the Bond movies' spectacular action scenes and its special effects orgies. While Bond's investigations take place in Jamaica (*Dr No*, 1962), Istanbul (*From Russia with Love*, 1963), and in Switzerland (*Goldfinger*, 1964), The Beatles' attempts to escape from the religious fanatics and the mad scientist take them to Obertauern, Austria, and to New Providence, Bahamas. The decision to film part of *Help!* on the Bahamas was partially motivated by financial reasons. Producer Walter Shenson as well as The Beatles had invested in a Bahamian company, and it is assumed that they wanted to demonstrate that they were "an asset to the Bahamian business community" ("Films" 2005).

The exotic settings, however, were not the only parallels to the James Bond movies. *Help!* is full of parodying references to the Bond movies, making fun of the stock characters appearing in these movies as well as elements of narrative construction, settings and equipment. The religious cult leader Clang and the mad scientist Professor Foot both feature traits of the typical Bond villain in the fashion of Goldfinger, while Ahme, the woman played by Eleanor Bron, fulfils a stereotype that corresponds to the character of Pussy Galore in *Goldfinger*. Neaverson points out that Clang, like Auric Goldfinger, "is both exotic and power-crazed" (Neaverson 1997: 38). while Ahme, the fickle heroine, resembles Pussy Galore, because "she switches sides to help the 'good guys' when she sees the error of her ways" (Neaverson 1997: 38). The movie also makes fun of stock characters typical of action movies. For instance, when the mad scientist Professor Foot fails to free Ringo from the ring, John is enraged and tells him: "You're nothing but a mad scientist."

Help! also sends up the Bond movies' obsession with scientific gadgetry, featuring numerous scenes which "ridicule the sophistication and ruthless efficiency of the hi-tech devices featured in *Goldfinger*" (Neaverson 1997: 38). What is more, *Help!* also includes scenes of relentless brutality, a fact which has been largely ignored by critics and scholars alike. For example, in the fight scene filmed at the Indian restaurant, several people are knocked out, and one man is even forced to put his head in a boiling pot.

Performance Scenes

The way The Beatles perform their songs in *Help!* parallels the semi-diegetic approach Lester had introduced in *A Hard Day's Night*. Again, the visualization of the songs is a mixture of performance footage and non-performance oriented action. The "Ticket to Ride" sequence parallels the "Can't Buy Me Love" sequence in *A Hard Day's Night*, similarly expressing a sense of fun and release, this time by showing The Beatles' first attempts at skiing. The scene was edited by John Victor Smith, who had previously edited a promotional film of The Beatles' "You Can't Do That". As pointed out by Bob Neaverson, "the 'Ticket to Ride' sequence is arguably the first time that the full potential of editing for pace and rhythm was prioritized above choreography in a pop film" (Neaverson 1997: 40). Similar to the "Can't Buy Me Love" sequence, "Ticket to Ride" includes segments filmed from a helicopter. However, for the most part "Ticket to Ride" shows quickly edited scenes of The Beatles fooling around in the snow. While the whole sequence is basically not performance-based, short sequences of The Beatles singing their hit song and playing a piano on a snowy mountain top add to the surrealistic quality of the whole sequence, which also includes totally disconnected footage of Paul McCartney riding a horse in the snow, and of all four Beatles riding on a train and sliding down the mountain on a sled. Typical of *Help!*, each Beatle wears a different outfit in this sequence. John, George and Ringo even wear different hats.

Although Lester chose to take a profoundly different route with *Help!*, compared to the semi-documentary style he had created in *A Hard Day's Night*, The Beatles are presented as musicians. They are even shown at work in situations ignored in *A Hard Day's Night*. Most importantly, *Help!* features a scene showing them in a recording studio, as they record their song "You're Going to Lose That Girl". However, the way Lester realizes this particular performance scene is far from the documentary-style he had developed in *A Hard Day's Night*. While Lester had experimented with the lighting in *A Hard Day's Night*, he took these experiments a step further in the sequence showing The Beatles' performance of "You're Going to Lose That Girl", as he made use of colored lighting to full effect. The lighting frequently changes throughout the sequence, mainly showing close-ups of The Beatles and their instruments in various shades of blue, red, and green.

The Beatles are also shown performing, albeit in a rather different manner than in *A Hard Day's Night*. While the diegetic performance scenes in their first feature movie had shown them playing for an audience, such as the girls on the train or the many fans in the television studio, they basically perform their songs for themselves in *Help!*. In addition, the level of surrealism is taken to another level in *Help!*. For instance, the group is shown recording George Harrison's song "I Need You" in the middle of a military training field, surrounded by soldiers of the Royal Army, who are ordered to protect the group from the religious fanatics trying to kidnap Ringo. The Beatles also perform the song "The Night Before" on the military training field. The performance is filmed in a quite similar way, with John Lennon playing electric organ instead of his guitar. The camera takes in various strange perspectives, and the scenes are cut extremely quickly and reflect the dynamics of the song. Edited in a break-neck tempo, close-ups of each Beatle and his instrument are intercut with scenes showing the cult fanatics' preparations for an attack. The picture is turned upside down more than once, adding to the surrealism of the scene. Suddenly the Indian fanatics attack, and the whole scene turns into a war scenario.

The performance of "Another Girl", filmed on the Bahamas, is equally surreal, with The Beatles switching instruments (Ringo Starr plays guitar, George Harrison plays McCartney's famous Höfner bass, while John Lennon is seen playing the drums), and Paul McCartney pretending to 'play' a girl instead of his bass guitar. The sequence shows The Beatles on a beach, where they mime the song. While it had been important to The Beatles to make performance scenes appear real in their first movie, the "Another Girl" sequence is realized in a way that makes clear that The Beatles are not really performing the song, as their electric guitars are not plugged in. A series of disconnected non-performance footage is intercut with the mimed performance of "Another Girl" and adds to the surreal quality of the segment. For example, one of the scenes shows The Beatles diving into a pool of sand.

In contrast, The Beatles' performance of "You've Got to Hide Your Love Away" is realized in a very conventional way, with all of The Beatles playing their respective instruments. With The Beatles miming to the playback of the song, the illusion of a diegetic performance is evoked. It is intercut with a few scenes of Clang, as he is approaching the house to steal the ring from Ringo. This, however, does not disturb the impression of a diegetic performance, as it works in the convention of parallel montage.

The Beatles' Image in *Help!*

Similar to *A Hard Day's Night*, Lester uses The Beatles' second movie to play with the group's image and their individual identities. This theme is introduced at the very beginning, when The Beatles are shown as they arrive at their house. Two women notice them and talk about them.

"First woman: Lovely lads, and so natural! I mean, adoration hasn't gone to their heads.
Second woman: So natural, and still the same as they was before they was."
(*Help!* 2000)

The scene seems to develop a joke introduced in *A Hard Day's Night*, where a reporter asks George Harrison whether success has changed his life, and he dryly replies "Yes." However, in *A Hard Day's Night*, The Beatles still project the image of being 'the boys next-door', while *Help!* shows them being rather spoiled and eccentric entertainers. The women's remarks are highly ironic, because as soon as The Beatles enter the house it becomes clear that they lead the most eccentric lives in a modern castle full of luxury and weird gadgets. There is even a lawn inside the house, which is taken care of by a gardener. Paul suddenly appears from the basement playing a spectacular organ on an elevator-like construction.

Instead of sheet music, several comic books, such as *Superman*, are placed on the organ. The comic books are a subtle hint at what Lester set out to create with *Help!*, which is basically a clever mixture of various elements of action comics and the James Bond adventures. Richard Lester's interest in the genre of comics and the references to comics in *Help!* have largely been ignored by most critics, even though John Lennon has pointed out Lester's pioneering role in adapting comics for the cinema. Visual references, elements of narrative construction and the use of color all indicate that Lester indeed intended to pay homage to the genre of action comics. Lester uses colors in a way that resembles the way comics are designed. For instance, the interior of The Beatles' house looks just like a comic panel, with bright colors decorating the walls as well as the floor. Ringo's corner in the house is colored blue, while John's area is brown; Paul's is white and George's is green. When Ringo wakes up his friends after Ahme tried to steal the sacrificial ring, each Beatle is seen wearing a pajama of the color corresponding to his area in the house.

Although there were still parallels to *A Hard Day's Night* in the way The Beatles were portrayed in *Help!*, one of the most obvious differences concerned The Beatles' outfit, which had played such an important part in the public perception of the group's collective image. The legendary mohair suits they had popularized between 1962 and 1964 were substituted by a range of suits and outfits that proved once again that The Beatles were trendsetters not only in music but also in fashion. Especially the clothes they wore in the scenes filmed in Obertauern, Austria, became quite well-known, as The Beatles decided to wear them at the photo session for the cover of the soundtrack album as well. It was a special wardrobe consisting of black skin-tight trousers and ankle-length ski boots in black sealskin. John Lennon sported a black cape lined with white satin, while Ringo Starr wore a tight fitting black sweater with white rings around the sleeves. George Harrison also wore a black sweater with a white stripe down each sleeve, while Paul McCartney wore a loosely-cut ski jacket in sealskin (vgl. Harry 1985: 29). Instead of the uniform outfit they had sported in *A Hard Day's Night*, The Beatles wear different clothes throughout *Help!*. In the course of the movie, they are seen in different-colored turtlenecks as well as in various suits. Changing their outfits is actually almost taken to an extreme in *Help!*, as The Beatles seem to wear different clothes in every other sequence. In this context, the cult leader Clang's comment "They all look the same" is highly ironic and anachronistic, as it reflects an attitude and opinion projected in the press as well as the public at the time of The Beatles' initial success.

The use of color is, however, not the only reference to comics. At several points in the movie, scenes are introduced by cards explaining the situation, such as "In the weeks that followed five more attempts were made to steal the ring" or "End of Part 1." While these explanations can be regarded as references to silent movies, they also work as narrative elements in the tradition of comic books, where individual panels often feature introductions or explanations. Richard Lester even referred to comics when he first described the movie to the press: "It's a comic-strip adventure; one long chase with Oriental church leaders who want to fill their temples with sacrifices and mad scientists who want to blow up the world" (Carr 1996: 73). Lester was very aware of the way he adapted comic conventions for the movie screen. Although not many critics have appreciated Lester's contribution to the genre of comic adaptations, some of the elements introduced in *Help!*, such as the use of colors and camera perspectives, as well as a surreal sense of humor, were popularized by the *Batman* television series a year later. In this context, it should also be noted that Richard Lester went on to direct two *Superman* movies in the early 1980s.

The differences between the four Beatles are even more exaggerated than in *A Hard Day's Night*. While the group's first movie defined each Beatle's public image, *Help!* pushes these images further apart (vgl. Yule 1994: 97). Even though *Help!* does not feature solo scenes comparable to the ones in *A Hard Day's Night*, one sequence allows Paul McCartney to compensate for the missing solo scene in *A Hard Day's Night*. Due to an accident, the shrinking serum intended for Ringo Starr to free him from the sacrificial ring, makes Paul shrink, and he ends up little enough to wrap a chewing gum wrapping paper around his body. While McCartney arguably played the least memorable role in *A Hard Day's Night*, his part in *Help!* finally establishes him as an equally important screen personality in The Beatles. His scene is even introduced with a title saying, "The Exciting Adventure of Paul on the Floor." George Harrison features in a wild action scene, which is particularly reminiscent of the car chases in the Bond movies. John Lennon does not feature in a solo scene, but he remains a dominant screen presence throughout the movie. However, the key role in The Beatles' second feature movie is again played by Ringo Starr. As with *A Hard Day's Night* and *The Beatles* cartoon series, Ringo Starr establishes himself as the most talented actor in The Beatles. His love for acting actually inspired Starr to pursue a rather interesting acting career, with Starr appearing in various independent films now considered cult movies, such as *Blindman*, *The Magic Christian*, *200 Motels*, *Lisztomania*, and *Caveman*.

Although Starr was almost universally accepted as the group's actor, Richard Lester considered John Lennon to be a rather talented actor as well and offered him the role of Sergeant Gripweed in his anti-war-movie movie *How I Won the War*, which was filmed in 1966. Even though Lennon's performance was quite convincing, he did not accept any acting roles after *How I Won the War*, since he found the experience of filming extremely tiring and boring.

It had been Brian Epstein's policy to project The Beatles' image of being four available young men, in order to attract as many female fans as possible. Even though it eventually became a well-known and publicized fact that John Lennon was married, and that the other Beatles had girlfriends, their image of being single was still promoted by their second movie. As with *A Hard Day's Night*, love and romance was entirely excluded from the film. There is only some light-hearted flirtation taking place between the band members and the character played by Eleanor Bron.

The Beatles were not as pleased with *Help!* as they had been with *A Hard Day's Night*. Especially John Lennon regretted that the band had not had any significant input in the making of *Help!*

"The movie was out of our control. [*Help!*] had nothing to do with the Beatles. They put us here and there. Dick Lester was good. With *Hard Day's Night*, we pretty much had a lot of input and it was semirealistic. But with *Help!*, Dick didn't tell us what it was about, though I realize, looking back, how advanced it was. It was a precursor for the *Batman* 'Pow! Wow!' on TV – that kind of stuff. But he never explained it to us" (Gross 1990: 24).

Paul McCartney has also stated that The Beatles had never really been interested in making the movie: "Basically we lost the plot, but I don't think there was much of a plot there to start with. It was this endless 'The ring must be found! Kali must be appeased.' Maybe that's why we didn't enjoy it. I've always felt we let it down a bit, but we just didn't care and that would fit more readily with a poor script" (Miles 1997: 42).

On 29 July, 1965, the world premiere of *Help!* was celebrated in London, where public hysteria again caused officials to shut down Piccadilly Circus for public traffic. On 11 August, 1965, the film opened at 250 theaters throughout the United States. It was the official British entry at the International Film Festival in Rio de Janeiro, where it won first prize. The movie was broadcast ten times on British television between 1971 and 1995. Similar to *A Hard Day's Night*, the television premiere of *Help!* put the soundtrack album back into the album charts, where it peaked at position 33. It was first released on video in 1990 and was part of a limited edition DVD release called *The Beatles DVD Collector's Set* in 2000. In November 2007, *Help!* finally saw its general release on DVD, storming the music DVD charts all over the world.

The Television Cartoon Series

Beatles for Children: Developing *The Beatles*

On 11 November, 1964, *Variety* announced that the US-based King Features Syndicate had secured the television animation rights to The Beatles. The article was already quite specific as to how ABC-TV envisioned the television series: "Projected cartoon series will follow the premise of the quartet's successful movie, *A Hard Day's Night*. The four lead characters will be based on the personalities of John, George, Paul and Ringo. On the soundtrack, The Beatles will perform a minimum of two songs in each half hour, some of them new, some Beatles classics" (Axelrod 1999: 23).

Television producer Al Brodax was the vital force behind the cartoon series. He developed the show's original format and retained complete control of the production. Brodax, who had produced numerous *Popeye* cartoons, had been trying to combine animation and original music in a creative way: "[T]he infusion of original music rather than the standard use of canned library music to score the *Popeye* animation, or for that matter any animation, would lift it out of the ordinary, enhance its storyline, it's action – would identify the uniqueness of each character. Disney's *Fantasia*, an extraordinary example of this" (Brodax 2004: 5). When Brodax became aware of The Beatles' music he realized that "the 'beat' of Beatle music [was] especially well suited to enhance an animated piece" (Brodax 2004: 11). Artistic considerations aside, The Beatles' enormous success in the United States in 1964 was probably the most important factor in developing a cartoon series featuring the group, in order to cash in on their recent popularity. Since *A Hard Day's Night* had been such a blockbuster, it was decided that The Beatles' characters in the television series would be built upon the public personae the group had embodied in their first feature movie. The stereotypes and character traits projected by the movie thus provided a useful framework for the development of the cartoon characters for the television series.

Al Brodax thought of the original concept for the show. Each half-hour episode would consist of two animated stories based on The Beatles' song lyrics and two Beatle 'sing-a-longs,' which were going to lead into commercials.

Brodax asked artist Peter Sander to create character models for the animated Beatles. The young artist based his designs on photographs he had collected of the group. Model sheets containing Sander's designs were distributed to the studios that were chosen to animate the Beatles series. These model sheets contained information about the basic features, gestures and tendencies of the characters to be animated (vgl. Axelrod 1999: 28).

"John, especially when delivering important lines, really looks the leader. Feet apart, hands on hips, chin up, looking down his nose. With a slightly mocking expression (This pose can also be used when he is pointing)
When facing front, he uses a sly, sideways look to talk to somebody.
Pulls funny faces, especially after orders, which he immediately wipes off. He also looks the other way before giving you an order.
Slightly queer 'showbiz' gestures can be used in long shot. Gives the feeling that John doesn't take his job as leader seriously.
John never sits, he slouches.
Paul is the most poised and stylish Beatle. When he talks, he uses his hands, with fingers spread, to express what he's saying. He always looks straight to whoever he is talking to. He is the one excited when John suggests anything. He doesn't really walk – he skips.
Paul sits as though he is ready to jump up and get on with whatever is happening.
When he is making his own suggestions and comments, especially ones suggesting mischief, he covers up by assuming a mock innocent look, eyes wide and head tilts to one side.
He tends to put his hand to his mouth when he is excited.
George never looks at who he is talking to. But his shoulders, which are hunched when he is in a standing or leaning pose, can indicate the direction.
Head always tilted forward.
George is the same height as Paul.
George is very loose-limbed and angular when he walks. Remember his legs are long and thin. Emphasis on the knees will help the angular appearance.
He often closes his eyes for short periods when he is talking.
George always gives the impression of frowning. This is because his eyebrows thicken as they reach his nose.
Notice distance between the nose and the mouth. His mouth is always lopsided.
George always leans against something. Shoulders hunched, hands in pockets, legs crossed.
Ringo is the nice, gentle Beatle, although he always looks rather sad.
Ringo always looks a bit disjointed whether walking or standing.
Ringo walks in a Groucho Marx pose.
Keep upper lip protruding. Keep Ringo's neck thin to help the disjointed look.
Keep hair, at back long and shaggy. Keep mouth in a wavy line.
When Ringo laughs, having made a funny remark, he squints.

His clothes tend to look as though they are a bit too big.
Normally Ringo is always deadpan, but should expression be required the main movement is arching the eyebrows."
(*Mojo* 35 1996: 19).

The animators were encouraged to watch footage of The Beatles' performances in order to become familiar to the band members' individual characteristics. Animator Dennis Hunt recalls, "We studied the movie and films of the Beatles performing. We would run the films backwards and forwards on the moviola [...]. We observed that John stood face on to the audience and bobbed up and down. George and Paul swung their guitars up high and leaned towards each other. Ringo shook his hair all over as he played his drums" (Axelrod 1999: 29).

On the one hand, *A Hard Day's Night* provided realistic models as to how The Beatles moved and behaved – although each character had to be portrayed in an even more stylized and exaggerated way than in the movie, in order to function as a cartoon character. On the other hand, the group's movie debut also inspired one of the most predominant themes in the series – the theme of escape. Throughout the series, the animated Beatles were constantly on the run from screaming fans or from some kind of monster or evil force. As in *A Hard Day's Night*, The Beatles hardly ever find a peaceful place to rehearse or to enjoy their holidays. Although *The Beatles* drew heavily from the stock repertoire of storylines and characters typical of cartoon series, the inclusion of screaming fans as a threat as well as emphasizing the group's lack of privacy were quite clearly influenced by the portrayal of the group in their first feature movie.

Again, Al Brodax was instrumental in the development of storyline ideas. In the course of three seasons he cooperated with four scriptwriters who were responsible for the stories to the series' 39 episodes – Dennis Marks, Jack Mendelsohn Heywood Kling and Bruce Howard (Axelrod 1999: 29). As each episode consisted of two adventures and two sing-a-longs, 78 storylines were developed by this team. While the stories were constructed very much in the tradition of conventional animated television series, it is quite obvious that *A Hard Day's Night* – and later *Help!* – contributed significantly to the thematic range and the choice of settings of the cartoon series.

As with The Beatles' movies, the production company treated the animated television series as a mere exploitation project. The budget was set at $32,000 per half-hour show, the bulk of which was basically financed through advertising. Regarding this kind of sponsoring, The Beatles' manager Brian Epstein was quite specific about what kind of sponsors to exclude from *The Beatles* series. According to Brodax, "commercials that have anything to do with depilatories, deodorants, etc. would be prohibited." After several potential sponsors declined to finance the new animation series, Brodax was able to find a toy train company in Chicago, A.C. Gilbert, which became the show's primary sponsor (vgl. Brodax 2004: 21). Other sponsors included the Quaker Oats Company and the Mars Candy Company (vgl. Axelrod 1999: 25).

Brodax also developed a rather innovative concept to realize the television series within the constraints of time and budget dictated by King Feature Syndicate. In order to meet the deadlines, Brodax cooperated with animation studios around the world instead of relying on King Features' partner studios in the United States. Therefore, the model sheets containing information as to how to draw and animate The Beatles were sent to animation studios all around the world. While outsourcing is now a common practice in the world of animation, it was Al Brodax who first thought of this way of producing animated films. Although employing studios in Great Britain, Australia, Canada and Holland was an efficient way to save time, Brodax and his production team had to find further solutions to keep to the tight budget. Brodax remembers the first meeting with two of the series' directors, George Dunning and Jack Stokes: "We then proceed[ed] to suggest techniques that [would] serve us well in our joint effort to produce an outstanding series on a miniscule budget: running cycles, cycle everything ... carefully filed and stored backgrounds for reuse, simply designed Beatle figures, extensive sound effects, undifferentiated blobs and splashes of paint [...]" (Brodax 2004: 28). Brodax indeed managed to keep the costs low. However, it proved to be rather impossible for him to produce what he had imagined to be an "outstanding series." Outsourcing the animation to studios in Australia and Great Britain actually meant that quite inexperienced teams of young animators were employed to work for the series. While The Beatles series prompted the evolution of an industry of animated films and television shows in both countries, the episodes produced there at that time were quite rudely animated and lacked the standards and continuity of American animated shows. In Great Britain, animation was still a very new industry. Basically, animation had been restricted to advertisements before The Beatles series, which was the first mass cartoon series produced, at least in parts, in Great Britain. In Australia, the situation was quite similar, as the Artransa Park TV Studios had previously not worked on a comparable project for television. Ron Campbell, who worked on the series as animator, storyboard artist and director, explains that "[t]o anybody viewing the show today, it's easy to tell the Australian episodes from the English. For example, if Ringo's nose was drawn too fat in one scene and too long in the next, the episode was made in Australia. If the inking wavered and seemed uncertain, or drawn with a too-heavy hand, it was made in Australia. If the backgrounds were minimal, it was Australian" (Axelrod 1999: 76). The episode "I'm Happy Just To Dance With You" is one of many examples of the series' low standards of animation. In this episode, a dancing bear falls in love with Paul and wants to cuddle and dance with him. Here the animation of the dance sequence completely lacks any sense of flow in the movement of the characters. What is more, the final sequence is animated in an extremely crude way, with characters suddenly popping up in the picture in the middle of a scene.

Songs and Stories

Not only was the animation below King Features' standards at the time, but also the storylines were rather simple and repetitive. The basic idea for many of the episodes was that The Beatles were at some remote place looking for some peace and solitude. However, they were always disturbed or followed by somebody who got them into trouble of some sort. In the end, one of their songs would always help them to get out of an unpleasant situation. For instance, in the episode "Not a Second Time," The Beatles fly to Africa to perform a concert there. They are followed by screaming fans, who make it impossible for The Beatles to rehearse. However, they manage to escape their fans and rehearse the song in front of an amphibian audience. In "I Should Have Known Better," The Beatles are in Rome looking for a place to rehearse for their evening performance. In the end, they rehearse in the Coliseum where they literally bring the house down (vgl. Axelrod 1999: 140-148). Other episodes show The Beatles fighting against evil forces, such as Dracula (in "Misery") or the mad Professor Psycho (in "Baby's in Black").

Although the animated band performances were inspired by The Beatles' performance in *A Hard Day's Night*, the animators realized most of these sequences in the 'musical'-tradition, with the band breaking into a performance at an apparently arbitrary point in the story. This way of integrating music in the narrative actually works in the tradition of classic animated movies, such as *Snow White and the Seven Dwarfs*, the first full-length animated feature, where Walt Disney introduced such musical elements in the world of animation. The difference, however, is the instrumentation. While the song performances in *Snow White* are largely without the accompaniment of musical instruments (except for the party scene at the dwarfs' house), the cartoon Beatles always have their instruments ready to perform. Here, the portrayal of the band roughly resembles the way Lester presents them in *A Hard Day's Night*, showing parts of The Beatles' instruments in detail. However, no great care is taken in the way this presentation is achieved, as the animated Beatles often do not seem to be performing the specific song presented in a particular episode. Although the cartoon Beatles open and close their mouths and imitate certain movements of the real Beatles, the way they use their instruments seems quite primitive in comparison with Disney's or Warner Brothers' classic cartoons from the 1930's and 1940's. Considering the fact that the series was produced in the mid-sixties, The Beatles' and their manager's criticism concerning the animation is quite understandable. Especially the fact that the songs are often sung by the wrong Beatle must have annoyed The Beatles, who were always concerned about an accurate depiction of what each band member contributed to The Beatles' music. For example, Paul McCartney refused to watch the movie *Backbeat*, a fictional account of The Beatles' time in Hamburg, when he found out that the character playing John Lennon performs the song "Long Tall Sally" in the movie, because this was 'his' song. There are numerous examples of such errors in The Beatles series. For instance, in "I'm Happy Just to Dance with You" John Lennon is seen singing the song, although it is actually sung by George Harrison, while in "Mr. Moonlight" the Paul character sings the song originally sung by John Lennon.

Not all songs were presented as diegetic performances. In some cases they illustrate or contrast the animated action on the screen. Although this way of using The Beatles' music as a score may also have been inspired by Lester's visualization of "Can't Buy Me Love" in *A Hard Day's Night*, it is not always used to effect in *The Beatles* series. For instance, in "Anna", Paul is kidnapped by a female Japanese ghost, who keeps him on her ghost ship 'AH-NAH'. The Beatles' performance of Arthur Alexander's song is heard while the cartoon Paul worships the ghost. In this case, the lyrics do not have anything to do with what is shown on the screen. In other episodes, the songs are used in a more clever way, at least for comical effect. For example, in "I Wanna Hold Your Hand", The Beatles encounter a lovesick octopus, who eventually finds a girl-octopus to hold hands with.

The sing-a-longs are hardly ever performance-oriented. In most cases, they are simply animated visualizations of each song's theme. Sometimes the pictures tell a story that is related to the lyrics in some way or other. For example the sing-a-long for "Don't Bother Me" shows the character of Paul suffering from a broken heart. He seems to be stranded on a little island but refuses to be rescued, because he does not want to be disturbed. Often the lyrics are interpreted in a slightly surreal way, in order to create the sense of comedy necessary for an animated children's program. As pointed out by Axelrod, "in the first season of the series, the sing-a-longs were fun and ambitious. In the last two seasons, they became less of a Beatles adventure and more of a surreal piece of imagery. [Some s]ing-a-long segments, especially in the third season, didn't feature the Beatles at all. For the song "Girl" the names of each Beatle would slowly pass by as the song went on" (Axelrod 1999: 184). The lyrics to the songs are always shown on the screen to enable the children to sing a long at home.

Although the sing-a-longs were an effective idea to promote The Beatles' songs through low-budget animation, The Beatles were not pleased with the way King Features treated their recordings. In order to fit the two-minute time slot of each sing-a-long, the songs were heavily edited by the series' production team. A memo from King Features Syndicate to the animation studios is quite specific about the shortening of The Beatles' songs: "In some cases where the sound track is longer than 2 minutes and the music track has to be cut to accommodate a 2 minute song, it is advisable to use teenage audience screams to cover the cut in the track so that the music beats may match" (Axelrod 1999: 190). In actual fact, the songs were often cut in a rather arbitrary way, which simply destroyed the structure of the songs. This lack of respect to their work was another reason why The Beatles themselves did not support the series in any way.

Image and Ideology

In hindsight it is not surprising that The Beatles did not like the series and even prevented it from being shown in Great Britain. On the one hand, the series was not up to contemporary animation standards and did nothing to support the group's increasing reputation as innovative musicians and artist. On the other hand, the show significantly lacked sensitivity and tact in the portrayal of ethnic groups as well as in the portrayal of women. Even though an animated film or series is likely to project a certain set of stereotypes in the way different cultures are portrayed, *The Beatles* series lacked the charm and subtlety that might excuse the stereotypical depiction of nationalities, for instance, in Walt Disney's *Lady and the Tramp* or *Pinocchio*. In actual fact, many episodes of The Beatles cartoon series would probably disturb contemporary audiences, since society has grown quite sensitive to the issue of 'political correctness.' The show itself would probably not pass any contemporary broadcasting commission.

While not all the episodes are necessarily racist, it seems that especially the episodes produced in Australia featured a rather heavy dose of discrimination. As observed by Mitch Axelrod, "[t]he series was made right at a time when Australia was in the midst of a change in social thinking. Many episodes in the series featured cartoon African cannibals licking their lips and chanting 'Unga Bunga'" (Axelrod 1999: 78). Australian animator Ron Campbell points out that "Australia still had in force a racially motivated immigration policy. It had been written into law long before, and it permitted only Europeans to immigrate" (Axelrod 1999: 80). In the episode "Can't Buy Me Love" an African chief wants John to marry his daughter. The man and his whole tribe are portrayed in a rather offensive way, featuring many of the stereotypes that would simply be considered racist today. The chief looks outright silly with his huge earrings, enormous lips and savage outfit. Other Africans are portrayed in a way that is reminiscent of Hollywood movies of the 1920's or minstrel shows, where white people dressed up the way they imagined a black person, which made them look like bad caricatures. What is more, the chief's two assistants look completely identical, which reveals quite a lot about the way the animators envisioned African people. This inability to accept the individuality of people from different ethnic groups or countries is a rather dominant feature of the latent racism typical of the time. The animators would probably not have considered making white people look completely identical in the series. The discrimination in *The Beatles*, however, was not exclusively directed toward Africans. Many episodes also make fun of Asian people. For example, "No Reply" features the stereotype of a wise but very silly-looking old Japanese man, while a similar stereotype is used in "It Won't Be Long" – this time it is an old Chinese with his – again – two identical-looking assistants. While stereotypes are often necessary in short and simple storylines in order to enable a narrative without lengthy characterization, the portrayal of most ethnic groups in *The Beatles* is simply offensive. This probably did not amuse The Beatles who were quite aware of racial issues.

Although the portrayal of ethnic groups is far less than charming, the way women are presented in *The Beatles* is equally offensive from today's point of view. By 1965, the public had become used to the reports of 'Beatlemania' in the media, depicting and showing mostly teenaged girls on the verge of hysteria, screaming and running after The Beatles wherever they publicly appeared. Especially their concerts had become outlets for their screaming fans, making it impossible for The Beatles to hear the music they were playing. *A Hard Day's Night* had integrated this aspect of The Beatles' overwhelming success and showed hysterical fans at several points in the story. The whole issue was entirely ignored in

Help!, where The Beatles are followed by religious fanatics and a mad professor instead of hysterical teenagers. Since the animated series was pretty much based upon The Beatles' first feature film, it made use of the screaming fans-motif in excess, as this particular phenomenon could be used effectively in an animated series. However, while a bunch of screaming fans following The Beatles may have been a funny idea for a couple of episodes, the way these girls are portrayed is far from charming or entertaining. Screaming fans always appear in a group in *The Beatles*. Instead of talking they only scream "Beatles!" and run after their idols. They seem threatening, and it is not surprising that the cartoon Beatles want to escape from them. While the screaming fans are always encountered with humor and affection by The Beatles in *A Hard Day's Night*, their animated alter egos simply want to avoid their female fans, because they are annoyed by them. There are no other recurring female characters in the series except for the screaming fans. The only other role sometimes taken by a female character is the role of the villain. Throughout the series, The Beatles encounter numerous scary female characters, such as witches, girl vampires and ghosts. The way women are generally portrayed in the series is quite revealing as to the way the creators of *The Beatles* envisioned the group's fans. While the hysteria surrounding The Beatles' success lent itself to spoofery and pastiche, the way it was dealt with in *The Beatles* was rather cynical and lacked the charm of later spoofs, such as Eric Idle's fake-documentary *The Rutles – All You Need Is Cash*.

In addition to the flat portrayal of side-characters in *The Beatles*, the portrayal of The Beatles themselves was less than flattering. Although the show was reportedly modelled upon *A Hard Day's Night*, the production team of *The Beatles* failed to adapt The Beatles' good-natured humor and their clever banter for the television screen. In *The Beatles*, the humor is pretty much reduced to slapstick situations and clumsy imitation of The Beatles' natural humor. Most of the comedy revolves around the character of Ringo, who is basically depicted as a good-natured fool. Similar to the feature movies starring the real Beatles, Ringo becomes the main character in the series. It is quite easy to imagine a child audience empathising with the cartoon Ringo, and he actually became the kids' favorite Beatle at the time. Although each Beatle is allowed to feature in the different episodes, Ringo draws most of the attention to himself, with his naivety and silly laugh, which – probably intentionally – resembles the way Walt Disney's beloved character Goofy laughs. In addition to being the most endearing character in the series, Ringo plays another dominant role in the segments introducing the sing-a-longs in each show. Before each sing-a-long there is an introduction where either John,

George or Paul encourage their child audience to sing along. As the property man is ill, Ringo sits in for the prop man and is requested to come up with the right decoration and equipment for the song. Ringo, of course, basically causes chaos with the equipment he provides.

During the making of *The Beatles* series conflicts arose at the very first stage of production. Since it was made clear to the producer that The Beatles themselves would not be interested in lending their own voices to their cartoon doubles, the production company insisted on dubbing the cartoon series with American actors. As this was totally against Brian Epstein's and The Beatles' interest, Al Brodax found a solution which seemed reasonable at the time: "English speech is often too difficult for Americans to decipher [...]. Since the series' initial airing will be to an American audience, I insist upon a split cast, that is one American, one Englishman, to give the audience at least a fifty-fifty chance of comprehension" (Brodax 2004: 29). American actor Paul Frees lent his voice to the cartoon Lennon and Harrison, while English actor Lance Percival took on the voices of McCartney and Starr. For The Beatles themselves, however, the cartoon series was always a rather controversial issue. They were not satisfied with the quality of the animation and did not like the fact that their voices had been 'Americanized.' In addition, the image projected in the cartoon series was not compatible with the image the band had in the United Kingdom. While the American public still considered The Beatles mainly as boy-group phenomenon, they had already become respected artists to a wide-ranging audience in Britain. Therefore, it had been clear from the very beginning that *The Beatles* would not be broadcast in Great Britain. John Coates, the Managing Director of TVC Animation Studios, recalls that Brian Epstein was particularly concerned about the dubbing: "[I]t was because of the voices picked, that the Beatles cartoons were not allowed to be shown in England. The decision was made by none other than Brian Epstein himself" (Axelrod 1999: 55). The Beatles have distanced themselves from their animated television show ever since. Although George Harrison admitted to like the series in a *Billboard* interview in the 1999, the group excluded the whole issue from their own Beatles history project, *The Beatles Anthology*.

The Beatles on TV

The Beatles' cartoon show premiered on September 25, 1965, at 10 a.m. Eastern Standard Time on ABC. It consisted of two five and one half minute episodes, the plot of which was based upon the lyrics of a Beatles song featured in each adventure. In between the two adventures, the cartoon Beatles introduced two 'sing-a-longs,' which consisted of animated sequences showing the lyrics of two of The Beatles' songs. All in all, seventeen episodes of The Beatles' television series were produced for the first season.

The show was an instant success, opening with a share of 51.9 per cent of the viewing audience. In the United States, it became the second most successful Saturday morning show of the season (vgl. Axelrod 1999: 107), encouraging ABC to order thirteen new episodes for a second season. The great success of *The Beatles* cartoons inspired Al Brodax to consider the production of similar television shows designed to revolve around the band lives of British beat bands such as Herman's Hermits and Freddie and the Dreamers (vgl. Axelrod 1999: 122). While Brodax failed to convince television companies of his idea, the show inspired a whole genre of television cartoons in the 1970s, when animated shows such as *The Jackson Five*, *The Osmonds* and *The Brady Kids* invaded American homes via television. Like *The Beatles*, these shows featured bands getting into mischief and rescuing themselves with the power of their songs (vgl. Axelrod 1999: 128).

By the end of the second season, ratings had diminished significantly. This was reportedly caused by the emergence of another extremely successful cartoon series called *Space Ghost*, which introduced a whole new trend in Saturday morning television. CBS, ABC's greatest rival at the time, recognized the growing interest in superheroes and began to focus on the genre, airing animated children's series, such as *Frankenstein Jr.*, *The Impossibles*, *Superman*, *Mighty Mouse and The Mighty Heroes*. *Space Ghosts* was slotted opposite *The Beatles* and reached a 44% share, compared to *The Beatles*' 36% share (vgl. "The Beatles" 2005). Although this was still a reasonable result as to market shares, some rather clumsy programming decisions were made by ABC Television, as recalled by Edwin Vane, the Director of Daytime Programs at ABC, which added to the series decline.

"[We ordered only thirteen episodes] so that we could run them clean through the fourth quarter of 1966. Then for repeats, we'd mix in some of the original seventeen with the new thirteen to put a little distance between re-runs. However, you can't fool the kids. When they watched "Roll Over Beethoven" the first time, they thought it was hysterical. By the sixth time, it wasn't quite so funny. And that's why the ratings went down" (Axelrod 1999: 124).

For the third season only nine new episodes were ordered in 1967. Despite the decision to mainly broadcast re-runs of early episodes, ratings were still fine and ABC-television kept the show alive for yet another season. However, the fourth season consisted entirely of re-runs, which means that the production of *The Beatles* cartoon series was cancelled. On April 20, 1969, ABC-television aired the last *Beatles* episode.

The initial success of *The Beatles* animated series also introduced a whole new branch of Beatles merchandise in the shops. In addition to the official and unofficial band merchandise products sweeping the American teenage market between 1964 and 1966, the likeness of the cartoon characters was licensed to numerous companies. Beatles candy sticks, cups and hand puppets were among the officially licensed merchandise products destined for the young target group addressed by the cartoon series. Companies such as Lux and Nestlé also cashed in on the Beatle craze and offered inflatable Beatles dolls to their loyal customers (vgl. Axelrod 1999: 112-121). In 2004, McFarlane, an American producer of toys, acquired the rights to produce a new set of Beatles merchandise based upon the cartoon characters featured in the television show.

As mentioned above, The Beatles and Brian Epstein prevented the show from being aired in Great Britain at the time it was produced. In 1980, *The Beatles* finally debuted on British television, when it was featured on early morning television on Granada Television. In 1988, the full series was featured on ITV's *Night Network* magazine show.

Although *The Beatles* series was shown on various TV programs around the world in the 1980s, it has disappeared from public awareness since The Beatles' company Apple bought the rights to the series in the early 1990s. Apple has prevented the show from being shown anywhere in the world, and since it was not even mentioned in The Beatles' official autobiography *Anthology*, it is not clear whether the series will ever be commercially released. However, with Paul McCartney's and Ringo Starr's latest excursions into the world of animation[8] and The Beatles' more recent effort to project a timeless image of the band, it is possible that Apple will compile a DVD featuring the better episodes of the series. In fact, the series could become an important means to introduce The Beatles to new generations of fans. Similar to the way The Beatles' film *Yellow Submarine* has attracted children in the last four decades, *The Beatles* series could contribute to preserving The Beatles as a timeless phenomenon. Despite its flaws, the animated series was an important factor in keeping a certain facet of The Beatles' image alive already in the mid-sixties. Tony Barrow, the group's press officer, points out that the

---

8   In 2004, Paul McCartney released a DVD called *The Music and Animation Collection*, featuring three animated short films produced by his company MPL. In January 2005, it was announced that Stan Lee, the creator of cartoon heroes such as *Spiderman* and *Hulk*, was developing a multimedia franchise in which Starr would play a superpowered animated version of himself.

animated series was quite important in terms of medial presence and image perseverance.

"Whilst generally helping to sustain The Beatles' record sales at a healthy level between concert tours (and beyond that short-lived era), the cartoon programs also preserved in Peter Pan fashion the early carefree and playful "Four Mop Tops" image, which children loved and parents approved of [...]. This crucial aspect of the Al Brodax venture was not even considered, let alone appreciated, by Brian Epstein, but the rest of us saw it as a significant factor in prolonging the career of The Beatles in the commercially important teenyboppers' sector" (Hieronimus 2002: 32).

BEATLES HISTORY - PART TWO: 1964-1966.
A CONTEXTUAL INTERPRETATION OF THE BEATLES' IMAGE CHANGE IN 1966

The Beatles followed the release of *A Hard Day's Night* with their first tour through the United States in August and September 1964. In October, Brian Epstein published his autobiography *A Cellarful of Noise*. In December, The Beatles released their studio album *Beatles for Sale* in the United Kingdom, while Capitol Records released a slightly modified version of the album under the name *Beatles '65* in the United States. By Christmas The Beatles again topped the charts on both sides of the Atlantic.

In 1965, The Beatles filmed *Help!*, toured North America and Britain again, and continued to be virtually omnipresent in all kinds of mass media. As their enormous success constituted a significant economic factor in Great Britain, they were awarded Membership of the Most Excellent Order of the British Empire in the Queen's Birthday Honours list, which upset several previous recipients of this award (vgl. Lewisohn 2000: 180). Despite these criticisms, the MBEs crowned the group's acceptance by the Establishment. The release of Paul McCartney's composition "Yesterday" on The Beatles' *Help!* album also introduced a major change in the way The Beatles were discussed by music critics and scholars, as many of whom had not taken them seriously before. The atmospheric recording of "Yesterday", the simple but haunting melody, as well as George Martin's arrangement of the song, featuring a string quartet, soon made the song the most popular Beatles song. In between filming and touring The Beatles wrote and recorded the songs for their albums *Help!* and *Rubber Soul*, which were both released in 1965.

Although The Beatles accepted their MBEs and the presence of members of the Royal family and politicians at their concerts and film premieres, they did not want to actually assimilate into the sphere of the Establishment. On the contrary, The Beatles had always encountered the representatives of the upper classes with their cheeky humor, and when they finally moved to London and became introduced to the city's underground art scene and various political, social and religious youth movements, they quickly absorbed a variety of ideas and contributed significantly to the popularization of countercultural ideology and aesthetics. Because of their enormous popularity and their sincere commitment, The Beatles became the spokesmen of a worldwide countercultural youth movement.

At that time various countercultural movements evolved from independent youth cultures in Great Britain and in the United States. While young people's social and political criticism had previously only reached a minority of the population in these countries, the 60s-movements managed to gain a much greater influence by appealing to a mass audience via the means of mass media. Previous countercultural movements, such as the Beat Generation in the 1950s, had never managed to cause mass interest. The hippies' ideology, however, was publicized in the media when young artists and stars made use of the media to propagate certain values and ideas.

"While most of the beatniks' thoughts and ideas were adopted by the hippies, the main difference between them lies within the structure of both movements itself: although the beatniks formed a radical critique of what they found was wrong with society, they simultaneously withdrew from society and detested it only among themselves; they sought individual and theoretical solutions rather than collective solutions. The hippies, in contrast though, represented a 'generational unit', looking for collective solutions or alternatives to social traditions of career or life-style" (Kolloge 1999: 147).

While the beatniks remained an underground movement, intellectual American folk singers, such as Bob Dylan and Joan Baez, adopted many elements of the beatniks' ideology and represented this countercultural value system. However, these folk singers still only reached a limited audience, as folk music only appealed to a certain target audience. When pop musicians such as The Beatles became interested in youth culture movements, they were able to convey their messages to a mass audience, as their popularity enabled them to communicate their opinions through the mass media. After numerous pop groups, such as the Byrds, the Hollies, and Peter, Paul and Mary, had released commercial cover versions of Bob Dylan's songs, Bob Dylan became finally known to a larger audience. While most pop musicians lacked the creativity to formulate and express intellectual concerns in their original songs, The Beatles began to use their music and films as media to express actual experiences, observations, criticism, and philosophical concepts. As their musical and intellectual interests had developed quite rapidly, they were able to include a wide range of ideas, sounds and images in their popular music recordings as well as in their promotional films and movies. Their 1966 album *Revolver* can be regarded as their first attempt at intellectual pop music, as the album consists of a variety of entirely different sounds, musical styles and lyrical forms, which are used intentionally to communicate a certain world-view. On the other hand, the massive popularity of The Beatles' music inspired Bob Dylan to make his recordings more accessible by arranging his songs in a more commercial way. Their mutual influence on each other as well as their ability to adapt to recent musical developments made Bob Dylan and The Beatles the outstanding personalities in the genre of popular music in the 1960s. They were the first artists to consciously use popular music as a medium to convey and propagate certain ideologies. Even though conservative critics tried to undermine the emerging hippie movement, The Beatles' overpowering popularity allowed them to voice the concerns and ideas of youth movements they identified with in the mass media.

In 1966, The Beatles absorbed a variety of philosophical concepts and musical ideas. Their album *Revolver* mirrors these personal developments which were significantly influenced by countercultural youth movements. As The Beatles had access to the key figures in the spheres of art, music, protest movements, religion, and philosophy, they were able to gather a conclusive knowledge of recent trends and developments in these matters and incorporated concepts, approaches, recording techniques, and film aesthetics in the production of their works at the time.

For instance, Paul McCartney had developed a profound interest in classical music. As a result, he included elements of classical music in the arrangements of Beatles songs, such as "For No One" and "Eleanor Rigby". In addition, he wrote the score for the movie *The Family Way*, which was arranged by The Beatles' producer George Martin. McCartney also became actively involved in London's underground and avant-garde scene. For example, he financially supported and contributed to the underground magazine *International Times*, he helped establishing the Indica Gallery and held occasional meetings with the likes of Allen Ginsberg, Andy Warhol, and Bertrand Russell.

George Harrison, on the other hand, became interested in Indian music and culture, and began to integrate Indian instruments and arrangements in The Beatles' songs, such as "Nowhere Man" and "Love You To". His involvement with Indian culture, music, and philosophy, as well as his support of the Maharishi Mahesh Yogi and Ravi Shankar eventually made him one of the key figures in introducing and popularizing Indian culture in the Western hemisphere.

Just like his songwriting partner Paul McCartney, John Lennon also established his initial contact with the avant-garde art in 1966, when he first met Yoko Ono, one of the most prominent representatives of the 'Fluxus' movement. He supported one of her exhibitions in London and went on to initiate a variety of art projects with Ono, whom he married in 1969. While all of The Beatles were interested in underground films, only John Lennon actually released some of his films in the late 1960s.

Their involvement with opinion leaders in the various contemporary youth movements also marked a change in The Beatles' attitude toward expressing their own views on international politics and society. Although Brian Epstein had prevented them from communicating their political opinions, the American magazine *Datebook* managed to create an anti-Beatles hysteria by quoting John Lennon's view of Christianity out of context in the summer 1966. In an interview with Maureen Cleave from the *Evening Standard*, Lennon had discussed the decline of Christianity: "Christianity will go. It will vanish and shrink. I needn't argue with that; I'm right and I will be proved right. We're more popular than Jesus now; I don't know which will go first – rock and roll or Christianity" (Coleman 1992: 404). While Lennon's discussion of religion was largely ignored by the British public, who had become quite used to Lennon's critical and often flimsy statements, *Datebook* used the quotation as a headline for an article on The Beatles. The *Datebook* article suggested that Lennon was claiming that The Beatles were actually bigger than Jesus Christ. The reaction in America, especially in the area of the Bible Belt, was devastating. Lennon's comments were considered to be blasphemy, and he was denounced by many fervent believers. Journalist Ray Coleman remembers: "The Ku Klux Klan marched; there were bonfires of Beatles records; and an estimated thirty-five radio stations across America banned Beatles records" (Coleman 1992: 404). The Beatles' manager immediately travelled to the United States to explain the misinterpretation of Lennon's quotation. He was told that only a public apology from Lennon could save the situation for The Beatles, who had planned on going on a tour through America in August 1966. Lennon, who did not understand why anybody would expect an apology from him, tried to clarify what he had actually meant with his statement: "Look, I wasn't saying The Beatles are better than God or Jesus. I said 'Beatles' because it's easy for me to talk about Beatles. I could have said 'TV' or 'the cinema', 'motorcars' or anything popular and I would have got away with it. I'm not anti-god, anti-Christ or anti-religion. I was not saying we are greater or better" (Miles 2001: 240). In the end, the public seemed to accept Lennon's explanation, and the group went on their last American tour. However, instead of avoiding controversial issues, The Beatles voiced their opinions quite clearly from now on. John Lennon became the most political Beatle, composing songs such as "Revolution" and "Give Peace a Chance", supporting several radical groups and controversial individuals, as well as leading numerous campaigns for world peace between 1969 and 1972.

The "bigger than Jesus"-fiasco, as well as several other unpleasant occurrences in Japan and in the Philippines, prompted The Beatles' decision to quit performing live in 1966. On August 29, 1966, The Beatles performed their last ever concert in front of a paying audience at Candlestick Park, San Francisco. From now on, The Beatles existed only as a studio band. However, their newly discovered interest in different genres of music and art, as well as their increasing versatility in the recording studio encouraged them to produce several masterpieces of popular music, such as *Revolver* (1966), *Sgt. Pepper's Lonely Hearts Club Band* (1967), *The Beatles* (1968), and *Abbey Road* (1969).

THE BEATLES ON FILM - PART TWO: 1965-1970

Promotional Films 1965-1967

During the making of *A Hard Day's Night*, Richard Lester had filmed The Beatles performing their song "You Can't Do That" at the Scala Theater in London. The whole sequence, however, was excluded from the film, because Lester thought the concert would seem too long. When Lester was working on his movie *The Knack...And How to Get It* in late 1964, he was asked to forward a clip of the performance footage of "You Can't Do That" to the *Ed Sullivan Show*. Lester did not have the time to edit the film, so he asked John Victor Smith to compile a promotional film of the footage (vgl. Yule 1994: 103). The result was a quite compelling clip showing The Beatles' performance of "You Can't Do That". The way Smith edited the footage, it could easily have been included in *A Hard Day's Night*. For the first time The Beatles did not appear personally on a television program to promote a record, and sent a promotional film instead. It was a pattern they would develop in the following years.

On 23 November, 1965, The Beatles filmed ten promotional films for their latest releases at Twickenham Studios, London. The idea was to provide television programs all around the world with these performances which were to promote their recent single "Day Tripper / We Can Work It Out." This way The Beatles were able to perform in front of a worldwide audience without having to leave London. In addition, the group would not be restricted to only a few television shows, as these promotional films could potentially be shown on any entertainment program.

All in all, The Beatles filmed three versions of "We Can Work It Out" and "Day Tripper," two versions of their previous single "I Feel Fine," and one version each of "Help!" and "Ticket to Ride." The films were directed by Joe McGrath, a television director and producer, whom The Beatles had first met in April 1964 (vgl. Harry 2000: 755). They were produced by the British company Intertel and financed by The Beatles' management agency NEMS, which was owned by Brian Epstein. As pointed out by film scholar Bob Neaverson, these ten promotional films occupy a unique position in television history.

"[T]hey were the first independently produced pop films to be made and distributed specifically for the international market, anticipating the beginning of contemporary pop video. Moreover, while their ultimate raison d'être (to allow the Beatles total control over their image and to be seen simultaneously all over the world) closely mirrors that of the group's move into feature films, so does their form. Unlike the performance-oriented construction of contemporary pop shows, several of McGrath's promos partially disposed of this notion, the most notable example being the "I Feel Fine" clip, which features the group miming into a punch-bag while Ringo rides an exercise bicycle" (Neaverson 1997: 40).

Although all of these promotional films feature lip-synching, some of them also contain elements of semi-diegetic performance, apparently determined to break from the realism of traditional television show performance (vgl. Neaverson 2000: 155).

The three promos of "We Can Work It Out" are basically three different takes of The Beatles miming their single hit. Two of the films feature The Beatles wearing black turtlenecks, while the third clip shows them wearing the uniforms they had worn at their famous performance at Shea Stadium on 15 August 1965, where they had played in front of 56,000 people. As all three versions of "We Can Work It Out" were edited the exact same way, it is quite certain that the performance had been storyboarded or rehearsed before the actual shoot. In all of the three versions of "We Can Work It Out" John Lennon plays an organ, while the other Beatles play their usual instruments. Paul McCartney, the lead singer on this recording, is shown in several close-ups, while the other Beatles are shown in medium shots. The performance is filmed in a more conventional way than The Beatles' song performances in their feature movies *A Hard Day's Night* and *Help!*, although the way The Beatles present themselves deviates from Hollywood perfectionism. Although The Beatles seem to enjoy themselves in all of the promotional films filmed on 23 November, John Lennon almost manages to interrupt the performance by fooling around on the organ. In the third version of "We Can Work It Out", in which The Beatles wear their Shea Stadium outfits, Paul McCartney seems to be on the brink of laughing several times; and at the very end he eventually loses control and breaks out in a laughter. Lennon apparently had a very good day and can be detected fooling around in all of the promotional videos. For instance, in "Ticket to Ride" he and George Harrison intentionally mess up the miming, and Lennon pulls faces and smiles at the camera in all of the films. While "We Can Work It Out", "Day Tripper", and "Ticket to Ride" are otherwise rather traditional television performances, "I Feel Fine" shows The Beatles surrounded by sports equipment. John Lennon, Paul McCartney, and George Harrison play their guitars, while Ringo rides an exercise bicycle. George Harrison, again, mimes intentionally badly, and sings into a punch-bag. The third version of "Day Tripper" is similarly surreal, with George Harrison and Ringo Starr barred 'inside' a 2-dimensional train wagon, while John Lennon and Paul McCartney stand behind the painting of an aeroplane. The Beatles were quite clearly moving away from mere performance films.

BBC's *Top of the Pops* premiered two of the new promotional films, "Day Tripper" and "We Can Work It Out," on 2 December, 1965, and showed excerpts from the other promos on 25 December, 1965 (vgl. Miles 2001: 220). Later, several clips were shown on *Thank You Lucky Stars* in Great Britain. In the United States, "Day Tripper" and "We Can Work It Out" premiered on 6 January, 1966, on the show *Hullaballo*, while "I Feel Fine" was apparently not screened in the United States until the 1990s when The Beatles' company Apple provided MTV with these videos of The Beatles in order to promote the re-release of their compilation *The Beatles 1962-1966* as a double CD set in 1993.

In 1965, it was quite unusual for entertainers to promote their songs with promotional films instead of personal appearances on television shows. Tony Barrow, The Beatles' press agent at the time, released the following statement: "The boys would normally have appeared on television themselves to plug their new single, but they have been busy preparing an entirely new stage act, featuring all new numbers from their forthcoming album for their tour [...]" (Miles 2001: 215). It almost seems as though The Beatles felt the need to apologize for not personally appearing on TV.

To promote their single "Paperback Writer" and its B-side "Rain", The Beatles taped several promotional films in both black and white and color on 19 and 20 May 1966. The clips were directed by Michael Lindsay-Hogg, an experienced television director who had directed the popular weekly television show *Ready, Steady, Go!* on which The Beatles had appeared several times. Filming took place at Chiswick House and at EMI's Abbey Road Studios, where the group was recording their album *Revolver* at the time. According to Bill Harry, one of the color performance clips was especially produced for use on *The Ed Sullivan Show*, featuring a short introduction by Ringo Starr apologizing for them not being there in person (vgl. Harry 2000: 889). The black and white clips were probably destined for British television shows, which were still broadcast in monochrome. The promotional videos filmed in the studio were aired on various British television programs, such as *Thank You Lucky Stars,* *Ready, Steady, Go!,* and *Top of the Pops.*

The color clips as well as the black and white clips filmed at Abbey Road were simple performance films showing The Beatles miming the songs featured on their latest single. The promos filmed at Chiswick House, however, consisted of performance footage intercut with sequences showing The Beatles hanging out at the park. In this context it is interesting that The Beatles do not project their previous 'happy Mop-Top' image and appear rather cool and detached in these promotional films. Instead of fooling around in front of the camera, they are shown in a way resembling the contemplative image projected by the early photographs taken by Robert Freeman. In 1966, The Beatles were indeed striving for acceptance as artists rather than pop singers. Their varied interests in avant-garde music and films, classical and Indian music, art films and exhibitions as well as their political commitment all contributed to a significant change in the way The Beatles projected their image to the world.

In 1967, the British Musicians' Union issued a rule preventing performers from miming to their records on television (vgl. Harry 2000: 457). Therefore, The Beatles had to find an alternative way of visualizing their latest single release, the double-A sided "Strawberry Fields Forever / Penny Lane." Although they had pioneered non-diegetic promotional films with previous clips, such as "Rain," the Union's ruling now entirely terminated the possibility of mimed performance videos.

Having lost interest in simple performance videos anyway, The Beatles decided that they wanted a more artistic quality to their new promo clips in order to match the groundbreaking sounds of "Strawberry Fields Forever" and "Penny Lane." Klaus Voormann, their friend from Hamburg, was playing bass guitar with Manfred Mann's Earth Band at the time and recommended Swedish director Peter Goldman to the group (vgl. Voormann 2003). Goldman had worked with Manfred Mann's Earth Band as well as with The Troggs, The Hollies and Donovan (vgl. Harry 2000: 457). In an interview Goldman explained that he had actually been inspired to become a director by The Beatles' first movie, *A Hard Day's Night*: "Originally, my enthusiasm for presenting English groups on TV in Sweden was fired by Dick Lester's fine film of the Beatles in *A Hard Day's Night*. I thought that was fantastic and wanted to try to present this music in an original and interesting manner on TV" (Sutherland 106). Filming took place in February 1967. As The Beatles were busy recording their album *Sgt. Pepper's Lonely Hearts Club Band*, they were not able to go to Liverpool to film their parts on authentic locations. Instead, they filmed their parts at Knole Park Estate, near

Sevenoaks in Kent, and in London. A film team was sent to Liverpool to shoot some scenes at the locations described in the songs. The scenes of Liverpool were later spliced into the films. The promotional film for "Penny Lane" seemed to portray John Lennon wandering through the streets of Liverpool, although these scenes were actually filmed in London and were later intercut with footage shot in Liverpool (vgl. Harry 2000: 457). With "Strawberry Fields Forever" and Penny Lane", The Beatles took the genre of promotional films to new heights. While "Penny Lane" worked well in the tradition of surrealistic films the group had created since *A Hard Day's Night*, "Strawberry Fields Forever" was especially innovative, as Peter Goldman used techniques borrowed from underground and avant-garde film, such as reversed film effects, dramatic lighting, unusual camera, and rhythmic editing. Created at the height of the psychedelic music period, these promotional films "are among the very first purpose-made concept videos that attempt to 'illustrate' the song in an artful manner, rather than just creating a film of an idealized performance" ("Music Video" 2005).

Magical Mystery Tour

Production History

The idea for The Beatles' project *Magical Mystery Tour* evolved in April 1967, when Paul McCartney and the group's manager Brian Epstein first discussed the possibility of producing a television special around some new songs provided by the band. Since The Beatles had quit touring they had been looking for alternative ways of how to stay in touch with their audience and to promote their recordings. According to The Beatles' press agent Tony Barrow, the group was considering to send out "homemade musicals and comedy shows occasionally to the world's theatres or television stations. This grand-scale global exposure would help to promote their albums and maintain a next-best-thing-to-touring link between The Fab Four and their millions of faithful fans" (Barrow 1999). The idea was inspired by Elvis Presley, who relied on the cinema and on television to remain in the eyes of the public after he had retired from touring.

Originally, it had been planned to produce a film to accompany the band's most extravagant album release to date, *Sgt. Pepper's Lonely Hearts Club Band*. Aware of the fact that it was impossible to reproduce the complex sounds of *Sgt. Pepper* on stage, The Beatles wanted to provide their audience with an adequate performance on film. Every song of the album was going to be visualized in a short film, similar to the way the promotional films for "Strawberry Field Forever" and "Penny Lane" had been made. Tony Bramwell, one of Brian Epstein's staff members, even filmed the recording sessions for the song "A Day in the Life." However, this project was abandoned, as the group was mainly concerned with recording the music for their album. The promotional film for "A Day in the Life" remained in The Beatles' archive and was eventually screened in 1983, when Abbey Road Studios opened their doors to the public for an exhibition called The Beatles at Abbey Road.

In April 1967, The Beatles were already busy recording the soundtrack for their next project, *Magical Mystery Tour*, although their latest achievement *Sgt. Pepper's Lonely Hearts Club Band* had not yet been released. The concept of the planned film had been developed by Paul McCartney, who had heard of Ken Kesey and the Merry Pranksters, a hippie-community that had painted an old school bus and had traveled across the USA, dispensing LSD along the way. The trip had been filmed but the film was never released, although Tom Wolfe later wrote *The Electric Kool-Aid Acid Test* about it (vgl. Miles 1997: 350-351).

Thinking about a way of realizing the concept of a psychedelic bus journey in a British setting, McCartney remembered a certain kind of traveling that had been common in the Liverpool area.

"It used to be called a mystery tour, up north. When we were kids, you'd get on a bus, and you didn't know where you were going, but nearly always it was Blackpool. From Liverpool, it was inevitably Blackpool and everyone would go, "Oooo, it was Blackpool after all!" Everyone would spend time guessing where they were going, and this was part of the thrill" (Miles 1997: 350).

According to McCartney's official biographer Barry Miles, Brian Epstein began to organize the production of the television special soon after McCartney's and Epstein's initial discussion (vgl. Miles 1997: 350). Unfortunately, however, Epstein was not to oversee the production anymore (vgl. Miles 1997: 352). When The Beatles were residing in Bangor, Wales, in order to learn about the Maharishi Mahesh Yogi's technique of Transcendental Meditation, Brian Epstein was found dead in his London house on August 27, 1967. While Epstein's sudden death caused a number of wild rumors to be publicized, his personal assistant Alistair Taylor confirms that Epstein had died because of an accidental drug overdose: "He died from the cumulative effect of bromide in a drug he had been using for a long time. The drug was Carbitral. The amount of bromide in him was only enough to be described as a 'low fatal level' but Brian had taken repeated 'incautious self overdoses' which added up enough to kill him" (Taylor 2003: 194).

The Beatles were still in a state of shock when they came together to discuss their future on September 1, 1967. They decided that they would continue their *Magical Mystery Tour* project and look for a reasonable solution as to the management of their business affairs. Having starred in two feature movie productions, The Beatles were convinced that they had learned enough about the film business to try and write, produce and direct their own film. As they had become the most successful songwriters and performers in the history of popular music, they believed that their approach to creating music could also be applied to the art of filmmaking. This approach seemed justified, since John Lennon and Paul McCartney had become the most prolific songwriters of their generation without having had any conventional musical training. They had demonstrated to a generation of young people that anybody can achieve public recognition regardless of their social backgrounds. Richard Lester, the director of The Beatles' movies *A Hard Day's Night* and *Help!*, recently commented on how the group's impact on culture and creative approach influenced the traditional class system in Great Britain:

"I think they were the first to give a confidence to the youth of the country, which led to the disappearance of the Angry Young Man with a defensive mien. The Beatles sent the class thing sky-high; they laughed it out of existence and, I think, introduced a tone of quality more successfully than any other single factor that I know. Eventually it became taken for granted that they were single-handedly breaking Britain's class system without the benefit of an education or family background. They were, of course, much more middle class than most people admitted" (Yule 1994: 12).

While Lester neglects the contextual factors enabling The Beatles to represent a certain attitude and image, it is certainly true that they contributed significantly to the way popular music was perceived in the 1960s. Having celebrated such huge success as artists and having taken popular music to a different level by integrating elements from classical music, world music, and from the contemporary avant-garde, The Beatles wanted to produce their new film in a similar, easygoing way. All of The Beatles had been interested in the film business and, as with their music, were intent to contribute to a way of changing public perceptions. For instance, in 1966, John Lennon had starred in Richard Lester's anti-war-movie movie *How I Won the War*, which had shocked the audience with its inventive combination of surrealism, comedy, and Brechtian drama in a World War 2 setting. Around the same time, Paul McCartney created his own avant-garde home movies, which he liked to present to his friends. Two of these films, *The Defeat of the Dog* and *The Next Spring Then*, were described in *Punch* magazine at the time. The description provides a rather interesting insight to McCartney's mid-60s films which would finally culminate in The Beatles' *Magical Mystery Tour*.

"They were not like ordinary people's home movies. There were over-exposures, double-exposures, blinding orange lights, quick cuts from professional wrestling to a crowded car park to a close-up of a television weather map. There were long still shots of a grey cloudy sky and a wet, grey, pavement, jumping Chinese ivory carvings and affectionate slow-motion studies of his sheepdog Martha and his cat. The accompanying music, on a record player and faultlessly synchronised, was by the Modern Jazz Quartet and Bach" (Miles 1997: 297).

In early 1967, Paul McCartney explained his approach to music and film to Barry Miles:

"With everything, with any kind of thing, my aim seems to be to distort it. Distort it from what we know it as, even with music and visual things, and to change it from what it is to what it could be. To see the potential of it all. To take a note and wreck it and see in that note what else there is in it, that a simple act like distorting it has caused. To take a film and superimpose on top of it so you can't quite tell what it is any more [...]. The only trouble is, that you don't have the bit that you did when you were a kid of innocently accepting things. For instance, if a film comes on that's superimposed and doesn't seem to mean anything, immediately it's weird or it's strange, or it's a bit funny to most people [...]" (Miles 1997: 301).

Denis O'Dell, who was to produce the film, remembers The Beatles' rather naïve do-it-yourself approach to filming: "They had absolutely no idea that studios have to be booked weeks or even months in advance, that contracts and union terms have to be negotiated with cast and crew, that locations have to be prepared and all manner of other things arranged" (Neaverson/O'Dell 2002: 66).

According to John Lennon, Paul McCartney asked his band mates to contribute ideas to the formless screenplay: "Paul would say, 'Well, here's the segment, you write a little piece for that" (Carr 1996: 116). Consequently, all group members came up with ideas for little sequences and fragments that were going to be filmed in the following weeks. However, none of the ideas were actually written down in a conventional screenplay. As pointed out by Paul McCartney, the group was striving for spontaneity: "I thought, well, we could just go places [...] and cobble together some sort of story as you went along, because, after all, the theme of a mystery tour is just that: that you don't know where you're going anyway. So we thought we'd take this to the extreme and literally not know what film we were making" (Miles 1997: 366).

Without a proper script and without having finished the soundtrack recordings, The Beatles started filming their *Magical Mystery Tour* on 11 September, 1967. Their assistants Alistair Taylor, Neil Aspinall and Mal Evans had hired a coach and painted a "Magical Mystery Tour" logo on its side. The Beatles had chosen several actors from a casting magazine, *Spotlight*, and had invited some members from The Beatles' fan club to join them on their tour. The film crew consisted of four cameramen and a sound man, a technical adviser and various technical assistants (vgl. Miles 1997: 360). All in all, 43 passengers were on The Beatles' *Magical Mystery Tour* bus when it left London for five days of filming. The party first drove to Teignmouth, Devon, where they stayed the first night of their trip. On September 12, they continued their journey to Newquay, Cornwall, where they filmed several sequences at the Atlantic Hotel. They spent two more days on the road, capturing some surreal moments of the journey on film. The following week The Beatles and their crew spent at West Malling Air Station, Maidstone, Kent, where they filmed most of the more memorable scenes of *Magical Mystery Tour*, such as their performance of "I Am the Walrus", the car race, and the grand finale, with The Beatles trooping down a staircase singing "Your Mother Should Know" (vgl. Miles 2001: 278-280). This location was agreed upon, when The Beatles found out that film studios had to be booked in advance. Denis O'Dell, the producer of *Magical Mystery Tour*, recalls that "I was frequently forced to improvise second-rate solutions at the last minute. An example of this was when I had to book an old disused air hangar at West Malling for the [musical] sequences because it was impossible to obtain any studio time at Twickenham, Pinewood or Elstree. We also shot the marathon sequence there" (Neaverson/O'Dell 2002: 68).

On September 25, 1967, Roy Benson, who had been one of the film editors on *A Hard Day's Night*, began editing the filmed material at Norman's Film Productions in London. The Beatles had originally set aside two weeks to edit the film, but due to the disorganized way the whole project had been filmed, it finally took eleven weeks for Roy Benson to edit the ten hours of material down to 53 minutes. The Beatles were involved in the editing process to varying degrees and informed Benson what to use in the film and what to leave out. Since the film had been Paul McCartney's original idea, he spent quite some time with Roy Benson at the editing suite.

While Benson was busy editing the movie, The Beatles finished recording the soundtrack for *Magical Mystery Tour* at Abbey Road Studios, London. When The Beatles realized that they had not filmed a suitable sequence for Paul McCartney's song "Fool on the Hill," McCartney spontaneously decided to fly to Nice, where he, his personal assistant Mal Evans and the cameraman Aubrey Devon spent a day filming an ad-libbed sequence for the movie on October 30, 1967.

Most accounts of the making of *Magical Mystery Tour* neglect Ringo Starr's contribution to the project. While his colleagues had been exploring different musical areas in 1966, Starr had become fascinated with photography and experimental films. At his home he developed and printed his own films and experimented with the technical aspects of photography. According to biographer Alan Clayson, Starr was well informed about the versatility of delayed-action shutters and different kinds of lenses (vgl. Clayson 1996: 157). His outstanding contribution to *Magical Mystery Tour* was the sequence showing George Harrison playing "Blue Jay Way": "[There's] a scene with George where I put him in my living room and projected slides on him. It's nothing new. It was done back in 1926 or so – but I happened to be a camera buff, and I think it came out fine" (Clayson 1996: 157). Honoring his creative contribution to *Magical Mystery Tour*, Ringo Starr was half-jokingly credited as 'director of photography' under his birth name, Richard Starkey, M.B.E.

Magical Mystery Tour and Swinging London

The Beatles were among the most fashionable young men in the mid-sixties. Having set contemporary fashion trends with their unique Cardin suits and their 'Beatle boots' at the early stages of their career, they were also the leading characters in fashion during the 'Summer of Love', 1967, which constituted the climax of 'psychedelia'. For the release of their *Sgt. Pepper* album, The Beatles appeared in colorful uniforms, kaftans, and other embroidered outfits. Although *Magical Mystery Tour* itself represented the psychedelic youth culture in the way it projected an escape into a bizarre dream world, some of the costumes The Beatles used in the movie were in complete contrast to what had been worn in London in the summer. The movie marked another change in The Beatles' outer appearance. For instance, John Lennon and Paul McCartney had shaved off their *Sgt.Pepper* – moustaches, which had shocked The Beatles' fans, when the group had first sported them in the promotional videos for "Strawberry Fields Forever" and "Penny Lane".

For no specific reason, The Beatles had decided to wear suits reminiscent of 'gangster suits' featured in old Hollywood movies. The Beatles' press officer Tony Barrow recalls, "For the coach trip, the group's film outfits recalled Chicago's legendary gangland heydays. George changed out of a favourite old blue denim jacket and into a big blue suit with black tie. John wore a brown pin-striped suit and feathers in his hat. Paul chose a pullover which was predominantly orange-red while Ringo went along with the 'gangster's suit' theme" (Barrow 1999). *The Beatles Monthly Book* even speculated at the time that clothes designers in Carnaby Street were wondering whether The Beatles were about "to spark off a nationwide craze for gangster-style Al Capone clothes" (Barrow 1999). It should be pointed out, however, that The Beatles wore these clothes mainly in the scenes showing them on the bus. In the "I Am the Walrus" – segment, for instance, they decided to wear psychedelic hippie–outfits, and in the sequence accompanying "Your Mother Should Know" they wore white suits.

The choice of clothes was also interesting in comparison to The Beatles' earlier movies *A Hard Day's Night* and *Help!*, as their identical appearance was now definitely a thing of the past. While they had still sported uniforms on the cover of their summer release *Sgt. Pepper's Lonely Hearts Club Band*, they had now completed their image transformation from 'four-headed monster'[1] to four individual pop artists. This is also evident in the way the group presents its image in *Magical Mystery Tour*. Except for the performances of "I Am the Walrus" and "Your Mother Should Know", The Beatles do not appear as a band in this movie. They hardly ever interact – as they had in *A Hard Day's Night* – and appear quite independently throughout the movie. Considering the fact that George Harrison and John Lennon had come to dislike The Beatles' mop-top image by then, it is quite certain that this way of presenting the group was constructed deliberately to emphasize the beginning of a new phase in The Beatles' career. It is also interesting that The Beatles do actually not just play themselves in the movie but take on various roles. For instance, John Lennon plays a travel agent, a waiter in Aunt Jessie's dream, and one of the magicians, while Paul McCartney impersonates a soldier, the 'fool' on the hill, as well as a magician. Film scholar Bob Neaverson points out that "[i]n this way, the viewer's perception of the group is constantly blurred by a series of dramatic and non-dramatic paradoxes which partially obscure any single and coherent image of the Beatles as a 'pop group'" (Neaverson 1997: 68). On the one hand, this enables The Beatles to satirize conventional modes of representation in showbusiness, while it also allows them to escape from the

---

1   The Rolling Stones' Mick Jagger has repeatedly called The Beatles a "four-headed monster", as they complemented each other so well, for instance, at press conferences.

group image that had been projected by *Help!* and *A Hard Day's Night*, which they found too restrictive at the time (cf. Neaverson 1997: 68).

Story and Aesthetics

The movie starts with a voice-over (John Lennon) telling the audience to get ready for a 'Magical Mystery Tour'. Ringo Starr buys tickets for himself and his aunt Jessie at a travel agency. The travel agent is played by a disguised John Lennon. They get on the tour bus, a big yellow vehicle with a blue stripe running horizontally along the side. The guests are welcomed by the courier, Mr. Jolly Jimmy Johnson, and the attractive tour guide, Miss Wendy Winters. As the bus rolls out, the other passengers are introduced. Among many others, all The Beatles are on board, along with a midget photographer, some old men, an actress, a little girl called Nicola, and Mr. Buster Bloodvessel, who believes he is the courier. Ringo is sitting beside his corpulent aunt, whose husband has just recently passed away. Ringo provokes a conflict when he points out that Jessie has been eyeing the men on the bus. The song "Fool on the Hill" suddenly starts to play. At first, Paul McCartney is still on the bus, smoking a cigarette, but suddenly he is shown wearing different clothes, standing on a mountaintop. The footage accompanying "Fool on the Hill" shows McCartney walking, running, and jumping around the French countryside. The sequence merely illustrates the song in a non-diegetic manner, as it does not feature any performance footage. Interestingly, The Beatles' *Anthology*-video project contains outtakes filmed for the "Fool on the Hill" – sequence, which show McCartney miming the words to the song. Consequently, it must have been a deliberate decision by The Beatles and Roy Benson to leave out the performance scenes in favor of non-diegetic footage illustrating the song. The other song sequences were "I Am the Walrus", "Flying", "Blue Jay Way," and "Your Mother Should Know".

During the making of *Magical Mystery Tour*, each Beatle was allowed to direct at least one sequence. According to editor Roy Benson, the performance of "I Am the Walrus" was John Lennon's directorial piece for the movie (vgl. *A Long and Winding Road* 2003: DVD 3). At first, the sequence had been planned to show a diegetic performance of Lennon's song. During the process of editing the piece, however, Benson and Lennon realized that they did not have enough usable material for the sequence. Lennon asked Benson to come up with some ideas, and Benson edited the sequence in a way that combined The Beatles' slightly surreal performance sequence with rather arbitrary footage The Beatles had filmed for the movie (vgl. *A Long and Winding Road* 2003: DVD 3). Interestingly, Benson's way of editing the sequence mirrored The Beatles' attitude toward the recording of John Lennon's psychedelic classic "I Am the Walrus". The lyrics to the song were reminiscent of nonsense poetry of the likes of Lewis Carroll, whose poem "The Walrus and the Carpenter" had actually inspired Lennon's lyrics. In addition to these obvious influences, journalist Ian McDonald has noted that "Lennon was satirising the fashion for fanciful psychedelic lyrics cultivated by Dylan's then much-discussed output" (McDonald: 1994: 215). The recording itself featured a rather conventional backing track, supplemented by John Lennon's voice, which was distorted by channelling it through the loudspeaker of a Leslie organ, a string arrangement by George Martin, and The Mike Sammes Singers chanting "everybody's got one/everybody's got one". What added to the recording's revolutionary impact on the psychedelic music of 1967 was The Beatles' use of a random radio scan that broke into a BBC broadcast of *King Lear*. This avant-garde technique of using coincidental and arbitrary sounds to complement The Beatles' performance was taken up by Roy Benson, who complemented the footage of diegetic song performance with random footage of The Beatles and their entourage.

The sequence accompanying The Beatles' only joint composition "Flying" features breathtaking footage of Icelandic landscapes presented in psychedelic colors. While, in the *Anthology,* Ringo Starr remembers that The Beatles had sent somebody to Iceland to film the sequence, the footage actually consisted of outtakes from Stanley Kubrick's movie *Dr Strangelove* (Neaverson/O'Dell 2002: 68). By suggesting that the color-filtered cloud formations and landscapes are seen by the people on the *Magical Mystery Tour*-bus, it is made clear that the bus really takes its passengers on a magical trip.

"Blue Jay Way", mainly directed by Ringo Starr and George Harrison, again emphasizes the psychedelic nature of the whole experience, with George Harrison performing his song on a keyboard painted on the floor of his garage. The performance is intercut with the aforementioned sequences of slides projected upon Harrison's face and footage showing The Beatles in John Lennon's garden, playing a white cello, and fooling around with a football. It has been pointed out that "[w]hile [Harrison] appears to be visibly 'tripping' (and therefore presenting himself as a Leary-inspired advocate of mind-expanding drugs), his 'lotus' posture also implies a contradictory advocacy of spiritual purity via transcendental mysticism and meditation" (Neaverson 1997: 69). Although Neaverson describes the atmosphere conveyed by the "Blue Jay Way" sequence in a quite adequate way, the statement referring to drugs is not correct, as the Beatles had never advocated the use of LSD and other psychedelic drugs. Although they supported a newspaper advertisement in favor of legalizing marihuana in July 1967, they later refrained from promoting the use of drugs, especially after George Harrison had witnessed the effect drugs had on American youth culture, when he visited a gathering of hippies in San Francisco in August, 1967. In The Beatles' *Anthology*, Harrison explicitly explains that he quit LSD after his trip to San Francisco (Beatles 2000: 259).

Therefore, it is simply wrong to suggest that The Beatles were advocating the use of drugs in *Magical Mystery Tour*. Although it was a colorful and mystical road movie with a hefty dose of surrealism, it was quite definitely not designed as a commercial for drugs. In contrast, George Harrison's encounter with eastern philosophy and transcendental meditation introduced a new phase in The Beatles' career, where they moved away from drugs – at least for a while – to explore alternative methods of achieving a heightened awareness. In February, 1968, The Beatles went to Rishikesh, India, where they studied the Maharishi Mahesh Yogi's technique of transcendental meditation. While Ringo Starr and Paul McCartney returned to England after a few weeks for various reasons, George Harrison and John Lennon stayed in Rishikesh for four months, during which they refrained from taking drugs and composed some of their best songs.

The film's final song sequence, accompanying "Your Mother Should Know", also constitutes a surprising finale for *Magical Mystery Tour*. The sequence, which unexpectedly follows a scene filmed at a striptease club, shows The Beatles on a lavish film set reminiscent of 1950s Hollywood musical sets, where the group perform a loosely choreographed dance down a big staircase to the music of Paul McCartney's dancehall song pastiche. By parodying the conventions of grand-scale Hollywood musicals and television gala shows, The Beatles pointed out that their far-out television special was intentionally designed to contradict the audience's expectations of old-fashioned show entertainment. It was a subtle criticism of established norms in show business and fit very well into the film's humorous view at the establishment, which The Beatles had always made fun of since the early stages of their career. Film scholar Bob Neaverson describes the way *Magical Mystery Tour* undermines established ideology.

"Perhaps the most poignant example of the mockery of state authorities is the sequence in which the party stop off in an army recruitment office, only to be confronted by a Sergeant (Victor Spinetti) who aggressively shouts abstract, meaningless orders at the entourage until Ringo gently asks 'why?' The scene then cuts to a similar sequence in which the same character is seen attempting to impose his gibberish orders upon a stuffed cow which is mounted on the back of a plank" (Neaverson 1997: 63).

The police as well as representatives of the Church of England are also ridiculed in several scenes. While the "I Am the Walrus" sequence features dancing policemen, the marathon sequence shows several vicars making objectionable gestures toward the winners of the race. (vgl. Neaverson 1997: 63). Moreover, the narrative form itself, the amateur aesthetics, as well as The Beatles' overall attitude toward the whole project reflect a desire to challenge social and moral norms, and the established system of values.

With the release of the movie's soundtrack, The Beatles also broke with conventional forms, as it was decided that they would release the six songs featured in *Magical Mystery Tour* on an unprecedented format – a double EP (Extended Player) instead of an album. The Beatles had released several EPs before, as this was a quite popular format in Great Britain. An EP usually consisted of four songs and, in The Beatles' catalogue, often contained exclusive recordings. The concept of a double EP was a first in the history of the British music business. In the United States, where EPs had never been a great success, Capitol Records insisted on releasing a soundtrack album. As The Beatles had only recorded six proper songs for their television special, Capitol Records added five songs The Beatles had released only as singles ("Hello Goodbye", "Strawberry Fields Forever", "Penny Lane", "Baby You're a Rich Man", and "All You Need Is Love").

The British EP release, as well as the American album release, contained an extensive 24-page full color picture book featuring a slightly different version of the movie's storyline, which was based upon The Beatles' original ideas. The differences reveal several changes made by The Beatles during the editing process.

"AWAY IN THE SKY, beyond the clouds, live 4 or 5 Magicians. By casting WONDERFUL SPELLS they turn the Most Ordinary Coach Trip into a MAGICAL MYSTERY TOUR. If you let yourself go, the Magicians will take you away to marvelous places.
Maybe YOU'VE been on a Magical Mystery Tour without even realizing it.
Are you ready to go?
SPLENDID! The story begins on Page 7...or 8...
1. RINGO AND AUNTIE JESSIE are always quarrelling about one thing or another. But they both agree it would be exciting to go on a Mystery Tour. 'Your Uncle Jack always liked a Charabanc Trip' says Auntie Jessie. 'And this is a MAGIC trip' adds Ringo.

2. A few days later, VERY early in the morning, they set off to start the tour. Auntie Jessie looks at the B-I-G bus and smiles: 'It's all yellow and blue! My favourite colours!' When everyone is ready JOLLY JIMMY JOHNSON (THE COURIER) climbs aboard.

3. 'Good Morning Ladies And Gentlemen, Boys And Girls! WELCOME TO MAGICAL MYSTERY TOUR! I am your Courier. All my friends call me Jolly Jimmy and YOU are ALL my friends! Everyone comfy? SPLENDID!'

4. Then Jolly Jimmy introduces the Tour Hostess, THE DELIGHTFUL WENDY WINTERS. 'And over HERE...' he goes on 'is our driver for the trip, a wonderful driver (WE HOPE!) whose name is ALF. Away-way-way we go, Alf! SPLENDID!'

5. Needless to say Auntie Jessie finds something to argue about. 'You ain't coming with me anymore' she tells Ringo. 'Who bought the tickets? I DID, DIDN'T I!' replies Ringo. 'Yes, YOU bought the tickets' agrees Auntie Jessie 'BUT I GAVE YOU THE MONEY!'

6. At the front of the bus sits a Sad Little Man in a funny old uniform. 'Who IS that man?' whispers Wendy Winters. 'That's Mr. Buster Bloodvessel' answers Jolly Jimmy 'He's quite harmless. He thinks HE'S THE COURIER! Last trip he thought he was THE DRIVER!'

THE MAGIC BEGINS TO WORK!

7. The other passengers are enjoying the bright sunshine, the green country-side. 'Excuse me' says LITTLE GEORGE to PAUL 'I'd like to take a photo-graph of your young lady.' 'O.K.' says Paul. 'All right' says MAGGIE, THE LOVELY STARLET.

8. 'This IS my lucky day!' chuckles Little George who loves to take LOTS of pictures. Click! Clack! CLICK! Meanwhile PAUL BEGINS TO DAYDREAM. His thoughts fly FAR AWAY. He is standing high up on a warm, grassy hill...

9. SUDDENLY Paul's daydreaming is over. He hears the delightful voice of the Hostess: 'I JUST WANTED TO SAY THAT IF THERE IS ANYTHING I CAN DO FOR YOU...YOUR WISH IS OUR COMMAND!' 'But I wonder where the MAGIC comes in?' thinks Paul.

10. Little does he know that THE MAGIC IS ALREADY BEGINNING TO WORK! Somewhere up in the sky, beyond the little white clouds, FIVE MAGICIANS study their mysterious maps and gaze into their magic telescope. They are CASTING WONDERFUL SPELLS.

11. At last one of the MAGICIANS looks up from his work: 'THE BUS IS TEN MILES NORTH ON THE DEWSBURY ROAD AND THEY'RE HAVING A LOVELY TIME!' he cries. The others dance with glee: 'THEY'RE HAVING A LOVELY TIME!!!'

12. Even as they dance THE MAGIC TAKES EFFECT and the bus is SPIRITED AWAY TO THE AMAZING MUSICAL LAND OF THE WALRUS! 'I AM THE WALRUS' says John. 'NO, YOU'RE NOT' cries Ni-cola, laughing at his funny feathery hat.

WHAT A MARVELOUS LUNCH!

13. NICOLA is the VERY YOUNGEST LITTLE GIRL on the bus. 'I'VE GOT A PRESENT FOR YOU!' says John. And he gives her a BIG RED BALLOON. She hasn't quite enough PUFF to blow it up for herself so JOHN and GEORGE help her.

14. In no time at all everybody is ready for lunch and the bus draws up beside a small cafe. Jolly Jimmy leads the way and all the people follow eagerly because they're HUNGRY! 'WHAT A MARVELOUS LUNCH!' says everyone. AND IT IS!

15. There is Chicken Soup followed by Roast Beef and Carrots with Thick Brown Gravy to go over the Potatoes! A small band plays Jolly Tunes in the corner of the room. Nobody is enjoying himself more than HAPPY NAT.

16. 'If I eat any more' says HAPPY NAT 'I SHALL FALL ASLEEP!' 'Then you'll MISS ALL THE MAGIC!' warns Little Nicola. While the waiters scurry away to get the pudding, the band plays a very exciting Spanish Dance.

17. 'I'm no Spanish Dancer but I certainly know my onions!' laughs HAPPY NAT. Up he gets from the table and becomes a FAMOUS SPANISH BULLFIGHTER. After all that eating and all that dancing no wonder Happy Nat nods off.

18. So while the others tuck into Strawberry Ice Cream or Aunt Mary's Apple Pie, HAPPY NAT has a HAPPY DREAM...all about his adventures with a bunch of pretty girls beside the seaside!
MEET MAJOR McCARTNEY & SGT. SPINETTI!

19. The sound of AUNTIE JESSIE PLAYING THE DRUMS brings Happy Nat's delicious dream to an abrupt end! Yes, there she is SITTING WITH THE BAND – banging away and singing at the top of her voice!

20. 'I suppose it runs in the family' suggests Happy Nat. 'I never knew she had it in her' replies Ringo. Soon the bus is on its way again and everyone congratulates Auntie Jessie because THEY didn't know she had it in her!

21. Presently Driver Alf brings his bus to a halt outside a STRANGE BUILDING. 'What a funny place!' remarks John. 'I don't like the look of it' adds George. 'WE'RE JUST PASSING THROUGH' says Wendy Winters reassuringly.

22. Before long Jolly Jimmy has led everybody into an Official sort of Office. Behind an old desk sits MAJOR McCARTNEY looking Very Important. Beside him stands SGT. SPINETTI looking over his shoulder.

23. 'Just follow me' whispers Jolly Jimmy 'and if they try to get you to join up DON'T TAKE ANY NOTICE!' Now that is easier said than done! Eventually they leave the Sergeant screaming about haircuts and Other Military Things.

24. 'Now!' says Wendy Winters 'We'll split into two groups. All the Ladies – THIS WAY PLEASE!' 'And ALL THE MEN should come with me' chortles Jolly Jimmy, a special twinkle in his eye 'I've got a NICE SURPRISE FOR YOU!'
THE GREAT MARATHON RACE

25. 'Hello!' says George 'We're going into a striptease club.' AND THEY ARE TOO! 'Whoops Johnny! Hey! Tee hee hee!' cries John. 'Front row seats for all you lucky lads!' shouts Jolly Jimmy ordering up the drinks.

26. 'Cheer Up Mr. Bloodvessel' says John giving him a friendly nudge 'Sup up your milk and enjoy the show!' Before the show is over Mr. Bloodvessel HAS FORGOTTEN ALL ABOUT HIS MILK!

27. When they are back on the bus all the Men look VERY PLEASED WITH THEMSELVES. So do the Ladies – but THEY don't say where THEY'VE been! After a while Jolly Jimmy jumps up again: 'NOW FOR THE MAGICAL MYSTERY TOUR MARATHON RACE!'

28. WELL! Have you EVER seen so many people IN ALL YOUR LIFE? Everyone lines up for the start – The Rugby Team, The Little Wrestlers, The Five Cheating Vicars and ALL the people from the bus. BANG! THEY'RE OFF!

29. It looks as though Five Vicars might win because they are cheating by RIDING BICYCLES. So some of the others use MOTOR BIKES and CARS which are MUCH BETTER ways of CHEATING!

30. GOOD OLD RINGO! HE finds the BEST WAY of cheating – BY DRIVING THE MAGICAL BUS! So the Mystery Tour Team wins the BIG RACE in the end WHICH SERVES ALL THE OTHERS RIGHT!!!

AUNTIE JESSIE'S DREADFUL DREAM

31. NO WONDER people are a bit sleepy after all that racing around! Poor Auntie Jessie nods off and has a dream ABOUT MOUNTAINS OF SPAGHETTI! 'Wake up Ringo! Wake up Auntie Jessie!' It is LITTLE GEORGE speaking.

32. 'NO MORE SPAGHETTI!' moans Auntie Jessie. 'Come on!' insists Little George. The rest of the party has already disappeared into a SMALL TENT standing in the middle of a meadow.

33. 'If we ALL manage to squeeze into THAT TINY TENT it will be MAGIC!' declares Ringo. I won't tell you the MARVELOUS and AMAZING things which happen in the tent BUT I WILL TELL YOU IT IS MAGIC!

34. By now the sun is setting behind the hills and it's time to head for home. SHIRLEY THE ACCORDIONIST plays Happy Tunes while everybody sings the words. Even MR. BLOODVESSEL! All the Magic has made him forget.

35. Funnily enough nobody notices the EXTRA PASSENGERS ON THE BUS. But there they are...THE FIVE MAGICIANS, SINGING AND LAUGHING ALONG WITH EVERYBODY ELSE! 'WE'RE HAVING A LOVELY TIME!' THEY CHANT.

36. Auntie Jessie and all the other people have NEVER enjoyed a Mystery Tour so much in their lives! Thanks to Jolly Jimmy, Wendy Winters AND THE FIVE MYSTERIOUS MAGICIANS. And, of course, THANKS TO JOHN, PAUL, GEORGE AND RINGO!!! WHOOPEE!

THE END."

(*Magical Mystery Tour* 1967).

While there are slight changes in the sequence of the scenes, the most obvious difference between the comic book version and the finished movie is the sequence titled "What a Marvelous Lunch" in the comic. The Beatles had filmed an extensive lunch scene at a hotel, which was almost completely cut from the film. Only short segments of this scene made it into the "I Am the Walrus" sequence. However, whereas it is easy to point out the marginal differences between The Beatles' outline and the finished result, it should be noted that – contrary to what some critics have claimed – The Beatles did have an idea of what the movie was supposed to be like.

Even though *Magical Mystery Tour* was clearly designed for a young, open-minded audience rather than for a general mainstream audience, the BBC decided to broadcast it at prime time. Denis O'Dell recalls his reaction when he found out about this.

"You can imagine my horror when BBC 1 screened the film on Boxing Day 1967 at 8.35 p.m. in black and white. The timing of the transmission could not have been more insensitive. Its screening, at a time traditionally reserved for more conventional forms of family entertainment, was totally inappropriate for an avant-garde film which would have been much more at home in a 10 p.m. slot on BBC 2. Worse still, the unfathomable decision to show the movie in monochrome totally undermined its swirling hallucinatory imagery, rendering its aesthetic raison d'être completely redundant" (Neaverson/O'Dell 2002: 70).

O'Dell's concerns were quite justified, considering the public reaction to The Beatles' first self-produced television special. The British press simply loathed the movie and slated it in their reviews. For instance, the *Daily Express* called it "blatant rubbish," the *Daily Mirror* criticized it because "it was chaotic," while the *Daily Mail* declared: "It's colossal, the conceit of the Beatles" (Sutherland 114). *Magical Mystery Tour* became The Beatles' first and only flop in Great Britain. The media's outrageous reaction to The Beatles' movie prompted Paul McCartney to release several statements justifying the group's first attempt at art films. On January 6, 1968, the *New Musical Express* published an interview with McCartney.

"We could easily have assembled a team of experts […] and asked them to come up with a first class show for Christmas which would star the Beatles. But that would have been easy. We wanted to try and do it ourselves […]. The mistake was that too many people were looking for a plot when there wasn't one. It was just a series of unconnected events which we thought would be interesting or humorous or just pleasant to watch" (Sutherland 114).

The film contributed significantly to The Beatles' departure from their early 'mop-top' image, which the group had gradually abandoned since their tour of America in 1966. John Lennon was quite aware of the public's conception of The Beatles, and commented on the way *Magical Mystery Tour* disappointed the public's expectations of The Beatles in 1968: "Sie hatten den Eindruck dass wir aus der Rolle fielen. Sie würden uns am liebstcn in den Pappanzügen lassen, die für uns entworfen wurden. Was auch immer für ein Bild sie für sich selbst haben, sie sind enttäuscht, wenn wir dem nicht entsprechen. Und das tun wir nie, also gibt es immer viele Enttäuschungen." (Beatles 2000: 274). While it was a critical flop in the United Kingdom, the whole project proved to be highly lucrative for the group. The film had cost £40,000 to make and reportedly grossed $2,000,000 in rentals to American universities and colleges alone (vgl. Neaverson/O'Dell 2002: 72). In addition, the soundtrack album grossed $8,000,000 in its first ten days of release (vgl. Miles 1997: 369).

Promotional Films 1967-1968

In 1967, The Beatles were invited to represent Great Britain at the first worldwide satellite television broadcast, *Our World*, which was going to be broadcast in June. The group accepted the invitation, and John Lennon wrote the song "All You Need Is Love" especially for the occasion. He was careful to use simple words in order to enable a worldwide audience to understand The Beatles' message. The band recorded a backing track for their television appearance two days before the show, and on June 25, The Beatles were shown in front of an audience of about 400 million viewers, as they performed a live overdub for "All You Need Is Love," which was also going to be their new single release. The event was filmed at EMI's Abbey Road Studios, where The Beatles had recorded most of their music up to then. The Beatles invited many of their famous friends to the broadcast, in order to create a party atmosphere that would appeal to the worldwide audience. Mick Jagger, Marianne Faithfull, Keith Richards, Keith Moon, Mike McCartney, and Eric Clapton were among The Beatles' guests and participated in the infectious chorus of "All You Need Is Love" (vgl. Lewisohn 2000: 260). With all these superstars in attendance, The Beatles proved once more that they were the world's leading pop group. The Beatles and their following sported lavish and colorful psychedelic outfits, although the audience could not see that, as the satellite transmission was in monochrome. With their landmark album *Sgt. Pepper's Lonely Hearts Club Band* released three weeks before the *Our World* performance, The Beatles had now become the beloved protagonists of Swinging London. When EMI released "All You Need Is Love" as a single on July 7, 1967, the BBC repeatedly screened The Beatles' performance of the song on various programs (vgl. Lewisohn 2000: 260). Therefore, it can be regarded as a promotional video. The single itself topped the charts worldwide in the summer of 1967.

According to film editor Roy Benson, who had worked with The Beatles on their *Magical Mystery Tour* television extravaganza, The Beatles wanted to use some of the outtakes of *Magical Mystery Tour* for a promotional film for their Christmas Single "Hello Goodbye": "After the *Magical Mystery Tour* was virtually completed, John wanted to use some of the unused footage for a full colour promo film for 'Hello Goodbye', so we put together about three minutes of film which included the luncheon at the Atlantic Hotel, footage shot in Nice, etc. To this day the film has never been seen" (Barrow 1999). Instead, The Beatles decided that they would produce a more conventional promotional video, which could also be shown on *The Ed Sullivan Show* in the USA. Consequently, on November 10, 1967, The Beatles met at the Saville Theater in London to film two promotional films for their forthcoming single release "Hello Goodbye." Paul McCartney had thought of the original idea of a performance video and directed the filming. The promo was to show The Beatles perform their new single on stage in order to undermine the BBC's regulations against musicians miming on television. However, the BBC noticed that The Beatles' did quite obviously not play the song live. The films were edited on November 12, and Paul McCartney supervised the process.

The Beatles wore three different outfits in the "Hello Goodbye" promotional films. One film showed them in their *Sgt. Pepper*-costumes, while they wore casual clothes in the second film. In addition to these contemporary outfits, the *Sgt. Pepper*-promo contained short scenes showing them in their collarless Pierre Cardin suits from 1962. A third promo clip was made up of out-takes from the other two films. One of the films was shown on November 26, 1967, on the *Ed Sullivan Show*, while the BBC decided not to show the band's promotional films. On December 2, 1967, *New Musical Express* reported that "The Beatles promotional clip of their new hit single 'Hello Goodbye' has been banned by BBC-TV. The last-minute decision by senior executives prevented the film from being screened in BBC-1's 'Top of the Pops' last Thursday. A Corporation spokesman explained that a 'minor portion of the film contravened the Musician's Union regulations concerning miming on television" (Sutherland 115).

On February 11, 1968, The Beatles intended to film a performance of their next single "Lady Madonna" at Abbey Road Studios, London. However, when the film team arrived, the group had decided to record a new song for the soundtrack of *Yellow Submarine*, "Hey Bulldog." They instructed the head of their own company Apple Films, Denis O'Dell and his assistant Tony Bramwell, to shoot footage during the recording of "Hey Bulldog" and to edit the filmed material in a way that would suggest that The Beatles were actually performing "Lady Madonna." Denis O'Dell recalls the situation: "We tried to edit the footage so that it echoed the rhythm of 'Lady Madonna' (which wasn't too difficult since the songs have roughly similar tempos) […]" (Neaverson/O'Dell 2002: 87). Interestingly, the result was shown on the March 14, 1968, edition of BBC's *Top of the Pops*, as well as on the next day's edition of *All Systems Freeman*, as the promo film did not violate the BBC's rules concerning miming on television – The Beatles were not seen miming "Lady Madonna", because they were actually playing a different song. Unintentionally, The Beatles undermined the BBC's and the Musician's Union's regulations.

While The Beatles were residing in India when "Lady Madonna" was released, they returned to London for the release of their first single on their own label Apple Records, "Hey Jude." In order to market their new single internationally, promotional films were required. Film editor Roy Benson was asked to design a storyboard for the promo film. Benson reportedly produced "an imaginative 38-scene storyboard idea" (Lewisohn 2000: 297). However, when The Beatles learned that it would take three days to shoot the film, they rejected Benson's idea. Denis O'Dell, who was still the head of Apple Films and produced the clips for "Hey Jude" and its B-side "Revolution", came up with an alternative. He remembers, "I felt that since the A-side was essentially a sing-along this should be echoed visually in the promo clip, with a studio audience joining in live for the final extended refrain" (Neaverson/O'Dell 2002: 129). Although it took some time to convince the group to stage a live performance of the song, they eventually agreed when their friend Michael Lindsay-Hogg, who had directed several of The Beatles' promos in 1966, was brought in to direct the films on September 4, 1968. As the group was not interested in a real live performance, only the lead vocals were sung live, while The Beatles, an orchestra and an invited audience basically mimed to their recorded tracks of "Hey Jude" and "Revolution". Lindsay-Hogg filmed three takes of "Hey Jude", which were later edited to two finished color clips. In addition, he filmed two almost identical versions of "Revolution". In the "Hey Jude" videos, Paul McCartney is sitting at the piano, John Lennon and George Harrison play guitars, and

Ringo Starr plays the drums. In the "Revolution"-videos McCartney plays his legendary Höfner bass guitar.

Popular television host David Frost was also at Twickenham Studios, where the filming took place, to tape an introduction to the songs for use on his Frost on Sunday program. While this gave viewers the illusion that The Beatles were playing live on David Frost's show, it also fooled the Musician's Union into believing that no miming was involved (vgl. Miles 2001: 309). "Hey Jude" became The Beatles' most successful single to date, selling more than six million copies in the first three months of the single's initial release.

Yellow Submarine

Since 1965, Al Brodax, the producer of the cartoon series *The Beatles*, had been negotiating the production of a feature length animated Beatles film with Brian Epstein and The Beatles. As the television show was quite a success, Brodax finally managed to convince Epstein and The Beatles of his idea in early 1967. Although the group had not particularly liked the television series, they thought that a cartoon feature was an easy way to fulfil their contract with United Artists, which obligated the group to participate in three movies, the first two having been *A Hard Day's Night* and *Help!*. Again, the production company insisted on a tight production schedule, as the producers were concerned that The Beatles' popularity might not sustain for a long time. Consequently, they only provided a budget of $1,000,000 and a time frame of eleven months to create the movie from start to finish (vgl. Hieronimus 2002: 33). Although The Beatles contributed four new songs to the soundtrack of the movie, they were not personally involved in the creation of *Yellow Submarine*, as pointed out by George Harrison in 1999: "The thing I liked the most about the movie was that we didn't really have anything to do with it. They just took our music, we met with them and they talked basically about what they were going to do and then Heinz Edelmann – who was fantastic – went off and created all these characters, showed them to us and that was basically it" (vgl. Hieronimus 2002: 53).

Brodax employed the London based TVC studios who had also worked on The Beatles cartoon series, and outlined the project together with the Canadian director George Dunning and line producer John Coates. Heinz Edelmann, now regarded as one of his generation's major contemporary graphic artists, was brought in to design the new cartoon Beatles and all the other characters for the movie. As The Beatles had undergone major image changes and had been broadening their musical horizon since the television series had first been broadcast, it was decided that the group was to be portrayed in an entirely different way compared to their cartoon series. After the creators of *Yellow Submarine* had been invited to listen to The Beatles' latest work, *Sgt. Pepper's Lonely Hearts Club Band*, they decided that it was necessary to develop the characters as well as the visualization, and to use a more contemporary, psychedelic setting for the movie's storyline, in order to be up-to-date with The Beatles present state of artistic awareness, their music and their public image. Because of the short production schedule, work on the movie began when the screenplay had not even been finished. This is a very unique situation for any film project, and it was a very particular situation for an animation project, as the recording of the soundtrack, i.e. the dialogues, are usually the first step in creating an animated film.

When *Yellow Submarine* went into production, numerous prolific writers were asked to submit treatments for *Yellow Submarine*, but The Beatles' manager Brian Epstein rejected all of them – most famously he turned down Joe Heller's treatment because he did not like the treatment's purple cover. Finally, The Beatles themselves were consulted and they agreed to a basic idea initially developed by Al Brodax and Lee Minoff, who had worked on Stanley Kubrick's most recent project *2001: A Space Odyssey*. The story, which was to be an "odyssey into the world of fantasy" (vgl. Hieronimus 2002: 190), was going to be based upon some of The Beatles' songs. According to Brodax, Ringo Starr suggested using The Beatles 1966 single release "Yellow Submarine," a song for children created by Paul McCartney and John Lennon, as the theme song for the animated picture.

More than a hundred people worked for more than ten months to realize this psychedelic odyssey that became *Yellow Submarine*. In order to proceed within the projected time frame, Brodax gave George Dunning, Heinz Edelmann and their team full artistic freedom to create psychedelic sequences for some of The Beatles' songs, which were later going to be fit into the storyline. In the meantime, Brodax' quest for the ideal screenplay led him to Yale professor Erich Segal, who was considered to be the right man for the project, because he had previously collaborated with Richard Rodgers on a musical. Segal joined the production team in London and wrote most of the screenplay for the movie within three weeks. When it was considered necessary to bring in a few more humorous ideas, i.e. Liverpudlian humor, Liverpool poet Roger McGough, who had been in the band The Scaffold with Paul McCartney's brother Michael, was brought in to help with the dialogue. Finally, California-based screenwriter Jack Mendelsohn was contacted to write, rearrange and edit several scenes of *Yellow Submarine*. While many parts of the movie were rewritten throughout the production process, most of the screenplay was finished when the movie was already in the fifth month of production. The film's eventual storyline was summarized in United Artists' official press folder.

"'Once upon a time – or maybe twice … there was a place called Pepperland'. On a peaceful day in this happy kingdom, a concert by Sergeant Pepper's Lonely Hearts Club Band is interrupted by an anti-music missile attack from the Blue Meanies. The Chief Blue Meanie, his assistant Max, and their 99 numbered henchmen turn their splotch guns on the docile Pepperland populace, determined to rid the world of music, happiness and love ('A World without music is a Blue World!')
Old Fred, conductor of the Band, flees to the old Lord Mayor, who puts him into the Yellow Submarine for a last-minute escape. The sub surfaces in Liverpool where Ringo wanders aimlessly in boredom. The sub, radar-like, follows Ringo to his house. Fred enters Ringo's house, explains the situation and enlists his aid. They proceed to round up the others.
John materialises out of a Frankenstein-like figure, Paul is found playing classical music, and George appears out of a haze of transcendental meditation.
Armed with a battery of puns and four new songs, the Beatles board the Yellow Submarine and head for Pepperland. They are detoured through the Seas of Time, Science, Monsters, Consumer Products, Nowhere, Phrenology, Green and Holes.
They undergo time warps, chase Lucy through her 'sky of diamonds'; climb clocks and soup cans; become ancient and infantile, molecularized, actually 'disappear up their own existence' and almost drown in the avalanche of apples, among other adventures.
Characters they encounter on their mad 'Modyssey' include the US Cavalry, Father Mackenzie, assorted monsters (including a vacuum-flask monster), cowboys, Indians, King Kong and several unidentifiable 'things'. Ringo takes a liking to the super-intellectual Boob (a poetic personification of the 'Nowhere Man') and takes him along on the trip: in the Sea of Green he is captured by a giant blue hand.
A Pepper-powered sneeze propels the Beatles through the Sea of Holes into occupied Pepperland, which has been almost completely drained of colour. The Lord Mayor is astonished at the resemblance between the Beatles and the original Sergeant Pepper Band. Disguised as an Apple Bonker, they infiltrate the musical instrument compound. Then it's Beatles versus Meanies, with guitars against splotch guns; the ferocious Flying Glove, the Butterfly Stompers, the Hidden Persuaders with guns in their shoes, the snapping Turtle Turks with their mouths in their bellies and the Count Down Clown with his nose-cone nose. A battle is waged to the tune of 'All You Need Is Love' and love becomes the overwhelming power. A surprise ending carries the fantastic fracas right into the theatre" (Harry 1985: 39-41).

The story of *Yellow Submarine* is very simple, but it contains several unconventional elements which complement the innovative animation. While there had not been any real antagonists in *A Hard Day's Night* and *Magical Mystery Tour*, *Yellow Submarine* works in the tradition of the oldest and most commonly used story-pattern – the eternal fight between good and evil. This particular pattern has evolved from mythic stories and constitutes the basis for most of today's popular culture narratives, such as movies, television series, comics, and novels. However, while most of the narratives in this tradition feature a brutal confrontation between the two Manichaean forces, the conflict is solved in a rather original way in *Yellow Submarine*, as The Beatles defeat their antagonists, the Blue Meanies, in an entirely peaceful manner with their song "All You Need Is Love". In the Beatles' world, love alone manages to save the beautiful Pepperland with all its surreal inhabitants.

With "All you Need Is Love" The Beatles instigate a symbolic social revolution by the powers of music instead of violent retribution (vgl. Neaverson 1997: 90). It is interesting that this movie was released at a point in history when many young people turned to radicalism and violence, in order to bring about social change, because they had been disappointed by Flower Power – ideology. While the movie's message seemed slightly anachronistic at the time, it was, however, the ideology The Beatles, i. e. John Lennon, still promoted at the time, while other rock stars, such as Mick Jagger from The Rolling Stones ("Street Fighting Man"), seemed to sympathize with a more radical approach. As pointed out by Neaverson, "[a]t no point in the film do the Beatles take punitive action against the Meanies; they merely want to re-establish the utopian peace of Pepperland" (Neaverson 1997: 90).

The animated Beatles' journey from Liverpool to Pepperland is basically realized in the tradition of famous odysseys, from Homer to Tolkien. Like the heroes of the great works of literature, such as *Odysseus* and *Gulliver's Travels*, The Beatles travel through several fantasy worlds and encounter numerous unexpected tasks and barriers. However, while the monsters and other opponents in the classics are usually defeated in a violent fight, even the most dangerous and unusual creatures in *Yellow Submarine* are presented in a humorous and loving way, which allows the audience to laugh at them rather than fear them. Using the artistic frameworks of fashionable and contemporary Pop Art and Psychedelia, Heinz Edelmann and his team create their own cosmos of monsters and surreal objects, which the animated Beatles encounter with surprising indifference.

During their voyage through the Seas of Time, Science, Monsters, Consumer Products, Nowhere, Phrenology, Green, and Holes, they encounter several dangerous situations, but they don't seem to be able to take anything seriously. For example, when Ringo accidentally ends up in the sea of monsters and is chased by an army of "Red Indians", the others stay quite cool:

"[George:] I don't half miss Ringo
[John:] He's far out there.
[Paul:] Always was.
Here comes Ringo!
[...]
[John:] There goes Ringo.
[...]
[George:] There goes Ringo again.
[John:] Rides well, doesn't he."
(*Yellow Submarine* 1999).

The dialogues were written in the style that had been characteristic of all of The Beatles' movies – except for *Magical Mystery Tour* – and was full of puns and good-natured banter. While the real Beatles had become slightly more serious in their public appearances, discussing drug abuse, politics, and civil rights issues, the cartoon Beatles' sense of humor and their continuous play with words resembled very much the way they were portrayed in *A Hard Day's Night*. Although The Beatles' contemporary activities and interests were also reflected in *Yellow Submarine*, the cartoon Beatles' innocence and humor connects it to *A Hard Day's Night* and *Help!* rather than The Beatles' self-produced *Magical Mystery Tour*. On the other hand, the development of the theme of escape in *Yellow Submarine*, which basically characterizes all of The Beatles' movies, makes it an almost logical sequel to *Magical Mystery Tour*, which also describes a kind of escape into a surreal world. In a way, The Beatles' bizarre bus trip resembles their cartoon counterparts' odyssey through fantastic dream worlds in their cartoon adventure.

The second distinctive feature that links *Yellow Submarine* with The Beatles' previous movies is the element of satire, which is realized in countless visual jokes as well as the way the characters are portrayed in the movie. Some of the characters the animated Beatles encounter on their quest to save Pepperland are exaggerated versions of certain social groups or movements. For instance, there is the Lord Mayor, who is a lovely caricature of the older generation, insisting on finishing his string quartet while under attack from the Blue Meanies. Another prominent example of send-ups in the movie is Jeremy Hillary Boob, a caricature of pseudo-intellectuals, who engages in some sort of conversation with the cartoon Beatles.

"[Jeremy:] Medic, pedic, zed oblique,
orphic, morphic, dorphic, Greek.
Ad hoc, ad loc and quid pro quo.
So little time, so much to know.
[John:] Can you tell us where we're at?
[Jeremy:] A true Socratic query that.
[John:] And who the Billy Shears are you?
[Jeremy:] Who? Who indeed am I? [hands out cards]
[...]
[Jeremy:] Eminent physicist, polyglot, classicist,
prize-winning botanist, hard biting satirist,
talented pianist, good dentist, too.
[John:] Lousy poet.
[Jeremy:] Critic's voice. Take your choice
[Ringo:] Must be one of them angry young men.
[Paul:] Or a daffy old creep."
(*Yellow Submarine* 1999).

It is quite interesting that the character of John Lennon engages in the conversation with Jeremy, since it was Lennon who was regarded as the intellectual Beatle. He had published two acclaimed books, and was now engaged in several avant-garde happenings with his future wife Yoko Ono. However, in 1967 and 1968, The Beatles were irritated by many critics and scholars trying to read impossible things into their work. Most of all, Lennon had recently been annoyed by people interpreting his song "Lucy in the Sky with Diamonds" as a direct reference to the drug LSD. As a defense he recorded the song "Glass Onion" in 1968, which ridiculed the cult concerning 'hidden meanings' in The Beatles' lyrics. In this context, the Beatles' encounter with the omniscient Jeremy can be regarded as a gentle retribution directed at all the intellectuals judging and interpreting their work.

The animated Beatles themselves are basically just caricatures of the 'real ones'. Their individual images are a slight development of what had been projected by *Help!* and *A Hard Day's Night*. Although the character developers integrated elements of The Beatles' more recent activities, the individual Beatles' characteristics are presented in a stereotypical way. The cartoon Ringo, who plays the most important role in the movie, is introduced in a way that is reminiscent of Ringo's solo sequence in *A Hard Day's Night*. As in The Beatles' first movie, Ringo feels lonely and left out as he wanders along a river bank. "Nothing ever happens to me," he complains, not noticing that a yellow submarine is following him through the streets of Liverpool. Paul McCartney is described by designer Heinz Edelmann as a "modern day Mozart" (*Yellow Submarine* 1999) – he is interested in classical music and is presented very much as 'the Cute One' throughout the movie. George Harrison appears on a mountain top, lost in transcendental meditation, which had fascinated The Beatles in early 1968. Harrison had introduced the sound of Indian instruments to pop music, and when he is introduced in the movie, the sitar sounds of his song "Love You To" contribute to the exotic flair of Indian culture, which he helped to popularize in the West at the time. John Lennon is introduced in a quite particular way in *Yellow Submarine*. Although all of the cartoon Beatles first appear in extravagant, surreal scenes, Lennon's entrance is the most spectacular, as he looks like Frankenstein's monster at first, and then transforms into a cartoon version of John Lennon. The creators of *Yellow Submarine* were obviously aware of the fact that Lennon's public image was by far the most controversial of all of The Beatles. He had caused quite a few scandals with his comments on society and religion, and he would cause even further provocations in the following years, when he engaged in several political movements in the United States.

While the characterization and the portrayal of the characters contained several unusual elements, the movie's animation itself was completely original at the time. Animated feature films had previously been released almost exclusively by Disney, whose *Jungle Book* had been a great success in 1967/68. With *Yellow Submarine*, the team around director George Dunning and designer Heinz Edelmann managed to break with most of the conventions of animated feature films in the tradition of Walt Disney. By integrating elements of contemporary art and aesthetics typical of genres outside of the Disney universe, the creators of *Yellow Submarine* demonstrated that animated films could also appeal to an adult audience. Dunning avoided the cuteness of Disney-style animation and substituted it with a more contemporary, artistic touch. Although Disney had used live-action footage as basis for several animated sequences in *Snow White* and *Bambi*, Dunning takes this a step further and includes photographic images and filmed material in some of the song sequences. For example, the "Eleanor Rigby" sequence contains cut-out photographs of houses and people in Liverpool, as well as short scenes of black-and-white footage. The animation of "Lucy in the Sky with Diamonds", on the other hand, was realized by the technique known as rotoscoping, which simulates animated drawings over live-action sequences (vgl. Neaverson 1997: 87). In a similar manner, countless scenes in *Yellow Submarine* combine elements of cartoon animation with still photography. As pointed out by Bob Neaverson, "the film is rooted in a range of sixties pop styles, and the eclecticism of its colour imagery [...] is derived

121

from a vast range of contemporary styles, including imagery culled from the pop art paintings, prints and designs of artists such as Peter Blake and Andy Warhol, the 'op' art of Bridget Riley, surrealist and expressionist art [...]" (Neaverson 1997: 84). What Neaverson forgets to mention is the fact that The Beatles themselves personally knew the likes of Peter Blake and Andy Warhol, with whom they engaged in discussions on underground culture and art.[2] As The Beatles became more involved in the process of making *Yellow Submarine* when they realized its innovative potential, it is quite possible that they contributed several ideas to the movie's style. Although most of the animation techniques and ideas had been realized in some way in art films, as well as in advertising, it was an entirely new idea to integrate these elements in a commercial feature movie. Similar to the way The Beatles used and popularized elements of the avant-garde and world music, the animators of *Yellow Submarine* pushed the boundaries of traditional standards of animation by approaching the project with a more artistic attitude. In a way, the impact *Yellow Submarine* had on the public conception of animation enabled artists, such as Terry Gilliam from Monty Python, to integrate avant-garde techniques in mainstream entertainment. For instance, Gilliam's animated contributions to the Python's television show *Monty Python's Flying Circus* featured a similar aesthetic to parts of The Beatles' "Eleanor Rigby" sequence, which combined photography and animated drawings.

On January 25, 1968, The Beatles filmed their cameo appearance, which constituted the finale of *Yellow Submarine*, at Twickenham Studios, London. It was only a short piece of live action with The Beatles encouraging a worldwide audience to sing along with one of the songs they had recorded especially for the soundtrack – "All Together Now."

The world premiere of *Yellow Submarine* took place on July 17, 1968, at the London Pavilion in Piccadilly Circus. All four Beatles attended the premiere and caused a traffic standstill, as more than 3,000 fans were awaiting their musical heroes around the cinema. While The Beatles had been heavily criticized for their own television movie *Magical Mystery Tour* only seven months earlier, the critics as well as the public reacted quite enthusiastically to The Beatles' cartoon adventure. For example, the *Daily Telegraph* commented: "Not since Disney's *Snow White* or *Make Mine Music* has a full-length animated film cartoon come upon us with such surprising skill and charm and freshness as this inventive little epic" (Harry 1985: 42), while the *Evening Standard* wrote: "*Yellow Submarine* is the key film of the Beatles era. It's a trip

---

2   Sir Peter Blake designed the cover for The Beatles' landmark album *Sgt. Pepper's Lonely Hearts Club Band* in 1967, while Andy Warhol was a personal acquaintance of both, Paul McCartney and John Lennon.

through the contemporary mythology that the quartet from Merseyside have helped create. It's a pop voyage – 'mod-odyssey' is the word, I suppose – that sails under the psychedelic colours of Carnaby Street to the turned-on music of *Sergeant Pepper's Lonely Hearts Club Band*" (Harry 1985: 43). The film was shown in only 50 cinemas in Great Britain, but it became a major commercial success in the United States, reportedly generating more than $8,000,000 on its original release (vgl. Hieronimus 2002: 303). Even more money was made through tie-in merchandising, which ranged from alarm clocks to lunch-boxes and toy models of the yellow submarine and The Beatles themselves. As pointed out by Denis O'Dell, the head of The Beatles' film company Apple Films, "the film was one of the first fully to realize the potential profits of associated products. Although movie merchandising was hardly new in 1968, the vast range of related items which the film generated [...] formed an important blueprint for the multi-marketing spin-offs of such seventies productions as *Jaws* and *Star Wars*, a tradition which continues to this day" (Neaverson/O'Dell 2002: 85).

In order to provide the fans with the songs featured in *Yellow Submarine*, The Beatles initially wanted to release a soundtrack EP, containing the four new songs they had provided for the movie – "Only a Northern Song", "It's All Too Much", "Hey Bulldog", and "All Together Now". For unknown reasons, however, this initial idea was rejected in favor of a soundtrack album featuring the four new songs, the title song "Yellow Submarine", the crucial "All You Need Is Love", as well as George Martin's instrumental film score. Interestingly, the album was released some five months after the movie had been released to the cinemas, in order to avoid an interference with The Beatles' double album release *The Beatles*. As their album *The Beatles* was still occupying the number one spot in the American album charts when *Yellow Submarine* was released, the soundtrack album became the first Beatles album release not to reach the top of the charts since 1964.

Yellow Submarine was first shown on British television in 1974 and has since been broadcast at least ten times. After its initial cinema release, The Beatles and their company Apple ignored *Yellow Submarine* for a long time, due to a long dispute over ownership rights. In 1999, however, after The Beatles had celebrated a tremendously successful comeback with their *Anthology* CDs and videos, *Yellow Submarine* saw its premiere on DVD. The release was accompanied by an unprecedented publicity campaign, including the official launch in Liverpool, where Lord Mayor of Liverpool, Joseph Devaney, declared Bank Holiday Monday August 30th, 1999, "Yellow Submarine Day". It was celebrated by approximately 300,000 people and captured the attention of the international media. The DVD soon topped the charts around the world, and a CD release, *Yellow Submarine Songtrack*, stormed the top ten in Great Britain. What is more, with the release of *Yellow Submarine* on DVD, the production of merchandise, such as toys, key-chains, mugs and badges, was revived and proved to be such a great success that new *Yellow Submarine* products have been released every year since. In September 2004, The Beatles' company Apple published a *Yellow Submarine* book for children in an attempt to introduce new generations of potential fans to the works of The Beatles. As pointed out by George Harrison, *Yellow Submarine* has been a quite effective vehicle to evoke the interest of young audiences: "I think each generation of kids enjoys it" (Hieronimus 2002: 49).

Let It Be

The Beatles had enjoyed the filming of the promotional films for "Hey Jude" and "Revolution" so much that they considered filming a concert for a new television special for Christmas 1968. In October and November 1968 newspapers and magazines reported that The Beatles were indeed preparing a concert at the Royal Albert Hall. Paul McCartney announced The Beatles' plans in an *NME* interview at the time: "What is probable is that before anything else, we will do our own TV show in which we'll perform numbers from the new album" (Sutherland 124). The new album was a double album simply called *The Beatles*, and it marked The Beatles' return to more straightforward rock music. When the album became their best-selling LP ever, The Beatles realized that there was no necessity to promote the album in a television special. Instead, they decided to stage a concert with entirely new material in early 1969. They wanted to prepare the concert in the first weeks of January. Denis O'Dell claims to have suggested filming the rehearsals for the concert at Twickenham Studios, in order to collect some footage for a possible television documentary about the concert performance (Neaverson/O'Dell 2002: 138). Michael Lindsay-Hogg, who had directed the promotional films for "Rain," "Paperback Writer," "Hey Jude", and "Revolution" was brought in to direct the filming of the rehearsals.

On 2 January, 1969, The Beatles met at Twickenham Studios, where they had previously filmed most of *A Hard Day's Night, Help!* as well as several of their promotional films, to select and rehearse the material for the planned concert. The first days of filming were spent writing and arranging some of the new songs The Beatles considered playing at their concert. In addition, the group, together with director Michael Lindsay-

Hogg and producer Denis O'Dell, discussed possible locations for the concert. However, it soon became apparent that Paul McCartney was the only Beatle really interested in the project. Ringo Starr was preparing for an acting role in the film *The Magic Christian* and refused to perform anywhere outside of London, while John Lennon had not composed many new songs since they had released their album *The Beatles*. George Harrison, who had initially tried to contribute several songs to the project, was becoming frustrated by Lennon's and McCartney's refusal to rehearse his material. On the seventh day of the rehearsals he quit the band after another disagreement with John Lennon. The three remaining Beatles continued the rehearsals for another two days. Finally, differences between the four Beatles were put aside at a band meeting on 15 January, 1969, and the group reconvened in front of the cameras at a studio owned by their own company Apple at Savile Row on 22 January, 1969. It had been part of George Harrison's terms for returning to the group to cancel plans for a live concert and end the filming at the rather uncomfortable Twickenham Film Studios (vgl. Miles 2001: 331). In 1970, John Lennon remembered the conditions at the Twickenham studios: "It was a dreadful, dreadful feeling in Twickenham Studio, and being filmed all the time. I just wanted them to go away, and we'd be there in the morning. You couldn't make music at eight in the morning or ten or whatever it was, in a strange place with people filming you and coloured lights" (Wenner 2000: 101).

George Harrison had invited Billy Preston, a legendary organ player The Beatles had known since their Hamburg days, to join them at their sessions. According to George Harrison, Preston's presence improved the atmosphere immensely, and The Beatles continued their jam sessions for another ten days of filming. In the last few days of January The Beatles also decided that they would not book any specific place for a performance. Because of Ringo Starr's commitment to begin work on the movie *The Magic Christian* in February, the group agreed to perform a surprise concert on the roof of their Apple Studio building (vgl. Sulpy/ Schweighardt 1997).

On January 30, The Beatles played a set of their new songs on the roof of their Apple building in Savile Row. Extra cameras had been ordered to film the event. The group performed for forty-two minutes and was finally stopped by the police because of the traffic chaos they had caused in the area (vgl. Miles 2001: 333). Nobody knew that they had just witnessed the last concert performance by The Beatles. On the next day, the group returned to the basement studio at Savile Row for one last time, as they wanted to film some proper performances of songs they had not been able to perform on the roof. Although The Beatles had enjoyed the final concert on the roof of the Apple headquarter, they were quite frustrated by the whole project and did not want to be involved in the process of compiling an album and a film out of the material they had recorded and filmed. Glyn Johns, who had produced most of the audio recordings, was initially asked to compile an album of the recordings they had made in January. However, as none of The Beatles was pleased with Johns' work, John Lennon and George Harrison decided to contact legendary record producer Phil Spector and asked him to supervise the production of this particular album.

Michael Lindsay-Hogg was left with the task of making an acceptable film of 29 hours of filmed material. As the original idea of filming The Beatles' sessions for a television documentary about The Beatles preparing a live concert, which was to be filmed and broadcast as another television special, had been abandoned midway in the production, Lindsay-Hogg was trying to arrange the filmed sequences in a way that would show The Beatles record an album and rehearse the live roof-top show.

The final result provides a rather interesting view of The Beatles' work as a recording band. In the tradition of cinema vérité, the film allows the audience to attend The Beatles' sessions, as they rehearse and perform a set of completely new songs. While most documentaries of this kind usually feature interviews and/or an over-narration voice, *Let It Be* breaks with these conventions and presents the band's rehearsals without commentary.

"As well as avoiding the classical documentary techniques of reportage and interview, the edited film lacks the traditional narrative signifiers of temporal construction, and although the audience must naturally assume that the acts of the triptych are presented chronologically, there are no titles or voice-over narration to clarify this. Indeed, beyond the 'correct' ordering of the sequences, the only other sense of temporal progression is provided by the increasingly accomplished musicianship of the Beatles [...]" (Neaverson 1997: 110).

In a way, *Let It Be* is what *A Hard Day's Night* pretends to be – a documentary about The Beatles' everyday life in their profession as rock band. However, many things had changed since the group's early success in 1964. In the meantime they had quit touring, they had recorded concept albums, and they had become less involved with each other. Since the death of their manager Brian Epstein, considerable tension had evolved over business matters. During the making of their double album *The Beatles*, artistic tensions had added to an unpleasant atmosphere within the group, and Ringo Starr temporarily left the band. Although he returned after a few weeks, the group was not able to sort out their problems within the band. With *Let It Be*, Michael Lindsay-Hogg manages to capture different facets of the band and achieves a seemingly honest portrayal of The Beatles at a critical point in their career. On the one hand, he presents a marvelous rock 'n' roll band, which is able to come up with numerous inventive ideas to improve their songs and their performance. On the other hand, Lindsay-Hogg also presents The Beatles at their worst, in moments of complete boredom and demotivation. Even though he does not include the scene where George Harrison leaves the group, he shows an argument between Paul McCartney and George Harrison, which added to the tensions at Twickenham Studios.

"[Paul:] I always hear myself trying to annoy you.
[George:] You're not annoying me. You don't annoy me anymore.
[...]
[George:] I'll play what you want me to play. I won't play at all if you don't want me to. Whatever it is that will please you, I'll do it."
(*Let It Be* 1970).

The film premiered in New York on 13 May, 1970 with none of The Beatles attending the occasion. While Paul McCartney was dissatisfied with Phil Spector's remixes of The Beatles' soundtrack, John Lennon criticized the film because in his opinion it portrayed Lennon, Harrison and Starr being McCartney's sidemen: "That film was set up by Paul, for Paul. That's one of the main reasons The Beatles ended [...]. And the camera work was set up to show Paul and not to show anybody else. That's how I felt about it. And on top of that, the people that cut it, cut it as 'Paul is God', and we're just lying around there" (Wenner: 2000: 23). Although Lennon's comment must be seen in the emotional aftermath of The Beatles' break-up, his observation that the movie focuses on Paul McCartney is quite accurate. Footage of the sessions, which was discovered years later and was included in The Beatles' *Anthology* shows The Beatles in many more pleasant situations, with everybody contributing ideas to the realization of their live show. When the movie was released, The Beatles had just disbanded, and John Lennon and Paul McCartney were at war with each other in the mass media. Therefore, many critics concentrated on the less pleasant aspects of the movie and declared it to be the document of The Beatles' break-up. Interestingly, this still seems to be the public conception of *Let It Be*. What is often forgotten, however, is the fact that the time The Beatles spent recording and filming *Let It Be* was another very productive period in their career. It must be noted that The Beatles only needed three weeks to write, rehearse, and record the songs for a whole album. Considering the fact that contemporary major pop artist spend three or four years recording an album, The Beatles' pace and energy are truly remarkable. Although the *Let It Be* sessions were probably not the most pleasant experience in The Beatles' history, the resulting movie offers a rare insight to the working methods of the group.

The movie was first shown on British television in 1975 and has been shown only three times since. It is the only Beatles movie that has never been released on video. However, when The Beatles released a re-mixed version of their *Let It Be* album in 2003, their company Apple announced that a *Let It Be* DVD was in preparation.

Promotional Films 1969-2005
and *Paul Is Dead*

The Final Singles

When The Beatles' single "Get Back" with its B-side "Don't Let Me Down" was released in April 1969, Apple distributed color promotional clips for both songs to television stations around the world. The footage consisted of scenes filmed by Michael Lindsay-Hogg for *Let It Be*. "Get Back" featured performance footage of The Beatles' rooftop concert, while "Don't Let Me Down" combined rooftop footage with segments filmed during the rehearsals at Twickenham Studios. Both promotional films featured footage not seen in *Let It Be*. The films were broadcast several times on the charts show *Top of the Pops* in Great Britain, while CBS-TV broadcast them in the United States (vgl. Lewisohn 2000: 313).

Although "Get Back" was still at the top of the charts in Great Britain, John Lennon insisted on releasing his song "The Ballad of John and Yoko" as a single on 30 May, 1969. Two almost identical films were compiled to promote the newest Beatles release on television. The films illustrated the lyrics of Lennon's song and featured footage of John Lennon and his wife Yoko Ono in Paris, Amsterdam, Vienna, at their London airport press conference, and traveling around Britain in their famous white Rolls Royce (vgl. Lewisohn 2000: 319). Only a few short segments show all four of The Beatles at the rehearsals for their *Let It Be* project; most of the footage presents just John Lennon and Yoko Ono. Although the footage works as an appropriate illustration of the song's lyrics, the song "Ballad of John and Yoko" and the accompanying promotional films marked a turning point in the way The Beatles, i.e. John Lennon, projected themselves to the world. While The Beatles had previously always appeared as a group in their promos, "The Ballad of John and Yoko" was clearly designed to concentrate on John Lennon's new personal and artistic partnership with Yoko Ono. It became clear that The

Beatles were now becoming more interested in their various solo projects instead of their work as a group. The fact that the recording of "The Ballad of John and Yoko" only featured John Lennon and Paul McCartney, and the rather ill-advised decision to release it when their previous single was still relevant on the charts can now be regarded as a clear signal that John Lennon was dissociating himself from his band, in order to pursue a new career with Yoko Ono. The couple's obsession to capture their artistic and private life on film found its first expression in the "Ballad of John and Yoko" films. In the following years, John and Yoko produced countless films of their happenings, their recording sessions, and their private moments. Their most famous films include *Imagine* (1972), a film accompanying John Lennon's landmark solo album, as well as the promotional film for Lennon's comeback single "Starting Over" (1980). The promotional films for "The Ballad of John and Yoko" were repeatedly shown on British and American television in 1969, supporting the single's way to the top of the charts in the UK.

In order to promote their double-A sided single "Something"/"Come Together", Neil Aspinall, the director of The Beatles' Apple company, produced a film showing each individual Beatle walking around in an English park with his wife. At that point, The Beatles would not even come together for the filming of their own promotional films anymore. Therefore, each Beatle's scenes were filmed separately at different dates and locations. Although the footage of The Beatles with their respective wives supports the lyrics of George Harrison's love song, it also clearly shows that each group member had now found a new partner, substituting band life with family life. "Something" was the first and only song by George Harrison to grace the A-side of a Beatles single.

To promote the single release of "Let It Be", Apple distributed color films of one of The Beatles' performances of the song at Apple Studios, London, on 31 January 1969. The footage was combined with footage of The Beatles' performance of "The Long and Winding Road" and "Two of Us", filmed on the same day. The promotional film was shown on major television programs worldwide, such as *Top of the Pops* in Great Britain, and *The Ed Sullivan Show* in the United States. When "The Long and Winding Road" was released as The Beatles' last new single for 25 years, a similar promo film was released in May 1970.

Single Releases after the Break-Up

On 10 April, 1970, Paul McCartney publicly announced that The Beatles had broken up. The following years the group's members were involved in unpleasant law-suits to legally dissolve their partnership. As soon as their recording contract had run out in 1976, EMI started to re-release The Beatles' classic recordings in various formats, which infuriated the group's ex-members, although this move made sure that a new generation of fans was introduced to the music of The Beatles. To promote a compilation called *Rock'n'Roll Music* on the radio, EMI released the song "Back in the U.S.S.R." as a single in Great Britain. A promotional video for the single was produced, helping it to reach #19 in the charts. The film featured footage of The Beatles in 1964, although the song was actually recorded in 1968. It showed several crucial moments in the group's career – their arrival in the United States, in Australia, in Liverpool, and in the Netherlands. It was clearly a very nostalgic perspective on The Beatles' most successful year, showing the group's impact on enormously large crowds of hysterical teenagers.

In 1982, a medley of some of The Beatles movie songs was released as a single to cash in on a recent trend of rock'n'roll medleys. The promotional film for the single, which was actually called "The Beatles Movie Medley", features scenes from all of The Beatles' movies, except *Yellow Submarine*. It starts with a scene taken from *A Hard Day's Night*, showing The Beatles being chased by a crowd of girls, and successively builds up to a performance of "Get Back" taken from the *Let It Be* rooftop concert. The video features some of the most legendary scenes from The Beatles' movies, including the semi-diegetic performance of "I Should Have Known Better" and the non-diegetic "Ticket to Ride" sequence showing The Beatles skiing in the alps.

In 1994, Apple released a collection of The Beatles' live recordings for various BBC radio programs as a double CD set called *Live at the BBC*. The release was promoted by a single, "Baby It's You", which reached #7 in the U.K. charts. The video for "Baby It's You" was surprisingly unspectacular, simply showing The Beatles travel around Britain in their van in 1963 as well as at the photo session for the picture that was used as the cover of *Live at the BBC*. The video promoted the group's image of their early suit-and-moptop era, which was a suitable representation of the period featured on the *Live at the BBC* album.

The Reunion. An Excursion into Beatles Fan Mythology: *Paul Is Dead*

In 1995, the three surviving Beatles, George Harrison, Paul McCartney, and Ringo Starr, came together to promote their band history project *Anthology* with the first new Beatles single in 25 years. It was called "Free as a Bird" and featured the voice of John Lennon, taken from a demo recording he had made around 1977. The single was co-produced by Jeff Lynne and the surviving Beatles, who worked together in a recording studio for the first time since 1970. In order to promote the single, which amazingly entered the top ten in the single charts around the world, a lavish video was produced by Apple, The Beatles' company still controlling all of The Beatles' output. The Grammy-Award winning video was directed by Joe Pytka, who had previously worked for Michael Jackson. It is filmed in a way that suggests a bird's perspective, with the camera floating over significant Beatles-related places in Liverpool and London. The video contains literally hundreds of references to various Beatles songs. Several segments were filmed in Liverpool and showed the places known from classic Beatles songs. For instance, there is footage shot at the Penny Lane roundabout, showing the barber, the fireman, and the nurse from the song "Penny Lane", while other scenes include footage of Strawberry Field. Digital picture processing allowed Joe Pytka to combine scenes filmed on location with historic footage featuring The Beatles in the 1960s.

On the one hand, the video for "Free as a Bird" contains a bulk of iconic Beatles footage and symbols related to the history and fan mythology of The Beatles. It is a clever collection of references to the group's songs, films, and history. On the other hand, it is interesting that the group's comeback video does not feature any footage of hysterical, screaming fans, or of The Beatles trying to escape from a mob of fans. This is all the more interesting, as footage of screaming fans has constituted a significant part in some of The Beatles' own film projects (*A Hard Day's Night*, *The Beatles* cartoon series, etc.), as well as in their autobiographical documentary series, where each episode begins with The Beatles' performance of "Help!" being drowned out by the sound of thousands of screaming fans. Hysterical fans were also the focus in EMI's 1976 promotional film for "Back in the USSR". Apple probably decided against the use of such footage, as it would not support the slow and atmospheric song.

The video's countless references to Beatles songs appeal to a particular target group of extreme Beatles fanatics who have been busy interpreting the group's songs and artwork in reference to The Beatles' own experience and history. These interpretations have developed into a set of myths which many Beatles fans and scholars mistake for reality. They often overlap with the band's actual development and have caused quite substantial confusion of facts and fiction in several representations of The Beatles' history.

The trend of scrutinizing The Beatles' lyrics started in 1967, when Lennon's song "Lucy in the Sky with Diamonds" was interpreted as a song about LSD, a popular drug in the psychedelic era, which The Beatles, in fact, consumed at the time. Although much was read into the song and its title, Lennon insisted that a drawing by his son Julian had inspired the lyrics (vgl. Everett 1999: 104).

It is quite interesting that the hype surrounding The Beatles' lyrics evolved at that particular point in time. No one has apparently realized the fact that The Beatles themselves actually initiated the interest in their lyrics by printing the words to their songs on the sleeve of their album *Sgt. Pepper's Lonely Hearts Club Band* (1967). This was a complete novelty and revolutionized the way pop songs have since been perceived. By printing the lyrics on the album sleeve, they gained significance and meaning, which the fans were eager to decipher. Although they had intended to elevate the status of their song lyrics, no one was more surprised than The Beatles, when fans and intellectuals interpreted the lyrics of "A Day in the Life" as a reference to heroin, while even the rather harmless "With a Little Help from My Friends" was thought to be about LSD.

Lennon was amused by the interpretations of his 1967 surrealist lyrics and wrote a song about the whole craze for The Beatles' album *The Beatles* aka *The White Album* (1968). In "Glass Onion", Lennon quotes several Beatles songs, claiming that there is no deep meaning hidden in their songs: "Yeah, I was having a laugh because there'd been so much gobbledegook about Pepper, play it backwards and you stand on your head and all that. Even now, I just saw Mel Torme on TV the other day saying that 'Lucy' was written to promote drugs and so was 'A Little Help From My Friends' and none of them were at all" (Wenner 2000: 86). With his sense of irony, Lennon sings "Here's another clue for you all/The walrus was Paul", a 'clue' which has kept Beatles fans and scholars busy for the past 40 years. Tragically, several songs on *The Beatles* were mis-interpreted by a group of deranged fanatics as an encouragement to commit several brutal murders. One of the victims was film actress Sharon Tate. The murderers claimed that The Beatles' songs contained secret messages inciting them to commit the murders (vgl. Harry 2000: 715). This time, The Beatles were shocked. In a tragic way, these incidents have evoked several unpleasant myths about The Beatles. For instance, it has been claimed that The Beatles were satanists, or the 'Riders of the Apocalypse,' announcing the end of the world. It is interesting that the band who pronounced "All You Need is Love" to the world would have to face such accusations.

The most popular Beatles myth, however, evolved in 1969, and, despite its complete absurdity, was believed by a considerable number of people – the "Paul is dead" myth. When The Beatles released their album *Abbey Road* in August 1969, it had become quite normal that fans would read meanings into the group's songs and cover artwork. In October, 1969, an American DJ jokingly announced in a bizarre Halloween radio show that Paul McCartney was dead, and that The Beatles had replaced him with a look-alike. A fantastic story was dreamed up, claiming that McCartney had tragically died in a traffic accident in 1966. The Beatles' lyrics and the album sleeves of *Sgt. Pepper's Lonely Hearts Club Band*, *Magical Mystery Tour*, and *Abbey Road* were reported to contain numerous hidden clues about McCartney's death.[3]

The story of Paul McCartney's death was the subject of a German movie called *Paul Is Dead* (2000). The movie, which was written and directed by Hendrik Handloegten, revolves around the adventures of a young Beatles fan, Tobias, who is quite surprised when the VW Beetle from the *Abbey Road* cover suddenly appears in a small German town in 1980. He investigates the matter and learns about the supposed death of Paul McCartney. He suspects the owner of the VW, who is now his English teacher, to be McCartney's murderer. When he finds out that the death of Paul McCartney was really just an invention by a radio DJ, he is terribly disappointed. Soon afterwards, his English teacher leaves Germany to go to New York City. One night, his brother wakes him up to tell him the shocking news that John Lennon has been shot dead in New York.

The charming low-budget production takes an innovative approach in dealing with the 'Paul is dead' myth, integrating all the elements of this supposed conspiracy, and taking it to a new level by the surprise ending, which establishes a connection with John Lennon's tragic death in 1980. Many famous Beatles-death clues are mentioned in the movie, with the protagonist finding the evidence increasingly credible as the story progresses. The boy's confusion of facts and fiction mirrors quite adequately the process of mythification of The Beatles' history in real life.

3　At least two books deal with this delightful chapter in Beatles mythology: R. Gary Patterson. *The Walrus Was Paul. The Great Beatle Death Clues.* New York: Fireside, 1998.
Andrew J. Reeve. *Turn Me On, Dead Man. The Beatles And The "Paul-Is-Dead" Hoax.* Bloomington: Authorhouse, 2004.

Promotional Videos 1996-2005

In February 1996, the release of The Beatles' second *Anthology* album was also accompanied by a new single, "Real Love", which was recorded in a similar manner to "Free as a Bird". The video for this single combined home-movie footage of George Harrison, Paul McCartney, and Ringo Starr recording their parts for "Real Love" with historic footage of The Beatles, and some sequences featuring computer-generated special effects.

The video for "Real Love" has got a unique standing in The Beatles' canon of promotional films, as it is the only video showing contemporary footage of George Harrison, Paul McCartney, and Ringo Starr recording their second 'reunion' song in McCartney's studio in Sussex, U.K. In addition, the directors Kevin Godley and Lol Creme, use digital video effects to quote and recreate one of John Lennon and Yoko Ono's better known films, *Two Virgins*, which features slow-motion footage of the faces of Lennon and Ono superimposed on each other. In the "Real Love" video, a similar effect is achieved, when new footage of Harrison, McCartney, and Starr's faces merge into each other.

Another narrative level of "Real Love" plays upon the idea of resurrection by having iconic Beatles-related objects ascend to the sky. The video starts with Lennon's famous white piano, which he used on the recording of his solo hit "Imagine", slowly flying above Liverpool. Later on, the *Sgt. Pepper* uniforms, The Beatles' famous instruments (Lennon and Harrison's Rickenbacker guitars, McCartney's Höfner bass guitar, and Starr's Ludwig drum set), and their album sleeves ascend to the sky. All these objects have played a quite important role in the history of The Beatles' image, and their inclusion in the "Real Love" video did not mark the first time they were featured in a video. Paul McCartney had previously produced two videos containing similar references to The Beatles' history. In his award-winning video for "Coming Up" (1980) he wears a collarless Beatles-suit from 1962-1963 and plays his Höfner bass for the first time in ten years, while "My Brave Face" revolves around the story of a Japanese Beatles collector, who tries to acquire Beatles-related objects, such as McCartney's blue *Sgt. Pepper* uniform and, again, the famous Höfner bass guitar, which McCartney revived on his album *Flowers in the Dirt* (1989) and during his world tour in 1989/1990. George Harrison's video for his single "When We Was Fab" also contains numerous references to The Beatles. The song itself is Harrison's humorous evocation of his time in The Beatles and features an arrangement consisting mainly of what have become Beatles-clichés, such as the sounds of sitars, distinctive harmony vocals, and a string arrangement resembling the arrangement of Harrison's Beatles song "Blue Jay Way" (1967). The video features a guest appearance by Ringo Starr, who actually plays the drums on Harrison's single, while the bass player in the video wears a walrus mask, which refers to Lennon's lyrics "the walrus was Paul" ("Glass Onion", 1968). Harrison also wears his *Sgt. Pepper* costume in one scene. It is quite remarkable that The Beatles' outfits, their instruments, as well as their album covers have become such iconic objects, which are instantly recognizable not only to The Beatles' fan community. No other act has got his or her public image tied to such an array of visual representations. As these images are persistently reinforced in accounts of The Beatles' history as well as in their group and solo videos, their status as symbols of not only The Beatles but the 1960s is continually confirmed.

In 2003, The Beatles released a re-mixed version of their *Let It Be* album, now called *Let It Be...Naked*. To promote the release, a video for the song "Two of Us" was produced by Apple. It was shown on music television stations around the world, and was available as a download on The Beatles' internet homepage. The video features footage of The Beatles' rehearsing the song for their *Let It Be* film. Instead of presenting a performance at the studio, however, digital video technology allowed the producers to cut out The Beatles and place them in a CGI surrounding.

The video for The Beatles' "Tomorrow Never Knows/Within You Without You", which was released to promote the remix album *Love* (2006), also featured various digital effects creating a visual representation of the recording's psychedelic soundscapes.

BEATLES HISTORY - PART THREE: 1970-2008

The Solo Careers

In September 1969, John Lennon told his musical partners at a business meeting that he was leaving The Beatles. It was decided that the split was to be kept secret until the group had secured a profitable new contract with EMI Records. In early 1970, The Beatles' staff prepared the release of *Let It Be*, which had been recorded in January 1969. As George Martin had lost interest in the production, American producer Phil Spector was asked to turn The Beatles' rough recordings into a valuable album. Spector's involvement, however, caused further friction between the band members, because Paul McCartney felt that Spector was ruining his song "The Long and Winding Road" with a lavish arrangement featuring an orchestra and a choir. In addition, the release of *Let It Be* collided with the release date of Paul McCartney's first solo album, *McCartney*, which was scheduled for 10 April, 1970. The conflicts within the band finally reached their climax when the other Beatles ignored McCartney's wish of removing Spector's orchestral arrangement from the recording of his song. Consequently, Paul McCartney decided to inform the public that The Beatles had disbanded. The promotional copies of McCartney's first album contained an interview, in which he stated that he did not want to work with The Beatles anymore, because of personal and musical disagreements. The release date of *McCartney* is therefore regarded as the date The Beatles broke up, although they legally existed as a band until 1976, when their contracts finally expired. The other Beatles, i.e. John Lennon, were enraged by McCartney's publicity stunt. In December 1970, Lennon commented on The Beatles' break-up, "Well, I said to Paul, 'I'm leaving.' [...] And then six months later Paul comes out with whatever [his announcement of leaving the band for a solo career]. A lot of people knew I'd left, but I was a fool not to do what Paul did, which is use it to sell a record" (Wenner 2000: 31-32).

In order to dissolve their songwriting partnership as well as their various contracts with Allen Klein, a New York business man who had taken on the role of The Beatles' manager against Paul McCartney's wish, McCartney was forced to sue his bandmates, which, according to McCartney, was one of the most difficult decisions in his life (vgl. *Wing-*

span 2001). The lawsuit Paul McCartney vs. John Lennon, George Harrison, and Ringo Starr became a favorite topic in the tabloids and finally led to a relentless war of words between McCartney and Lennon, which they fought out in the media as well as on their records. For example, McCartney's song "Too Many People" from his album *Ram* (1971) was a quite obvious criticism of Lennon's recent activities ("Too many people going underground [...]/That was your first mistake/You took your lucky break and broke it in two"), while Lennon's "How Do You Sleep" from *Imagine* (1971) was a rather fierce attack on McCartney's work as a solo artist ("The only thing you done was yesterday/And since you're gone you're just another day").

The lawsuits against each other took on quite absurd proportions, while The Beatles themselves reconciled in early 1972. In January 1972, John Lennon and Paul McCartney agreed to stop "slagging each other off in the press" (Badman 2001: 62) at a dinner in New York. In 1973, John Lennon, George Harrison, and Ringo Starr fired their manager Allen Klein, and all of the former Beatles contributed to Starr's hit album *Ringo*.

In the 1970s John Lennon, Paul McCartney, George Harrison, and Ringo Starr pursued successful solo careers as musicians. John Lennon continued to release albums until 1975, when he decided to temporarily retire from the music business to raise his son Sean Ono Lennon. His political commitment and his support of radical groups and human rights issues caused him quite some problems to obtain a Green Card in the United States, which he applied for in 1972, as he wanted to stay in New York City.[1] Lennon's most successful solo works include the albums *John Lennon/Plastic Ono Band* (1970), *Imagine* (1971), *Mind Games* (1973), *Walls and Bridges* (1974), *Double Fantasy* (1980), as well as the singles "Give Peace a Chance" (1969), "Cold Turkey" (1969), "Instant Karma" (1970), and "Power to the People" (1971). After a four-year long break from the record business, Lennon celebrated a successful comeback in 1980 with his single "Starting Over". He was planning a world tour, a musical, as well as a collaboration with Paul McCartney, when a deranged fan shot him in front of the Dakota Building in New York City on 8 December 1980.

Between 1968 and 1973, John Lennon also produced and directed numerous art movies with his wife Yoko Ono. Most of their avant-garde movies were originally screened only for a limited time at selected cinemas or at film festivals, and they attracted some heavy criticism at the

---

1   For a detailed discussion of John Lennon's political activities and his struggle against Richard Nixon and the F.B.I. see Jon Wiener. *Come Together. John Lennon In His Time*. London: Faber, 1995.

time they were released. Only recently Lennon and Ono's films have been re-evaluated by film critics and scholars alike, which resulted in a successful retrospective at the Viennale, the Austrian international film festival.

In addition to these non-commercial projects, Lennon and Ono were quite active producing promotional films for their record releases. Their 70-minute film *Imagine*, which was basically a visualization of Lennon's most successful solo album, premiered on television on 23 December, 1972. Their promotional videos for songs, such as "Give Peace a Chance" and "Woman" have seen various re-edits and re-packaging since Lennon's tragic death in 1980. Besides supervising a number of video- and DVD-releases, such as *Gimme Some Truth* and *Lennon: Legend*, Yoko Ono has also been involved in a couple of projects celebrating the life and career of her late husband, such as *Imagine: John Lennon* and *John & Yoko's Year of Peace*.

Ringo Starr released several successful albums in the early 1970s and pursued a rather successful career as an actor. He appeared in cult movies such as *The Magic Christian, Candy, Blindman, That'll Be the Day*, and *Caveman*. In addition to his appearances in various feature films and television productions, Starr also directed the documentary *Born to Boogie*, a film about the pop group T. Rex, and *Back Off Boogaloo*, a surreal story about the return of Frankenstein in the 1970s.

Starr's musical career waned in the late Seventies, when he lost himself in alcoholism. While he became known to a generation of children as Mr. Conductor on the children's television series *Shining Time Station* in the 1980s, he celebrated his comeback to the music business in 1989, when he went on his first tour with his 'All Starr Band'. He has continued touring and has released several successful albums throughout the years. Starr's most memorable releases include the albums *Sentimental Journey* (1970), *Beaucoups of Blues* (1970), *Ringo* (1973), *Goodnight Vienna* (1974), *Vertical Man* (1998), *RingoRama* (2003), *Choose Love* (2005), *Liverpool 8* (2008) and the hit singles "It Don't Come Easy" (1971), "Back Off Boogaloo" (1972), and "Photograph" (1973).

Paul McCartney is the most successful former Beatle. He has released more than twenty studio albums and more than fifty hit singles in the course of 38 years. In the 1970s he formed his new band Wings, with whom he managed to establish himself as one of the major rock stars of the 1970s. In the 1980s, he collaborated with the likes of Michael Jackson, Stevie Wonder, Carl Perkins, and Elvis Costello, and continued his run of hit records. In the 1990s, he toured the world twice, propagated vegetarianism, and expanded his musical activities in the field of classical music. After the death of his wife Linda McCartney in 1998, he returned to public attention with a variety of musical projects, including classical music, experimental music, and rock'n'roll. He has continued to stay in the limelight and has been setting new standards in the world of musical entertainment. In the *Guinness World of Records* McCartney holds the record of being the person holding the most world records.

After eye-witnessing the attacks on the World Trade Center in September 2001, he organized the Concert for New York, which united some of the world's biggest names in rock music, such as Mick Jagger, David Bowie, The Who, Elton John, and Billy Joel. He went on sold-out world tours in 2002/2003, 2004, and 2005 and recently confirmed his position as the world's most famous music celebrity when he opened and closed Live 8, the biggest concert event in history. His most successful releases contain *McCartney* (1970), *Ram* (1971), *Band on the Run* (1973), *Venus and Mars* (1975), *Wings at the Speed of Sound* (1976), *McCartney II* (1980), *Tug of War* (1982), *Flowers in the Dirt* (1989), *Flaming Pie* (1997), *Chaos and Creation in the Backyard* (2005), *Memory Almost Full* (2007) and the singles "Another Day" (1971), "Uncle Albert/Admiral Halsey" (1971), "My Love" (1973), "Live and Let Die" (1973), "Jet" (1974), "Band on the Run" (1974), "Silly Love Songs" (1976), "Mull of Kintyre" (1977), "With a Little Luck" (1978), "Coming Up" (1980), "Ebony and Ivory" (1982), "Say Say Say" (1983), "No More Lonely Nights" (1984), "My Brave Face" (1989), and "Hope of Deliverance" (1993).

In addition to his career in the music business, Paul McCartney has been linked to the film industry in various ways since the group officially split in 1970. He produced several short films in the 1970s, some of which have never been released. Since the early 1980s he has established himself as a producer of independent short films, such as *The Cooler* (1982) and *Daumier's Law* (1992). In addition to these smaller productions, McCartney also wrote the screenplay for *Give My Regards to Broad Street*, a light-hearted comedy starring Paul McCartney, his wife Linda, Ringo Starr, and Barbara Bach. Although the movie became McCartney's only financial flop in his entire career, he established a reputation of producing innovative videos at the time, winning several awards with the promotional videos for his songs "No More Lonely Nights" and "Pipes of Peace". He also produced and scored the highly successful animated short film *Rupert and the Frog Song*, which was the bestselling video in Britain in 1984. More recently, he has revived his interest in animated films and has produced several animated shorts, such as *Tropic Island Hum* and the award-winning *Tuesday,* which premiered in Cannes in 2001.

George Harrison was initially the most successful solo artist of the four Ex-Beatles. His triple album release *All Things Must Pass* (1970) and the single "My Sweet Lord" topped the charts worldwide, and his *Concert for Bangla Desh* (1972) was the first large-scale charity concert in the history of rock'n'roll. When his musical career stalled in the mid-Seventies, he became an important independent film producers in Great Britain with his company HandMade Films. In 1987, he celebrated a successful comeback to the music business, when his single "Got My Mind Set on You" topped the U.S. charts. He went on to form the 'supergroup' The Traveling Wilburys with Bob Dylan, Tom Petty, Roy Orbison, and Jeff Lynne, and toured Japan with Eric Clapton in 1991. In the 1990s Harrison endured an ongoing battle with cancer, which he seemed to have won in 1999, when an insane fan broke into his London home and stabbed him multiple times. After the attack, the cancer returned, and George Harrison died on 29 November 2001 in Los Angeles. His musical legacy contains the albums *All Things Must Pass* (1970), *Living in the Material World* (1973), *Thirty Three & 1/3* (1976), *George Harrison* (1979), *Cloud 9* (1987), *Traveling Wilburys Vol. 1* (1988), *Traveling Wilburys Vol. 3* (1990), *Brainwashed* (2002), as well as the hit singles "My Sweet Lord" (1970), "Give Me Love (Give Me Peace on Earth)" (1973), "All Those Years Ago" (1981), "Got My Mind Set on You" (1987), and "When We Was Fab" (1988).

While Starr, McCartney and Lennon all celebrated quite some success with their individual film projects, it was George Harrison who not only became the most active Beatle in the film business but also one of the most influential independent film producers in the British film industry since World War II. Initially created to help his friends from Monty Python to finance their movie *The Life of Brian*, Harrison's production company HandMade Films was responsible for some of the most successful and most respected British films in the last thirty years. Besides *The Life of Brian*, Harrison produced, among many others, the blockbuster *Time Bandits* as well as the critically acclaimed *Mona Lisa* and *Withnail and I*. After some personal disappointments and the financial disaster of *Shanghai Surprise*, a movie featuring Madonna and Sean Penn, Harrison lost interest in producing movies and sold HandMade Films in the early 1990s.

Beatles Projects after 1970

As early as 1969, Neil Aspinall, the director of The Beatles' company Apple, began to collect film material featuring The Beatles from TV stations and news archives all around the world. He compiled a two-hour film of the material, which spanned the whole career of the group, from their first televised performance at the Cavern club in Liverpool to the rather unpleasant recording sessions for their *Let It Be* project. A documentary about The Beatles was planned to be released in 1973. For legal reasons, however, the project was abandoned, and the film, which was called *The Long and Winding Road* at the time, remained in The Beatles' archives. Interestingly, the albums featuring the film soundtrack were released by Apple in 1973. The two double albums *The Beatles 1962-1966* aka *The Red Album* and *The Beatles 1967-1970* aka *The Blue Album* contained many of The Beatles' greatest hits and sold several million copies in the 1970s, introducing a new generation of music fans to the works of The Beatles.

In the second half of the 1970s, The Beatles did not have any control concerning EMI/Capitol's Beatles releases. In order to provide the public with Beatles products, the record company released several packages of re-releases without The Beatles' consent, e.g. *Rock'n'Roll Music* (1976), *Love Songs* (1977), *Reel Music* (1982), *20 Greatest Hits* (1982). In 1977, George Martin re-mixed live recordings he had made of The Beatles in 1964 and 1965 at the Hollywood Bowl, Los Angeles, and compiled the first Beatles live album, *The Beatles Live at the Hollywood Bowl*, which topped the American album charts in May 1977.

Various legal complications discouraged The Beatles from releasing any group projects in the 1970s. In fact, it took The Beatles until 1989 to resolve all the legal matters concerning their musical partnership, their contracts with EMI/Capitol Records, and their own business venture Apple. In 1989, a large crowd of reporters applauded Paul McCartney when he announced at a press conference: "I think we're settled. [...] Everything is there, ready to be signed, and we finally – after about twenty years – sorted it all out" (McCartney *Press Conferences* CD).

As soon as their legal difficulties had been overcome, the three surviving Beatles resumed the work on several group projects. In 1992, Apple started to film interviews with each individual Beatle for the documentary film *The Long and Winding Road*. When George Harrison vetoed the documentary's title, The Beatles decided to call their project simply *Anthology*.

In 1993, Apple re-released *The Red Album* and *The Blue Album* on CD, which generated quite some interest around the world. A year later, The Beatles surprised their fans with a double CD called *Live at the BBC*, which featured historical recordings of The Beatles' performances on various BBC radio shows. Finally, in 1995 and 1996, George Harrison, Paul McCartney, and Ringo Starr re-united for the release of their

Anthology project, which initially consisted of a television documentary, three soundtrack double CDs, as well as two new recordings featuring the voice of John Lennon, who had been murdered in 1980.

Further recent Beatles projects include the DVD release of *Yellow Submarine* (1999), *A Hard Day's Night* (2002), *The First U.S. Visit* (2004), and *Help!* (2007), as well as the album releases *Yellow Submarine* (1999), *1* (2000), *Let It Be...Naked* (2003), *The Capitol Albums Vol.1* (2004), *The Capitol Albums Vol. 2* (2005), and *Love* (2006).

SCREENING THE PAST: FILM AND HISTORY

All works of art and popular culture convey information about the condition of humankind at particular points in time, as each artefact is shaped by the cultural circumstances and dominant ideologies of the time it was produced. Consequently, the interpretation of a popular culture text in a historical context establishes relationships between the work and the social, political, and artistic developments at a certain time. While certain works are conscious reflections on contemporary historical and social developments, others convey dominant world-views in an unintentional or indirect way.

The study of mass media examines and interprets the influence of the mass media on our perception of reality. The matter has been approached in various academic disciplines, from sociology to literary criticism, and the research in this field has produced numerous insights as to how the media and contemporary societies interact in the creation of what we call reality. In order to convey content without the necessity of extensive explanation, the mass media make use of popular myths and stereotypes.

In every part of the world, traditional mythology offers symbolic and metaphoric explanations for the existence of human beings (vgl. Campbell/Moyers 1994: 42). Mythology is closely linked to religion and proposes certain value systems designed to guide people through life. Ancient stories convey moral guidelines and models of behavior, which have been repeatedly reinforced throughout the ages. Thereby, numerous myths have acquired a status of factuality for many people. For instance, in the United States, the widespread belief in the myth of creationism still poses a problem in the scientific debates about the evolution of the planet Earth. Consequently, once integrated in the common conception of reality, a myth can hardly be extinguished.

In the contemporary world of mass media, the dominant set of world views and beliefs in a society is repeatedly presented by all kinds of media. Roland Barthes describes how the continuous repetition of certain representations in mass media leads to the creation of contemporary myths. According to his theory, any kind of semiotic units, such as symbols, words, pictures, et al. can acquire additional connotations which 'charge' them with ideology (vgl. Biguell: 1997: 16). The set of values conveyed by these connotations constitutes modern mythology and represents the ideology of the dominant class in a society: "[M]yth consists in overturning culture into nature, or, at least, the social, the cultural, the ideological, the historical into the 'natural'. What is nothing but a product of class division and its moral, cultural and aesthetic consequences is presented (stated) as being a 'matter of course'" (Barthes: 1977: 165). This suggests that the pluralism of opinions in democracies is also always subordinated to a dominant system of values.

Every semiotic system is an expression of cultural, political, economical, and social myths in society. According to Barthes, the creation of these myths is a social phenomenon achieved by constant repetition and reinforcement of certain ideological messages (vgl. Barthes 1977: 165). People perceive everyday life 'filtered' by their basic value system.

Today, in our 'global village', film and television play an increasingly significant role in the way we perceive ourselves and the world around us. Most major blockbuster movies and television shows continually reinforce contemporary social values and conceptions, expressing as well as shaping the dominant value system of the social system they are part of. Dramatizations of history have always been among the most successful genres in the history of the moving image. From the classic *Gone with the Wind* to the more recent *Gladiator*, the movie industry has been a continuous re-interpreter and projector of history, feeding its audience with visions of the past, which have contributed considerably to the way we imagine what went before. Although many producers of popular culture texts dealing with the past like to point out that it is not their intention to re-create an authentic account of past events, because they mainly consider their products as entertainment, their influence on the audience's conceptions and imagination cannot be denied. John E. O'Connor explains how continual reinforcement shapes the public's notion of the past: "What a series such as *The Waltons* has to say about life in the Depression is likely to have a far more penetrating and long-lasting effect on the nation's historical consciousness than any number of carefully researched articles or books" (O'Connor 1983: xxxiii). While 'docudramas' may convey a certain flair of historical setting, historical films and television series are always limited by the conventions and codes of the genre they are part of. Therefore, they often merely represent stereotypical characters, settings, and storylines, which enable the audience to relate to what they see. Stereotypes, as defined by Walter Lippmann, are a form of "'ordering' the mass of complex and inchoate data that we receive from the world" (Dyer 1995: 11). This definition corresponds to Roland Barthes' definition of myths, as stereotypes are "a very simple, striking, easily-grasped form of representation but are none the less capable of condensing a great deal of complex information and a host of connotations" (Dyer 1995: 11). Consequently, a myth is a repeatedly re-inforced stereotype – a simplified representation of reality that becomes accepted by the audience as a natural fact. Seymour Chatman has called this process of accepting (literary) conventions as reality 'naturalization':

"Audiences come to recognize and interpret conventions by 'naturalizing' them [...]. To realize a narrative convention means not only to understand it, but to 'forget' its conventional character, to absorb it into the reading-out process, to incorporate it into one's interpretive net, giving to it no more thought than to the manifestational medium, say the English language" (Chatman 1980: 49).

In film, these conventions contain everything from the characterization of the individual characters to the way the plot is constructed. By using stereotypical elements of various kinds, the producers of popular culture texts enable the audience to relate to what is presented, as large segments of mass audiences have naturalized the conventions of the genres they prefer. Therefore, the audience will not be estranged by the way a story-line develops, or the way a protagonist is characterized. However, as pointed out by Richard Dyer, the need to order "'the great blooming, buzzing confusion of reality' is liable to be accompanied by a belief in the absoluteness and certainty of any particular order, a refusal to recog-nize its limitations and partiality, its relativity and changeability, and a corresponding incapacity to deal with the fact and experience of bloom-ing and buzzing" (Dyer 1995: 11). This means that the audience will ac-cept continually reinforced myths as reality, which is highly problematic in the context of representing history on the screen. O'Connor points out that "[r]ather than plumb the complexities of issues, analyze the contra-dictions of human motivation, and interpret events from various perspec-tives in the context of their own time, film and television producers work to reduce complex issues and motives to simple ones and to present one view of events in a context with which the audience will feel immedi-ately at ease" (O'Connor 1983: xxxvi). In film, history has always got a fictional dimension. Gaps in the historical record are filled, and ambigui-ties and complexities become polished (vgl. Carnes 1996: 9), in order to enable a conventional progression of the storyline and to meet the audi-ence's expectations. Laura Seger explains the difficulty of turning his-torical events and biographies into movies.

"Film is a story medium. Aristotle told us that drama is about 'one action,' one consistent story line. Clearly he wasn't thinking of the true-life story. There are many stories within one life; a life defies cinematic neatness and creates diffi-culties for anyone choosing which story to show. If you're doing a film on Mar-tin Luther King, Jr., for instance, are you going to tell his whole life story or only emphasize his part in the civil rights movement? Are you going to focus on his relationship with Coretta Scott King? Or perhaps it should be the story of the theological journey that led him to make a number of decisions about the relationship of religion and social action" (Seger 1992: 49).

In addition to the restrictions implied by a particular popular culture genre and the selective nature of biographical texts, historical accounts of a phenomenon such as The Beatles are also predominantly shaped by the particular point of view of who tells the story. In his recent cultural history of The Beatles, Steven D. Stark points out that one of the problems of re-creating the band's history is posed by the fact that The Beatles were already considered a historic phenomenon in their own time, and that it may be "close to impossible to write an objective history of the Beatles after 1963 that is unclouded by the revisionism of the participants, whether intentional or not. [...] Because of the group's unique kind of fame, those who knew the band tend to have an even stronger than usual stake in placing themselves at the center of the narrative" (Stark 2005: 7). Stark goes on to explain that the distortion of The Beatles' history was caused by the group's immense popularity.

"[T]here's a process with any historical figure by which those associated with the figure color their memories through the lens of subsequent events. With the Beatles, however, this process was exponential. The group reached a level of celebrity and adoration never seen before or since in modern times (Marilyn Monroe would be the closest, not Elvis). [...] Their aura was so blinding – they were just too famous and mythologized even then – that anyone around them formed impressions and recollections with the implicit awareness that these reminiscences would become instant fodder for the once and future gospel"(Stark 2005: 7).

As individual recollections of The Beatles' history are shaped or at least influenced by the impact of early mythologization, all histories of the band are to some degree clouded by myth. This is true for the countless books on the band as well as for documentaries and dramatizations of the band's history. While documentaries often contain interviews that express or reflect the particular point of view of the person interviewed, the producers of movies about The Beatles only consulted one or two people close to The Beatles at some point in their career, in order to emphasize the movie's authenticity. In fact, however, the choice of depending on the recollection of a few individuals limits a movie's objectivity. Although movies are generally not produced with the intention of educating the public's historical awareness, they literally project a vision of the past which is accepted as authentic history by large segments of the audience, because they may not have the opportunity or desire to compare what is presented in the movie with other historical accounts or alternative sources. As pointed out by O'Connor, the historical film does not question or explain what is presented. Instead, it "establishes relationships between the facts and offers a more or less superficial view of them" (O'Connor 1983: xxxvi). These simplified and often subjective accounts of history are accepted as authentic portrayals by a less critical audience because of the power of the visual media. O'Connor explains that "unlike the historical monograph that invites response and rebuttal, the completed film or broadcast docudrama has a more powerful presence – the quality of a final statement" (O'Connor 1983: xxxvii).

Taking into account all the factors mentioned above, the dramatizations of The Beatles' history are necessarily characterized by the limitations of popular culture genres, the distortion of historical facts by individual perspectives, over-simplification of facts due to the medium's restrictions, and the film teams' interpretation of the events and circumstances constituting the group's history. Consequently, they perpetuate different versions of The Beatles' history, contributing to the confusion of fact and fiction and to the creation and modification of contemporary popular cultural myths.

MOVIES ABOUT THE BEATLES

Early Beatles History: 1940-1964

Birth of The Beatles

In 1978, *Elvis – The Movie* premiered on American television. The production was a dramatization of Elvis Presley's life, featuring Kurt Russell as Elvis. His unexpected death the year before had revived the public interest in 'The King,' and countless biographies invaded the market. The movie spawned several fictional and/or biographical films about popular culture icons, such as Buddy Holly (*The Buddy Holly Story*, 1978) and The Beatles (*Birth of The Beatles*, 1979). In the 1980s and 1990s, only a handful of pop biographies were successful at the box office, i. e. Luis Valdez' *La Bamba* (1987) about Richie Valens, Oliver Stone's *The Doors* (1991) and Iain Softley's *Backbeat* (1993). More recently, Hollywood has produced a string of highly successful TV and cinema biographies of musical heroes. The most notable films and series are *The Rat Pack* (1998) about the lives and times of Frank Sinatra, Dean Martin, and Sammy Davis Jr., *Ray* (2004) about Ray Charles, *Stoned* (2005) about The Rolling Stones' Brian Jones, and – again – *Elvis* (2005). Starting with *Birth of The Beatles*, The Beatles' history has been dramatized in various forms for television as well as for the cinema. While The Beatles' early group history has been dealt with in *Birth of The Beatles* (1979), *Backbeat* (1993), and *In His Life: The John Lennon Story* (2000), John Lennon's private life was explored in *John and Yoko: A Love Story* (1985) and *The Hours and Times* (1991). *The Linda McCartney Story* (2000) focused on Paul and Linda McCartney, while *Two of Us* (2000) dramatized an encounter between John Lennon and Paul McCartney in 1976, six years after The Beatles had broken up.

Birth of The Beatles was produced by Dick Clark, an influential producer in the field of musical television shows and films in the United States. For this project, Clark teamed up with director Richard Marquand, who was going to direct George Lucas' *Star Wars: Episode VI – Return of the Jedi* in 1983. The Beatles' story from 1961 to 1964 was turned into a screenplay by Jacob Eskendar and John Kurland, while Ringo Starr's predecessor Pete Best was consulted as 'technical advisor'.

Although it is pointed out that the movie contained fictional elements, Pete Best's involvement was used as a way to sell the movie as an 'authentic' biographical picture. At the very beginning, the viewer learns that "[t]he following is a dramatization, using actors, of the early career of the Beatles. It is based on factual accounts including the recollections of former Beatle Pete Best, as well as other sources" (*Birth of the Beatles* 1979). Although *Birth of The Beatles* depicts many crucial events in The Beatles' early history, the movie fails to represent the group's way to success in an authentic way. Despite Pete Best's involvement, *Birth of The Beatles* is full of factual errors and clumsy editing decisions. In addition, the The Beatles' personalities are stereotyped in a way that is partly reminiscent of the portrayal of The Beatles in the American cartoon series.

The very first sequence already establishes a set of poorly researched details. The characters of John Lennon, Paul McCartney, and George Harrison are walking down a Liverpool street in 1961. They wear leather jackets, and George Harrison is playing a (naturally) un-plugged electric guitar while chatting to his mates. First of all, The Beatles did not own any leather outfits before their first trip to Hamburg later that year. This is an important fact, because the leather outfits contributed to the group's unique stage appearance after their return from Hamburg. Second, George Harrison – who is unlikely to have practiced guitar riffs while walking through the streets of Liverpool – did certainly not remotely talk the way actor John Altman imagined him to talk. The character's voice and intonation actually resemble the way the cartoon Harrison talked in *Yellow Submarine* rather than the real George Harrison. In addition, the character of John Lennon looks much older than Lennon at the age of 21, which diminishes the character's credibility throughout the movie.

As Pete Best worked as a consultant for the *Birth of The Beatles*, the Pete Best character in the movie is clearly designed to contradict the myth of Best being only a modest drummer and a loser type. In the movie, Pete Best is introduced in a scene portraying his audition to become The Beatles' drummer. He recalls the audition in his autobiography.

"First I had to audition at Allan Williams' Wyvern Club (later to become his popular Blue Angel Club). John was the only one there when I arrived. He played a couple of bars of Ramrod while I beat the skins, until George and Stu turned up and we had a further session. Paul was last, as usual, but once there they all joined in such numbers as Shakin' All Over. We played for about 20 minutes in all and at the end they all reached the same conclusion: 'Yeh! You're in, Pete!'" (Best/Doncaster 2001: 29).

Birth of The Beatles does not show a session as described by Best. Instead, the handsome Pete Best character performs an impressive drum solo, which the real Pete Best would probably not have been capable of performing at the time. While it has been suggested that The Beatles desperately needed a drummer and would have welcomed any half-decent rock drummer in their band, the movie makes it clear that Best was accepted in the group because of his outstanding drumming ability.

Many accounts of Pete Best's role in The Beatles early history point out that his good looks and moody manners made him very popular with The Beatles' female audience (vgl. *A Long and Winding Road* 2003: DVD 2). This is also the stance taken by *Birth of The Beatles*. When Best is replaced with Ringo Starr in the movie, the group is confronted with a crowd of girls chanting "Ringo never, Pete for Ever" at their first performance featuring Starr on drums. This particular incident was first described by manager Brian Epstein in Hunter Davies' book about The Beatles (vgl. Davies 1969: 150). Epstein also confirms Best's popularity at the time: "I knew how popular Pete was. He was incredibly good looking with a big following. [...] So I was very upset when the three of them came to me one night and said they didn't want him. They wanted Ringo" (Davies 1969: 151). Instead of marginalizing Pete Best's audience appeal, *Birth of The Beatles* quite accurately depicts Best as an important part of their stage presence from 1960 to 1962.

As *Birth of The Beatles* deals with The Beatles' history from 1961 to 1964, it contains their first engagement in Hamburg, their triumphant return to Liverpool, their meeting with Brian Epstein, their initial success in Great Britain, and their appearance on *The Ed Sullivan Show* in February 1964. In order to include all the important events of this period, the producers were forced to simplify several chapters in The Beatles' history. For example, instead of the group's five trips to Germany, the film only shows them return once. In addition, the portrayal of The Beatles' friends in Germany is rather superficial and flawed. The character of Astrid Kirchherr is never shown without her camera, and she is constantly taking pictures of the group at their live performances. In fact, Astrid Kirchherr's famous photographs of The Beatles in Hamburg were not performance pictures. She actually took many of her pictures of the band at the Hamburg fairground. Although performance photos from this period exist, they were taken by photographers Jürgen Vollmer, and Peter Brüchmann, among others. In addition, Kirchherr's influence on The Beatles' style is portrayed in an inaccurate way. Although it is true that Kirchherr practically invented The Beatles haircut, she initially only cut Stuart Sutcliffe and George Harrison's hair. Paul McCartney and John

Lennon's hair was cut this way months later when they visited their friend Jürgen Vollmer in Paris.

There are quite a few factual errors in the representation of The Beatles' Hamburg period. For example, the way The Beatles learn about the death of their former bassist Stuart Sutcliffe, who had also invented the group's name, does not correspond to the facts. In *Birth of The Beatles*, the group is getting ready for a performance at the Star Club, when Astrid suddenly appears to tell them that Stuart has died. The actual circumstances were, however, rather different to what is shown in the movie. In an interview, Pete Best talks about the way Sutcliffe's death was portrayed in *Birth of The Beatles*: "They've taken artistic liberties. What actually happened was we were met by Astrid at the airport and we were expecting to see Stu. This is when we went over to open the Star Club. When Stu wasn't there we asked where he was, and we were told he had died. It had only been a day or two before" (Giuliano/Devi 1999: 200). While the other films dealing with this period, *In His Life: The John Lennon Story* and *Backbeat*, portrayed the sad event as described by Pete Best, the producers of *Birth of The Beatles* opted for an alternative version, which is, interestingly, less dramatic than what really happened.

Bill Harry, Stuart Sutcliffe and John Lennon's friend from art college explains his disappointment with *Birth of The Beatles*.

"Apart from scores of trifling errors (the art college sequence was nothing like the real place and the fat model was like no model who ever posed there), the entire 'feel' was wrong. It was like watching fantasy which had bare association to what I had personally lived through. I understood the need to make the film dramatic, but the real events had seemed far more dramatic then the ones of the film, which seemed to 'lessen' the Beatles story" (Harry 1985: 145).

The movie was not a big success when it was first shown on American television in 1979. The audience, Beatles fans, and critics were quite disappointed by the movie, which did not manage to capture The Beatles' excitement and failed to represent their early career in an accurate way.

Backbeat: "I Didn't Want to Do a Bio-Pic"

Iain Softley's movie *Backbeat* provides a detailed depiction of The Beatles' time in Hamburg. The movie mainly concentrates on the relationships between John Lennon, Stuart Sutcliffe, and Astrid Kirchherr. Softley sets out to explore the intense friendship of Lennon and Sutcliffe, and how the appearance of Astrid Kirchherr and her 'existentialist' friends influenced the group's structure and image at a crucial point in their career.

In a recent interview, Iain Softley explains that he did not intend to make a strictly biographical movie: "The last thing I was trying to do is to tell a story about The Beatles in Hamburg from a sort of biographical point of view. [...] In fact, at one stage, I considered not mentioning the band as The Beatles, and not mentioning anybody's surname – to really make it like an everyman group" (*Backbeat* 2003). Despite Softley's focus on Lennon, Sutcliffe, and Kirchherr, the background story is quite well-researched and represents The Beatles' early history in Hamburg more adequately than *Birth of The Beatles*. In contrast to former movies about The Beatles, Softley spotlights the group's friends in Germany and manages not to over-simplify some of the facts that were quite misrepresented in *Birth of The Beatles* and *In His Life*. However, criticism of the movie has been targeted at the rather romantic representation of Hamburg's notorious Reeperbahn and the nostalgic and idealistic view of the 'existentialist' scene in Hamburg. For example, Horst Fascher, the group's friend and bodyguard from Hamburg, identified the movie's main deficiency being the reliance on only Astrid Kirchherr's memory and perspective.

"Astrid Kirchherr hat diesen Film so beraten, dass er so gedreht wurde, wie sie die Vergangenheit gern gehabt hätte. Das war's nicht. [...] Die Realität war eine andere. Wir waren damals rough, wir haben unsere Biere getrunken – die Beatles waren morgens genauso angetrunken wie die Gäste, und wir haben zusammen gesessen und haben irgendwo Hähnchen gegessen – wo's billig war, in so kleinen Restaurants-Ecken. [Dann sind wir wie] tot ins Bett gefallen, haben geschlafen, sind manchmal morgens ungewaschen und ungekämmt zur Arbeit gelaufen – nur die Mütze auf und dann zur Arbeit. Und manchmal sind die Beatles auch so auf der Reeperbahn rumgelaufen – dass ich gesagt habe: „You look like Penner!" Und dann haben sie gesagt: „But tonight, on stage, you will see the difference." Und das war so" (Fascher 2003).

However, Astrid Kirchherr has pointed out that the film would have looked different if she had had more influence on the project. She explains that a production of this kind demands certain compromises, in order to increase its potential at the box office, and that the producers always had the final say: "Ich hab' sehr viel gelernt bei dieser Filmproduktion – dass man ganz viele Kompromisse machen muss. Dass die Menschen, die das Geld haben, viel mehr zu sagen haben als die Künstler. Und dementsprechend war es für mich natürlich eine harte Sache. [...] Man hätte es, wenn man sehr, sehr viel Geld gehabt hätte, sehr viel besser machen können. Ich fand die Musik toll" (Kirchherr 2003).

The music was produced by Don Was, who assembled a 'super-group' consisting of some of the most prominent names in rock music in the 1990s. The group featuring Dave Grohl (Nirvana, Foo Fighters), David Pirner (Soul Asylum), and Mike Mills (R.E.M.) perform several songs from The Beatles' early repertoire, such as "Long Tall Sally," "Oh Carol," and "Money". Instead of reproducing the well-known sound of The Beatles' early records, producer Don Was and director Iain Softley decided to evoke the excitement of the early Beatles performances for the cinema audience with a more contemporary rock sound. Softley explains, "When we were thinking about the music for the film, I always wanted it to be – again – not a counterfeit band trying to imitate the exact voices of the different Beatles, or the exact sound, because I thought that that would kill what made them special, which is an attitude, and an energy, and an attack" (*Backbeat* 2003). The timing was right for the soundtrack, as rock music was celebrating a revival in the early 1990s, when the rock group Nirvana popularized the 'Grunge' sound.

The selection of the actors portraying The Beatles and their German friends was done more carefully than in the case of *Birth of The Beatles*, and although none of the actors would pass as a Beatles-lookalike, each of the characters manages to capture some essential quality of the real Beatles. Liverpool actor Ian Hart received very positive feedback for his portrayal of John Lennon. In fact, Hart had previously played John Lennon in a low-budget production by director Christopher Münch. Softley recalls the casting of the Lennon character: "I went to see a film that he'd done – where he'd also played John Lennon – called *The Hours and Times*. And I was sceptical after that, because, even though he's fantastic in the role, it's a very, very different Lennon to the Lennon that we had in *Backbeat*" (*Backbeat* 2003). The John Lennon in *Backbeat* is a witty, arrogant, and aggressive person, trying to hide his fear of losing his best friend to Astrid Kirchherr behind an angry macho attitude. His remarks and behavior are characterized by a violence, which cover up his inner sadness. At one point the character of Astrid Kirchherr says to him, "Why are you so angry? You are the angriest person I have ever met" (*Backbeat* 2003). Later, she manages to bring out his gentler and vulnerable side during a conversation in a lighthouse, when they talk about their relationships and John admits that he is not just jealous of Astrid but also of Stuart, because he has fallen in love with a girl that embodies John's ideal.

The characters of Astrid Kirchherr and Stuart Sutcliffe were played by American actors Sheryl Lee and Stephen Dorff. Both prepared their roles for a very long time, consulting several of the people originally involved with The Beatles as well as voice coaches, in order to increase the level of authenticity of the performance. Sheryl Lee's voice and the German accent she developed for the role strikingly resemble Astrid Kirchherr's, although the few German sentences she says in the movie sound quite awkward to native speakers. Stephen Dorff, who worked very hard to substitute his American slang with an authentic Liverpudlian 'Scouse' accent – which he manages very well, may have been quite disappointed when Stuart Sutcliffe's sister pointed out to him that her brother did actually not talk the way the other Beatles talked: "When Stephen Dorff came to see me he told me he was working with a voice coach – he had to be taught how to talk Liverpool. I said, 'Why bother?' If anything, Stuart had more of a soft Edinburgh accent. But for the movies they all had to be Scousers, didn't they?" (Sutcliffe/Thompson 2002: 220). Stuart and Pauline's parents had both grown up in Scotland. Although it was not the director's intention to recreate every detail in an authentic way, this minor inaccuracy may have a quite lasting effect as to how Stuart Sutcliffe will be remembered. In fact, the movie may have been an important factor why Sutcliffe's role in The Beatles has not been 'air-brushed' out of the band's official history the way, for instance, Alistair Taylor or Alf Bicknell have been. Liverpool journalist and editor Paul Du Noyer has pointed out that Stuart Sutcliffe "was somewhat rescued from obscurity by the film *Backbeat* [...]" (Du Noyer 2004: 34). While Stephen Dorff's portrayal of Stuart Sutcliffe emphasizes the character's intelligence, artistic talent, and 'coolness,' the movie's overall air of nostalgia and idealization tint this particular account of The Beatles' early history, despite its high standard of factual accuracy.

Although they do not play central roles in *Backbeat*, the characters of Paul McCartney, George Harrison, Pete Best, and Ringo Starr are portrayed in a considerably more credible way than in *Birth of The Beatles* and other dramatizations of the group's history. For example, the Paul McCartney in the movie, played by Gary Bakewell, is much more convincing in *Backbeat* than the one in *Birth of The Beatles*. On the one hand, his criticism of Stuart Sutcliffe's musicianship expresses his musical professionalism as well as his jealousy of Sutcliffe's role in John Lennon's life. On the other hand, he is also shown as a sensible and caring person who manages to calm down a drunk and raging Lennon, and takes him home.

Reality vs. Movie Myths: How Stuart Sutcliffe Died

Backbeat, *Birth of The Beatles*, and the television production *In His Life: The John Lennon Story* all include a sequence showing a violent confrontation of Stuart Sutcliffe and some jealous Teddy Boys in Liverpool. After flirting with some girls in the audience during an early Beatles performance, Sutcliffe was beaten up by a group of young men. Sutcliffe's sister Pauline describes the incident in her biography *The Beatles' Shadow*.

"George and Paul were beaten up at Hambleton Hall in Huyton, and Stuart received a severe beating at Lathom Hall, Seaforth, Liverpool, on 30 January, 1961. The group were helping Neil Aspinall load equipment through a fire door at the back of the stage and into their van. Stuart was on his own when he looked up and there were a crowd of toughs. They had waited until John and the others had gone back inside the hall. Stuart said he was punched in the stomach so hard he rolled on to the ground and his glasses fell from his face. He had one hand on his head and the other between his legs as he was kicked and punched. John was alerted by a couple of girls and rushed out to help. He ran into the thugs and the punching and kicking went on. John sprained his wrist and broke his finger and it might have been much worse but Pete Best, the true hard man of the group, arrived and the odds became too intimidating for the hooligans, who ran off. 'John and I doubled back and charged into the fray, freeing Stu and collecting our fair share of knocks along the way. Lennon broke a finger belting a Ted and had to play guitar for a while wearing a splint.' Stuart's face was smothered in blood" (Sutcliffe/Thompson 2002: 117).

In *Birth of The Beatles*, the scene is based upon Pete Best's account of the incident. The Pete Best character defeats the Teddy Boys only with the help of John Lennon, while *In His Life: The John Lennon Story* has John Lennon and Paul McCartney turn up and rescue Stuart Sutcliffe, while the producers of *Backbeat* decided to create a new version of the story, where Sutcliffe and Lennon insult a group of dock workers in a bar and are chased and beaten up by them. Here it is again Lennon who rescues his friend. The decision to re-invent the story in *Backbeat* and to focus it on John Lennon and Stuart Sutcliffe alone makes sense from a dramatic point of view, as the movie revolves around the relationships between John Lennon, Stuart Sutcliffe, and Astrid Kirchherr. By making John Lennon Stuart's rescuer in the first narrative scene of the movie, their close friendship is established for the audience. To have the character of Paul McCartney help rescue Sutcliffe, however, does neither reflect the historical account of the event, nor does it work very well in the way of characterizing the McCartney character, who later heavily criticizes Sutcliffe's musical abilities. Paul McCartney's critical view of Sutcliffe's limited musicality has been quoted in numerous accounts, including The Beatles' autobiography *Anthology*. While McCartney now prefers to describe his disagreements with Sutcliffe as quite harmless, Hunter Davies' authorized Beatles biography makes it quite clear that Sutcliffe and McCartney did not get along very well at all.

"The relationship between Paul and Stu, the petty jealousies and rows, is not too difficult to explain. In a way, they were both competing for John's attention. Paul had had it for a couple of years, until Stu came along. Stu was obviously very talented, more mature, more in touch. Even Michael McCartney, Paul's younger brother, remembers how in Liverpool Paul had been a bit jealous of Stu" (Davies 1969: 97).

The injuries Sutcliffe received when he was beaten up by a gang of Teddy Boys were later believed to have contributed to his early death. After enduring several months of severe headaches and collapses, Stuart Sutcliffe died of a brain haemorrhage in Hamburg, Germany on 10 April 1962 (cf. Lewisohn 2000: 56). While all the movies dealing with The Beatles' early history include Sutcliffe's death, it is certainly staged as the dramatic climax in *Backbeat*. In one of the movie's last sequences, the characters of Stuart Sutcliffe and Astrid Kirchherr are excited about The Beatles returning to Hamburg. Stuart looks exhausted and ill, but he is enthusiastic about The Beatles' progress, and he is convinced that they will be famous. Astrid wants to 'surprise' Stuart and undresses in another room, when Stuart suddenly screams and collapses in the attic of Kirchherr's house, which had been his studio.

In the TV production *In His Life: The John Lennon Story* (2000), Sutcliffe collapses after reading a letter from John, telling him about their recent progress in Liverpool, where they had just topped a poll in Bill Harry's magazine *Mersey Beat*. In both movies, the juxtaposition of The Beatles' success and Stuart's death expresses the tragic irony of the fact that Stuart Sutcliffe, one of The Beatles' original members and the inventor of their name, would never know that his friends were about to become the biggest attraction in show business since Elvis Presley.

In *Birth of The Beatles*, the producers opted for a different portrayal of Sutcliffe's death. Here, Stuart Sutcliffe breaks down while dancing with his girlfriend Astrid Kirchherr. However, none of these depictions come even close to the actual circumstances of Stuart Sutcliffe's death. Pauline Sutcliffe reconstructs the dramatic events in her biography of her brother.

"He was alone in the attic at Astrid's where he painted. Astrid's mother Nielsa was startled by a shout-scream. Stuart was writhing on the floor and Nielsa could not get his emergency medication into his mouth as his teeth were shut. She called the emergency services [...]. Nielsa telephoned Astrid but when she got home Stuart was in a coma. Astrid sent a telegram to my mother warning that her son was desperately ill. The paramedics got Stuart from the downstairs bedroom and into the ambulance, but getting him to Heidbert Hospital became academic.

Astrid had his head in her hands. She said he had a smile on his face, which was nice of her. At 4.45 p.m. Stuart died on his way to hospital. His body was taken to the forensic department of the University Hospital, Eppendorf, for autopsy, which concluded that the cause of death had been cerebral haemorrhage in the right ventricle of the brain" (Sutcliffe/Thompson 2002: 166-167).

Since John Lennon's death in December 1980, several authors have suggested that John Lennon had severely injured Sutcliffe in a fist-fight and was therefore partly responsible for his death (cf. Goldman 2001: 117-120). Although Lennon was known to be aggressive at times and made headlines in 1963 when he beat up Liverpool DJ Bob Wooler at Paul McCartney's 21st birthday party, clear evidence of this confrontation ever taking place is missing, as neither Sutcliffe nor Lennon ever mentioned the incident in their letters, and McCartney, who reportedly witnessed Lennon's violent outburst has also never suggested that this incident ever took place.

Lennon's reaction to learning of Stuart Sutcliffe's death has been described differently in several accounts. While some authors claim that Lennon laughed hysterically when he learned that his best friend had died, others maintain that he became apathic, in a state of shock. It is not clear how these stories came about, since The Beatles themselves, including Pete Best, remember the incident quite well. Pete Best has said that "[f]or the first time I actually saw him physically break down and shed tears. The rest of us, too, had tears in our eyes. John respected Stu as an artist. I think it hurt him a lot more than us" (Giuliano/Devi 1999: 200). *Birth of The Beatles* and *Backbeat* show the character of John Lennon shocked by the news, embracing Astrid Kirchherr. Here Lennon's reaction is probably portrayed in a more accurate way than in *In His Life: The John Lennon Story*, where Lennon almost aggressively tells Kirchherr to stop crying and to carry on with her life; then he orders some whiskey in a bar at the airport.

Historical Accuracy in Biographical Movies

John Lennon's First Guitar(s)

In His Life: The John Lennon Story is a NBC television production focusing on John Lennon's life in Liverpool from 1956 to 1963. Although the movie does not offer a new perspective on The Beatles' rise to fame, it is the only film dramatizing Lennon's first attempts as a musician with The Quarry Men. It also depicts Lennon's first encounter with Paul McCartney at the Woolton Garden Fete. Even though the events leading up to The Beatles' breakthrough had to be simplified, in order to function in the context of a semi-fictional movie, the producers tried to keep to the facts, drawing a rather accurate picture of John Lennon as a young man. The drama was shot entirely on location in Liverpool, which adds to its air of authenticity.

The film starts with a scene depicting an auction in London on 14 September 1999, where "the first guitar ever owned by John Lennon" (*In His Life* 2000) is auctioned. This auction actually took place at Sotheby's in 1999, although the guitar, which was finally sold to a Beatles fan in New York City, was, in fact, John Lennon's second guitar. Although the auction sequence makes a very effective opening for the movie, establishing and explaining the historical importance of its protagonist, the confusion surrounding Lennon's first instrument has become a common source of errors in many Beatles biographies. It may seem to be only a minor inaccuracy in John Lennon's biography, but it is of great significance when considered in the context of The Beatles' history, which has become subject of many history books and exhibitions, claiming to inform the public with academic accuracy. Instead of scrutinizing and verifying the data found in many biographies of The Beatles, scholars and contemporary historians often seem to simply copy and quote the information provided by some authors who have gained the reputation of being experts on The Beatles. For example, Hunter Davies' biography *The Beatles* (1968) was long considered to be the most reliable source of information on the group. However, the book contains various factual errors, and – despite its merits – has certainly contributed significantly to the confusion of many dates and events in The Beatles' history. For instance, Davies provided a wrong date for the first encounter of John Lennon and Paul McCartney: "I have to admit, with a shamed face, that in my so-called authorised biography of 1968, I gave the date of this momentous event as June 15, 1956. A whole year and three weeks out. Shows the quality of my research [...]" (Davies 2001: 55). Although many errors have been corrected in more recent editions of the book, it would be quite interesting to know how many scholars and students have quoted the wrong date in their books and papers.

The confusion surrounding John Lennon's first guitar serves as a rather good example of how history is distorted and partly invented in history books and biographies. In *The Beatles*, Hunter Davies briefly describes how Lennon acquired his first guitar:

"He took a guitar off a boy at school one day but found he couldn't play it so he gave it back to him. But he knew that his mother, Julia, could play the banjo, so he went to see her. She bought him a second-hand guitar for £10. It had on it – ,guaranteed not to split'. He did go for a couple of lessons, but never learned. Instead Julia taught him some banjo chords. The first tune he learned was 'That'll Be the Day'" (Davies 1969: 27).

Davies' account is consistent with what Lennon recalled in 1963: "Anfangs lieh ich mir eine Gitarre. Ich konnte nicht spielen, aber meine Mutter kaufte mir eine von einem dieser Versandhäuser. [...] Meine erste Gitarre kostete zehn Pfund" (Beatles 2000: 11). Lennon's half sister Julia Baird also remembers that "we never saw John without his guitar, the one our mother had bought him for £10 which was now well battered from use" (Baird/Giuliano 1988: 29).

Ray Coleman, whose biography *Lennon* is one of the bestsellers in the genre, reconstructs the story in a rather similar way: "John [...] decided to send away for his first [guitar] himself. From a mail order advertisement in the *Daily Mail* he ordered a £5 10s ($9) model, 'guaranteed not to split,' and was canny enough, at this stage, to have the guitar posted to Julia's address where he would run less risk of a scolding" (Coleman 1992: 137). While most authors agree with the fact that John Lennon's aunt Mimi Smith was initially against Lennon's aspirations to become a guitarist, some Beatles historians claim that it was Smith who bought Lennon's first guitar. Mark Lewisohn, who is now regarded the leading Beatles historian, writes that "In March 1957, having finally persuaded his guardian, Aunt Mimi, to buy him a £17 guitar, he decided to form a skiffle group" (Lewisohn 2000: 12). Bill Harry, another leading authority on The Beatles, writes that "Mimi did not entirely approve of his interest in rock'n'roll music and attempted to dissuade him, but on realising that he was so determined, she bought him a guitar at Frank Hessy's music store for £18 when he was seventeen" (Harry 2000: 1008). Barry Miles, who has also published several accounts of The Beatles' history, finally offers a combination of the two basic versions: "John's Aunt Mimi lent him the money to buy a £17 Gallotone Champion guitar, complete with a sticker promising that the instrument was 'Guaranteed not to split'" (Miles 1997: 9). Although it seems natural to trust John Lennon's own memory in this respect, the question remains how all this confusion came into existence, and whose version we can completely trust. While all the great Beatles experts fail to provide a complete history of Lennon's first guitar, his former bandmate Rod Davis recently pointed out that Lennon owned two guitars in 1957: "I was in the USA in August 1999 with The Quarrymen and phoning home. I was astounded to learn that John's guitar was coming up for sale at Sotheby's. The guitar was the one he was playing in Geoff Rhind's famous photo; a Gallotone Champion, actually the second guitar he had ever owned, the first one being an Egmond [...]" (Davis 2001: 260).

The stories of how Lennon acquired the two guitars were simply mixed up in various ways over the years. Mimi Smith's claim that she was the person buying Lennon's first guitar probably contributed to this confusion. With the help of Rod Davis, one can now reconstruct Lennon's situation in 1957: As his aunt Mimi did not support his ambition of becoming a guitarist, he asked his mother Julia for a guitar. Julia, who was an amateur musician herself, agreed, and bought him a cheap Egmond guitar by mail order. When Mimi Smith realized that Lennon was a talented guitarist and that he would need a better instrument in order to improve, she agreed to buy him a second hand Gallotone Champion guitar at Frank Hessy's music store in Liverpool.

Auditioning for Larry Parnes

An important step in the history of The Beatles was their audition for Larry Parnes in 1960. Parnes was one of the most successful managers in the entertainment business at the time. According to Paul Du Noyer, Parnes "would sign up young boys wherever he went and launch them into showbusiness with thrusting new names – Tommy Steele, Vince Eager, Marty Wilde, Duffy Power [...]" (Du Noyer 2004: 12). One of Parnes' singers was Billy Fury, one of the few successful pop stars from Liverpool prior to The Beatles. Allan Williams, The Beatles' first manager, remembers how this audition came about: "Larry told me [...] that he was looking for a backing group for Billy [Fury]. He wanted me to round up as many of the Liverpool groups as I could muster and arrange an audition which he and Billy could attend" (Williams/Marshall 1977: 30). Williams held the auditions at his own new club, the Blue Angel, and invited several of Liverpool's top groups, including Rory Storm and the Hurricanes (featuring Ringo Starr on drums) and Derry and the Seniors. When it was The Beatles' turn to play, Parnes was quite impressed with the group, although their drummer, Tommy Moore, arrived late for the audition. However, Parnes was not impressed with Stuart Sutcliffe's bass playing and requested The Beatles to perform a song without him (vgl. Williams/Marshall 1977: 35). When The Beatles refused to perform without Sutcliffe, they lost their chance of backing Billy Fury on a national tour. Instead, they were hired to back another young singer from Liverpool called Johnny Gentle on a tour through Scotland. It was The Beatles' first engagement outside the Liverpool area, and they all re membered the experience with fondness, despite the modest payment they received for the tour (vgl. Beatles 2000: 44).

As the audition for Parnes marked a turning point in The Beatles' career, it is shown in *Birth of The Beatles* as well as in *In His Life: The John Lennon Story*. In *Birth of The Beatles*, the group already calls themselves The Beatles, while they are still called Johnny and the Moondogs in *In His Life*. In actual fact, however, the group was called The Silver Beetles at that particular time (vgl. Lewisohn 2000: 19). In both movies, Larry Parnes' rejection of Stuart Sutcliffe bass playing is described. The particulars of this event were first described in detail in Allan Williams' first book *The Man Who Gave The Beatles Away* (vgl. Williams/Marshall 1977: 29-37). Although both movies apparently gained their information about the audition from Williams' book, neither features Williams as a movie character. In fact, *Birth of The Beatles* shows Larry Parnes offering The Beatles an engagement in Hamburg, although the real Larry Parnes did not have anything to do with The Beatles' move to Germany. In *In His Life*, Parnes suggests to Johnny and the Moondogs that they "find a new name" (vgl. *In His Life* 2000), although, in reality, The Beatles had already found their new name. It is rather interesting that all the dramatizations of The Beatles' history neglected and erased Allan Williams's vital contributions to the group's early career, although Williams' own biography would make a rather entertaining movie.[1]

Brian Epstein, Alistair Taylor, and Raymond Jones

The way Brian Epstein's interest in The Beatles was initially evoked has become one of the many mysteries in The Beatles' history. *Birth of The Beatles* and *In His Life: The John Lennon Story* provide slightly different versions of this chapter in The Beatles' story. In *In His Life*, Epstein tries his best to help a customer looking for the record "My Bonnie" by The

---

1   In fact, Allan Williams' life has recently been the subject of a play, *The Man Who Gave the Beatles Away* (2002), written by Irish playwright Ronan Wilmot. In addition, journalist Lew Baxter published a delightful account of Williams' anecdotes in 2003. Lew Baxter. *Allan Williams is...The Fool On The Hill...how the beat went on after his BIG BEATLES blunder*. Wirral: Praxis, 2003.

Beat Brothers. Epstein has not heard about the group and asks his shop assistant Linda if she knows them. Linda points out that he must be talking about The Beatles, who regularly perform at the Cavern, which is located right around the corner from NEMS, Epstein's store. Epstein decides to go there at a lunch-time session and is welcomed by the DJ. He meets up with Linda and expresses his enthusiasm for the group.

In *Birth of The Beatles*, a similar scene has a young man asking for the single "My Bonnie" by The Beatles in Epstein's music store. When two girls turn up talking about the "fab" and "gear" Beatles, Epstein decides to go and see the group at the Cavern. He goes to an evening session with his personal assistant, who is annoyed by the loud music and leaves again soon.

Both movies basically reconstruct the official version of the story as provided by Brian Epstein in his autobiography.

"On Saturday, October 28, [1961], I had just come back from a long holiday in Spain during which I had wondered how I could expand my interests. And then, suddenly, though quite undramatically, a few words from Raymond Jones brought the solution. The words, of course, were "Have you got a disc by the Beatles?" [...] The name "Beatle" meant nothing to me though I vaguely recalled seeing it on a poster advertising a university dance at New Brighton Tower, and I remembered thinking it was an odd and purposeless spelling" (Epstein 1998: 94-95).

More recently, several other versions of how Epstein became aware of The Beatles have appeared. Bill Harry, whose magazine *Mersey Beat* was on sale at Epstein's store NEMS, says that he was surprised when he read Epstein's account in his book *A Cellarful of Noise*, as he was discussing The Beatles and his paper *Mersey Beat*, which often featured The Beatles on the cover, with Epstein as soon as July, 1961: "It was obvious in *Mersey Beat* that they were the number one group" (*A Long and Winding Road 2003*: DVD 2).

Other people claiming to have made Epstein aware of The Beatles include Liverpool promoter Sam Leach, who says that he put up a poster announcing a Beatles show at the Tower Ballroom in Epstein's music store (vgl. Leach 1999: 125-127), and Epstein's personal assistant Alistair Taylor, who came up with one of the most fantastic stories in recent Beatles mythology: "I got so fed up with people asking if we had a record of 'My Bonnie' by the Beatles and having to say No that I put through an order for it myself under a name I simply dreamed up. [...] The famous story is that a guy called Raymond Jones came into the shop and asked for a record by the Beatles. I know that I invented the name and put it into the order book" (Taylor 2003: 16). However, Taylor's version of the story is highly improbable. In the 1990s, when he started claiming that he made up the name Raymond Jones at Beatles conventions around the world, Beatles experts doubted his claim, and Spencer Leigh, a renowned Beatles biographer and Merseyside radio presenter, finally managed to find the real Raymond Jones, who was now living in Spain. He quotes Jones in his book on Liverpool DJ Bob Wooler.

"I used to go to NEMS every Saturday and I would be buying records by Carl Perkins and Fats Domino because I heard the Beatles playing their songs. My sister's ex-husband, Kenny Johnson, who played with Mark Peters and the Cyclones, told me that the Beatles had made a record and so I went to NEMS to get it. Brian Epstein said to me, 'Who are they?' and I said, 'They are the most fantastic group you will ever hear.' No one will take that away from me that it was me who spoke to Brian Epstein and then he went to the Cavern to see them for himself" (Leigh 2002: 155).

Although the producers of *Birth of The Beatles* and *In His Life* realized Epstein's initial encounter with The Beatles in a way that resembled the manager's recollection of the event, the alternative versions have been presented in various unauthorized documentaries, such as Brian Epstein. *Inside the Fifth Beatle*, and *A Long and Winding Road*.

The Hours and Times: Was John Lennon Gay?

Albert Goldman's biography *The Lives of John Lennon* introduced the rumor of John Lennon's bisexuality in the world of Beatle-myths (Goldman 2001: 140). Since the book was first published in 1988, the topic has been exploited in various poorly researched and highly speculative biographies and documentaries. Most of these accounts focus on the particular relationship between John Lennon and The Beatles' manager Brian Epstein. Much has been made of the fact that Lennon went on a short vacation with Epstein in April, 1963, only weeks before Beatlemania would sweep Great Britain. Only days after the birth of his son Julian, Lennon left Cynthia and their new born baby for four days, to enjoy a short vacation in Barcelona, Spain. Despite Paul McCartney's insistence that Lennon was not a homosexual, and that Lennon probably went on a holiday with Epstein because he wanted to confirm his position as the leader of the group, this particular trip became one of the most mystified chapters in The Beatles' history, although it was probably one of the less spectacular events. Lennon recalled the trip in the famous interview he granted Jann S. Wenner for the *Rolling Stone*.

"And I just went on holiday. I watched Brian picking up the boys. I like playing a big faggy, all that. [...] It was enjoyable, but there [were] big rumors in Liverpool. It was terrible. Very embarrassing. [...] I was pretty close to Brian because if somebody's going to manage me, I want to know them inside out. And there was a period when he told me he was a fag and all that. I introduced him to pills [...] to make him talk – to find out what he's like. And I remember him saying, "Don't ever throw it back in me face, that I'm a fag." Which I didn't" (Wenner 2000: 63).

Rumors about a secret homosexual relationship between Lennon and Epstein were circulating in Liverpool as soon as they departed for Barcelona. Having just established his own family with Cynthia and Julian, Lennon was particularly enraged by these rumors. When Liverpool DJ Bob Wooler made a remark about Lennon and Epstein's vacation at Paul McCartney's 21st birthday party in June, 1963, a drunk Lennon lost control of himself and beat up Wooler, who had been one of the group's fervent supporters on the Liverpool music scene. The fight caused the first mention of The Beatles in the national press (cf. Harry 2000: 1169). Even though Lennon later reconciled with Wooler, the whole incident further fuelled the rumors surrounding Lennon and Epstein's trip to Spain. The violent confrontation between Lennon and Wooler is reconstructed in *In His Life*, where Lennon almost kills Wooler. The scene evokes what actually took place at McCartney's party in an authentic way. Years later, Lennon recalled the incident: "The first national coverage was me beating up Bob Wooler at Paul's 21st party because he intimated I was homosexual. I must have had a fear that maybe I was homosexual to attack him like that and it's very complicated reasoning. But I was very drunk and I hit him and I could have really killed somebody then. And that scared me" (Badman 2001: 98).

In 1991, *The Hours and Times*, an hour-long movie by Los Angeles filmmaker Christopher Münch premiered in the United States. *The Hours and Times* explores the possibilities of what might have happened during Lennon and Epstein's vacation together. It depicts the complex homoerotic relationship between the characters of John Lennon and his manager Brian Epstein. Münch, who wrote, produced, and directed *The Hours and Times*, shot the black-and-white movie in 1988 and spent two years on the post-production, because of financial reasons.

The *Hours and Times* is a very different kind of movie than all the other dramatizations of The Beatles' history, as it is not restricted by the conventions of commercial cinema, nor was it made to cash in by sensationalizing a controversial chapter in the group's history. Christopher Münch was able to exercise complete freedom and independence in the way the film was shot and edited. Münch had full control over every aspect of the movie, which, he claims, he initially made only for himself (vgl. *The Hours and Times* 2002). In contrast to most of the other films about The Beatles, Münch and his actors succeed in the creation of full-rounded characters, who, however, do not necessarily resemble the real Lennon and Epstein in every detail. Similar to Iain Softley, Münch explains that he had considered making a movie without The Beatles connection. In contrast to *Backbeat*, which is much more tied to The Beatles' history than Iain Softley would want to admit, *The Hours and Times*, with its three-dimensional characters and the simple but strong story, would also work if the characters were not associated with The Beatles. However, had the characters been named differently, the film would probably not have reached a more general audience. On the other hand, the choice of making a fictional movie about Lennon, which portrays him as a man with bisexual interests, poses the problem of reinforcing a set of myths about Lennon.

John Lennon is played by Liverpool actor Ian Hart, who manages to capture and interpret some of the real Lennon's most notorious features, such as his restlessness, his mercurial temper, as well as his ability to entertain and charm the people around him. Lennon is also presented as a rather relentless playboy, who proves to be rather insensitive when he talks to his wife Cynthia on the telephone. He also flirts with an attractive flight attendant, with whom he subsequently has an affair in Barcelona. While Lennon is known to have had numerous affairs in the early years of The Beatles' success, this particular incident is completely fictitious. In *The Hours and Times*, the affair serves as some sort of reassurance after Lennon's first homo-erotic encounter with Brian Epstein in the bathroom. He apparently feels uncomfortable after having kissed Epstein and needs to be with a woman to convince himself that he is not really gay.

The character of Brian Epstein, played by David Angus, also captures many of the real Epstein's traits. He is portrayed as a flamboyant gentleman of excellent manners, who has got a secret crush on John Lennon. Epstein's feelings for Lennon cause some tense situations and encourage Lennon to direct some cynical comments toward his sensitive manager. Finally, however, Lennon surrenders to his curiosity and his own latent feelings for 'Eppy', and he sleeps with his manager. While David Angus manages to convey the real Epstein's elegance and sophistication, his interpretation of Epstein's personality appears to be much less self-assured and complex than in real life.

Ian Hart's convincing portrayal of Lennon and David Angus' re-interpretation of Epstein's sensitive features seem to justify the choice of having the story revolve around historic characters instead of completely fictional characters. Despite the fictional dimension of the movie, Münch apparently researched Epstein's background quite thoroughly, and includes a few personal details about Epstein, such as his obsession with bull-fighting and his overwhelming personal concern for The Beatles.

Although the topic of homo-eroticism would lead itself to a sensationalist approach in the context of Lennon and Epstein's biographies, Münch describes the relationship between the characters in a sensitive and tasteful way and avoids the danger of stereotyping the characterization of the two friends.

Beatlemania and Beyond: 1964 to the Present

Back to Beatlemania:
Robert Zemeckis' *I Wanna Hold Your Hand*

In 1978, Steven Spielberg co-produced a movie called *I Wanna Hold Your Hand*. The film was directed by Robert Zemeckis, who would later direct the *Back to the Future* trilogy (1985, 1989, 1990), *Who Framed Roger Rabbit* (1988), and *Forrest Gump* (1994). The story, written by Zemeckis with his long-time collaborator Bob Gale, revolves around the adventures of a handful of Beatles fans, who are going to New York to see The Beatles' performance at the *Ed Sullivan Show*. While most of the movies about The Beatles fail to convey a convincing impression of The Beatles because of poorly selected actors, Zemeckis avoids the danger of disappointing the audience with Beatles impersonators by never showing their faces. Instead, The Beatles themselves rarely appear throughout the movie. At one point, however, the camera takes in the subjective point of view of a fan hidden underneath one of The Beatles' bed in the hotel room, and The Beatles' feet are shown. Another fan witnesses them as they leave the building, but she – and the audience – only gets to see their backs. Instead of actually showing The Beatles, the group is in one scene only represented by their iconic instruments which make one of the fans faint in the hotel room when she finds them.

I Wanna Hold Your Hand is less a celebration of The Beatles' music or their history than a subjective view of their initial, overwhelming impact on the American youth at the time of their first arrival in the United States. The film works very well without The Beatles being embodied by actors. Instead, the hype surrounding the group's 'invasion' of the United States is re-created, and the fans' reaction is shown from their own perspective. By taking in the subjective position of the fans, *I Wanna Hold Your Hand* breaks with the tradition of juxtaposing footage of The Beatles with footage of the fans' reactions, which characterizes most of the concert footage featuring The Beatles. The only notable previous instance where a camera is placed in the audience had been Richard Lester's portrayal of the concert scene in *A Hard Day's Night*. Because of its closeness to the fans, who are the film's protagonists, *I Wanna Hold Your Hand* evokes the excitement The Beatles generated at the height of Beatlemania. Zemeckis provides a very accurate portrayal of the circumstances surrounding the group's arrival in the United States and includes many details, which contribute to the authentic overall impression of *I Wanna Hold Your Hand*. For example, the film shows the fan crowd outside the Plaza Hotel singing "We love you Beatles", the actual fan club song at the time, and refers to the almost surreal craze for Beatles memorabilia and merchandise – a Beatles fan wants to sell pieces of the bedsheets used by The Beatles to other fans. In actual fact, a similar occurrence took place in 1964, when a business man dreamed up the idea of selling small pieces of The Beatles' used bed-sheets. Capitol Records' advertising strategies are also shown in the movie, where a record sales manager wears a Beatle-wig at a store in New Jersey. Zemeckis' movie also includes a tribute to the radio stations' effort to promote The Beatles, as radio DJ Murray the K, who called himself 'the fifth Beatle', appears as himself in the movie.

The authentic sets also feature an exact replica of the stage at The Beatles' first appearance on *The Ed Sullivan Show*. In addition, an Ed Sullivan look-alike introduces The Beatles with the exact same wording as in 1964, which has become a popular quotation in many documentaries and reports on The Beatles. The camera then focuses on the audience, with archive footage of The Beatles' actual performance of 1964 visible on a few camera screens. This is actually a subtle reference to the concert sequence in *A Hard Day's Night*, where Richard Lester partly shows them on the director's control monitors.

I Wanna Hold Your Hand depicts The Beatles' arrival in the United States from the point of view of the American public. The movie expresses a generation's recollection of The Beatles' first U.S. visit and evokes their initial impact on the American youth by taking in a perspective close to a gang of five Beatles fans. The way of representation and the selection of events included in the narrative correlate to the common perception of this particular episode in The Beatles' career, which is often considered as their peak concerning commerciality and popularity. The Beatles' first arrival in the United States was already mythologized at the time of its occurrence, because of the enormous, immediate impact the group had on the American public and popular culture. *I Wanna Hold*

Your Hand recalls the circumstances surrounding their break-through in the United States and supports the mythic character of the event.

"You and Me. And Everything Between Us": Paul and John in 1976

In 1999, VH-1, one of MTV's adult-oriented TV channels, produced the telefilm *Two of Us*, a fictional movie depicting an encounter of John Lennon and Paul McCartney in New York in 1976. *Two of Us* was directed by Michael-Lindsay Hogg, who had previously directed The Beatles' promotional films from 1968, their documentary *Let It Be*, as well as a video for Paul McCartney's 1978 single "London Town". Aidan Quinn (*Looking for Richard*, *Legends of the Fall*) plays the character of Paul McCartney, and Jared Harris, who had portrayed Lennon's friend Andy Warhol in *I Shot Andy Warhol*, embodies John Lennon in VH-1's third movie production.

Two of Us begins with a statement saying "Legend has it that in 1976 – six years after the bitter break-up of The Beatles – Paul McCartney paid a surprise visit to John Lennon at his apartment in New York City" (*Two of Us* 2002). The film basically displays screenwriter Mark Stanfield's fantasy of what a mid-Seventies meeting of the two former Beatles may have looked like. Although the movie was carefully researched and included a lot of authentic information and locations, the movie's basic theme of two estranged friends recovering their friendship did probably not mirror reality at all. May Pang, who was John Lennon's personal assistant from 1970 to 1974, explains that John Lennon and Paul McCartney were still close friends when they met in the mid-Seventies.

"I thought the premise for this movie was odd, considering the fact that John, Paul, Linda and I spent quite a bit of time together, both in Los Angeles and at our apartment in New York. I was amazed that they picked up their friendship as if nothing had happened between them. They were instantly comfortable. Just before John returned to the Dakota, we had planned on joining Paul and Linda in New Orleans at the recording sessions for Paul's *Venus and Mars* album. John was excited about possibly writing with Paul again. Sadly, it was never to be. I think the movie would've been better had it explored what actually did happen" (Pang 2003).

While John Lennon and Paul McCartney may have been much closer than depicted in *Two of Us*, the movie works against the popular belief that the former songwriting team were bitter enemies throughout the

1970s. After they had overcome their initial conflicts concerning The Beatles' break-up, Lennon and McCartney revived their friendship around 1973-74. In 1974, they even recorded some songs together with Harry Nilsson and Stevie Wonder. However, this rather rough recording of rock standards, such as "Stand By Me" and "Midnight Special" was never intended for release. The tapes featuring this secret recording session surfaced in the 1990s and have since been bootlegged.

After a surprise visit around Christmas, 1975, Paul and Linda McCartney again visited John Lennon and Yoko Ono in their apartment in New York City in April, 1976. It is this meeting that inspired the movie *Two of Us*. Even though there is no way of knowing what exactly occurred at Lennon and McCartney's private get-togethers, both, Lennon and McCartney later talked to the press about a particular episode which took place at Lennon's apartment on 24 April, 1976. Lennon and McCartney were watching the show *Saturday Night Live*, when Lorne Michaels, the show's creator, suddenly made the following announcement:

"Lately there have been a lot of rumours to the effect that the four of you might be getting back together, that would be great. In my book, The Beatles are the best thing that ever happened to music. It goes deeper than that, you're not just a musical group, you're a part of us, we grew up with you. It's for this reason that I'm inviting you to come on our show. Now we've heard and read a lot about personality and legal conflicts that might prevent you guys from reuniting, that's none of my business. You guys will have to handle that. But it's also been said that no one has yet come up with enough money to satisfy you. Well, if it's money that you want, there's no problem here. The National Broadcasting Company authorises me to authorise you a cheque for $3,000. [...] The Beatles for $3,000" (Badman 2001: 181-182).

When this announcement was made on the popular comedy show, Lennon and McCartney considered surprising not only the team of *Saturday Night Live* but the whole world by actually accepting the offer and going to the studios, where the show was broadcast live. The studio was only a few blocks away from John Lennon's apartment. In 1980, John Lennon recalled this episode in an interview: "Paul was visiting us at our place in the Dakota with Linda. He and I were watching it and we went ha-ha, wouldn't it be funny if we went down and we almost went down to the studio, just as a gag. We nearly got into the cab, but we were actually too tired" (Badman 2001: 182). The incident inspired the climax of *Two of Us*, when the characters of Lennon and McCartney decide to go there and perform. The McCartney character briefly goes downstairs to his limousine to get his guitar. When he returns, Lennon is engaged in a telephone conversation with Yoko Ono, and McCartney realizes that they will not do their surprise performance on *Saturday Night Live*. The two friends wave at each other, and the movie ends with McCartney calling his wife Linda to tell her about his exciting day with John.

The portrayal of the two protagonists is surprisingly stereotypical, considering the fact that director Michael Lindsay-Hogg had previously worked with the real Beatles. The character of Paul McCartney is considerate, reasonable, and sentimental, while John Lennon is portrayed as a rather aggressive and unpredictable cynic. The character of John Lennon's appearance is modelled upon Lennon's outfit during his *Imagine* period (1971), while the McCartney character's looks resemble the real McCartney's appearance in the early 1990s rather than his 1970s outfits, haircuts, and manners. In addition, the McCartney character's mannerisms, such as scratching the side of his nose during interviews, are inspired by the way McCartney presented himself to the media in the 1990s. The behavior of Lennon's character oddly resembles rock singer Liam Gallagher's mannerisms, which are, in turn, modelled upon the way he imagines John Lennon. [2]

One of the movie's main functions is the explanation of John Lennon and Paul McCartney's friendship on the grounds of their traumatic childhood experiences and their difficult relationships with their parents. John Lennon is described as a tortured man, hurt by the fact that his parents abandoned him when he was a little child and by his mother Julia's untimely death when he had just begun to re-establish his relationship with her in 1958. The character of Paul McCartney contrasts Lennon's inability to lay the past to rest. While Lennon uses his pain as an excuse for his eccentric behavior, McCartney has managed to overcome his equally unpleasant past by establishing a family, raising his children, and by resuming his career as rock musician. He does not see a point in sharing his pain with the world. Instead, he has opted to provide pleasure to his fans through his music. Throughout the day they spend together, they discuss their problematic relationships with their respective parents and the pain of losing their mothers at a young age. In actual fact, both, Lennon and McCartney, have pointed out that the fact that they had both lost their mothers when they were teenagers had cemented their friendship and established a bond between them that was never broken (vgl. Miles 1997: 49).

The movie contains a sentimental scene, pointing out another connection between them, which revives their emotional understanding of

---

2   Liam Gallagher is the singer in Oasis, a rock'n'roll group from Manchester, celebrating their greatest success in the mid-1990s. They are known for being great Beatles fans and imitating The Beatles' sound, manners, and styles.

each other and serves as a defining scene for the resurrection of their friendship in the movie. In this particular sequence, they tell each other that their fathers had recently died. Again, this correlates to reality, as both, James McCartney and Alfred Lennon, died in 1976. By discussing and contrasting their different relationships with their fathers and the way they deal with their loss they re-discover the faith in each other and admit an emotionality which makes their friendship so special. While the death of Paul McCartney's mother Mary is mentioned in connections with a dream McCartney has had of her – an idea inspired by the fact that the real McCartney wrote The Beatles' last UK single "Let It Be" after his mother had appeared in a dream –, the death of John Lennon's mother Julia is recalled in a more detailed way, as he is still haunted by the tragedy. When Lennon and McCartney are stopped by two policemen in Central Park, Lennon cannot help but to provoke them because he has hated policemen ever since the death of his mother, who was run over by a car driven by a drunk policeman.

The movie also introduces quite common misconceptions and stereotypes connected with the personalities of John Lennon and Paul McCartney. In *Two of Us*, Lennon is a recluse, living a boring life in his New York apartment, which he apparently never leaves. When the McCartney character suggests going for a walk, Lennon replies, "A walk? Out there?" In actual fact, the assumption that Lennon lived his final years in seclusion and boredom is another myth that has evolved since Albert Goldman published his Lennon biography in 1988. While it is true that Lennon and Ono spent the years from 1976 to 1980 away from the eyes of the public, they were far from inactive. They went on several trips around the world, visiting Japan, Egypt, and the Caribbean, they attended a few official occasions, such as Jimmy Carter's Presidential Inauguration Ball in 1977, and they recorded many demo tapes of songs for their comeback album *Double Fantasy* (1980).

Despite these factual errors, *Two of Us* sets out to explore the foundation of the close friendship between two of the driving forces in 20th century popular culture, and their different kinds of motivation for their creative endeavor. While the idea of a psychological exploration of Lennon and McCartney may be appealing, the sentimental way it is dealt with in this particular production diminishes the movie's credibility.

The Beatles and Women

Brian Epstein's Regulations

When Brian Epstein took on the management of The Beatles, he insisted that The Beatles were not to be seen with their girlfriends in public, in order to convey the impression that they were single and available. He was convinced that this would contribute to increasing their popularity, as the largely female fanbase would not have to face a 'real' rival. As this PR-tactic had previously worked for other male pop singers, such as Cliff Richard and Elvis Presley, The Beatles's strength was that their fans were able to choose their favorite Beatle out of four. Therefore, The Beatles' appeal and their potential impact on their fans was theoretically much higher than only one singer's. Although the principle seems easy, Brian Epstein and George Martin's decision to allow The Beatles to represent themselves as a group of four equal members revolutionized the pop business and has become the standard way of designing 'boygroups' in popular music.

The illusion of The Beatles being singles – although they were dating girlfriends – worked well for quite some time. When John Lennon's girlfriend Cynthia Powell, whom he had dated since his time at the Liverpool Art College, became pregnant in the summer of 1962, they decided to marry. The wedding took place in secrecy and was paid for by manager Brian Epstein. As The Beatles were now on the brink of nationwide success, Epstein insisted that Lennon's marriage be kept a secret. However, soon after Cynthia and John's son Julian was born, the press found out about their marriage and publicized pictures of Cynthia Lennon and her child. While the Lennons' marriage became headline news in several tabloids and teen magazines, it did surprisingly not diminish the groups or Lennon's popularity. Epstein arranged that the press stayed away from Lennon's private life and that his marriage was not highly publicized in the following year. For example, when the Maysles brothers filmed their documentary of The Beatles' first U.S. visit, they were asked to keep Cynthia Lennon and any girlfriends out of the movie (vgl. Stark 2005: 160). Marriage was also not talked about at press conferences. In his autobiography *A Cellarful of Noise*, Epstein points out what the public expects of The Beatles: "A Beatle must not marry. It is very well if one is married before one is a fully grown Beatle, but a fully grown Beatle must stay single" (Epstein 1998: 188).

Fans simply got used to the fact that Lennon was married and had a child. Although the other Beatles still pretended to be available for a while, the media soon reported that Paul McCartney was dating actress Jane Asher. McCartney's decision to make the relationship known to the press caused an argument with manager Brian Epstein, who feared that the fans would be offended (vgl. Stark 2005: 164). George Harrison had fallen in love with model Pattie Boyd, who had been an extra in *A Hard Day's Night*. He married her in January, 1966, while Ringo Starr married his long-time girlfriend Maureen Cox in February, 1965. Geoffrey Ellis, one of Brian Epstein's employees, remembers the way Epstein tried to keep their marriage a secret: "When the date for their wedding was decided on, [...] Brian helped to plan the affair like a military operation. I was particularly intrigued by the detail that even the name of the London Hotel where Maureen's parents, Mr and Mrs Cox, were to stay when they came from Liverpool for the wedding, was kept a secret: the press were not to know even this" (Ellis 2004: 48).

Initially, the female fans were jealous of The Beatles' wives and girlfriends and assaulted them quite fiercely. For instance, Pattie Boyd was attacked when she attended The Beatles' Christmas Show in 1964 (vgl. Harry 2000: 199). After a while, however, the fans accepted The Beatles' partners. While Cynthia Lennon and Maureen Starkey decided to stay out of the limelight, Jane Asher and Pattie Boyd became popular public figures. Pattie Boyd, in particular, became very interested in spiritual matters around 1966 and was the first in The Beatles inner circle who attended a lecture by Maharishi Mahesh Yogi, who became The Beatles' spiritual guide from 1967 to 1968. Cultural critic Steven D. Stark points out that an "increased public focus on the Beatles' fashionable girlfriends also helped cement their appeal at this time" (Stark 2005: 164).

Despite occasional press reports about The Beatles and their partners, manager Brian Epstein wanted The Beatles to be portrayed as available young men in their movies. Both, *A Hard Day's Night* and *Help!* shows The Beatles flirting with young ladies, but it is clear that they are not romantically involved. In contrast, Elvis Presley's movies always feature a female protagonist, who falls in love with the King, in order to provide an opportunity of identification for the female audience. This approach, though effective, was out of the question for Epstein and The Beatles, because it was thought that it would not work well with four lead characters.

The Ballad of John and Yoko: *A Love Story*

John Lennon left his wife Cynthia when he became involved with Yoko Ono, a Japanese artist, who had acquired quite a reputation in the New York art scene, where she had been instrumental in the Fluxus movement. Lennon and Ono made use of the media to stage what has now become one of the great love stories of the 20th century. In films, songs, exhibitions, newspapers, as well as at press conferences and in TV shows they exposed and discussed mainly their relationship and, therefore, controlled much of the information about them in the press. They became very much a "public couple," (Pang 2003) as pointed out by May Pang, their former personal assistant, and established the myth of an apparently perfect relationship. They promoted their relationship in this way until 1973, when Lennon left Ono for a period of 18 months to live with May Pang in Los Angeles and New York. Soon after Lennon and Ono had reconciled, their son Sean was born. Lennon retreated from public attention for more than four years to be a house-husband. When he returned to the music business in 1980, the comeback album *Double Fantasy*, a collaborative effort of Lennon and Ono, projected the myth of marital bliss to the world in rather personal love songs. The publicity campaign surrounding Lennon's comeback was dominated by Lennon and Ono's views of their own relationship and their family life.

It is not surprising that a movie was made about one of the 20th century's most famous couples. In 1985, *John & Yoko: A Love Story*, a television production written and directed by Sandor Stern premiered on American television. The movie concentrates on the couple's relationship, beginning in 1966, when they first met at the Indica Art Gallery, and ending with Lennon's violent death in 1980.

The movie is rather well-researched and depicts all the famous incidents in the lives of the eccentric couple in an authentic way. What distinguishes the movie from many other accounts is the fact that it includes Yoko Ono's side of the story as well. For example, the movie contains scenes portraying her involvement with John Cage, Ornette Coleman, and the Fluxus movement in New York City. Yoko Ono, who was never a popular figure with many Beatles fans, is depicted as a talented, intellectual, and sensitive artist. *John & Yoko: A Love Story* also contains some less publicized chapters in the couple's history, such as Ono's two miscarriages, and aims at a rather factual portrayal of their love story.

Despite the production's merits, some unfortunate decisions in the way the side characters are presented drastically reduce the movie's credibility. For example, the other Beatles do not resemble Lennon's real band mates in any way. In fact the misplaced artificial moustaches and hair make them look rather ridiculous. In addition, Lennon's first wife Cynthia is portrayed in a way that is hardly realistic. She is depicted as a housewife, knitting while Lennon is reading Ono's book *Grapefruit*. Considering the fact that Cynthia Lennon was a graduate from the Liverpool College of Art, it seems rather odd to portray her as a knitting housewife.

While *John & Yoko: A Love Story* marginalizes and stereotypes many of the side characters, the portrayal of Lennon and Ono is rather three-dimensional and much less idealizing than the couple's own PR or the documentaries endorsed by Yoko Ono after Lennon's death.

Whereas Lennon is often portrayed either as a saint or as an aggressive cynic in other movies and documentaries, *John & Yoko* manages to present John Lennon in a more balanced way, including his sincere commitment for humanity as well as his sometimes frantic behavior. For instance, the film includes a rarely publicized episode, depicting John Lennon's despair when Richard Nixon is re-elected president of the United States in 1972. Angry because his campaign against the Nixon legislation had failed – Nixon had become Lennon's personal enemy and wanted to see him deported -, he gets terribly drunk and has sex with a young woman, while Yoko is waiting for her husband in a room next door. While this dark chapter in the couple's history is hardly ever mentioned in official biographies, it was a defining moment in their marriage, as it marked the point when this reportedly 'ideal couple' started to drift apart, resulting in an 18-months long separation from 1973 to 1975.

John & Yoko: A Love Story was not designed as a sensationalist exploitation of Lennon's life. Instead it is a rather accurate portrayal of Lennon and Ono's personal and artistic history from 1966 to 1980 in the form of a television dramatization. Unfortunately, the production has not stood the test of time, and its overtly 1980s TV aesthetics, the rather unfortunate props, and the superficial and sometimes ridiculous portrayal of the side characters look quite dated in 2008.

The Linda McCartney Story

1966 was not only the year John Lennon met Yoko Ono; it was also when Paul McCartney first met Linda Eastman, a photographer from New York City, whose pictures had been published in various magazines such as *Rolling Stone*. She had taken pictures of rock groups like The Rolling Stones and The Doors and was looking for an opportunity to photograph The Beatles in London, where she happened to meet Paul McCartney at a nightclub in Soho. They stayed in touch, and Linda Eastman was one of the few photographers invited to the press launch of The Beatles' landmark album *Sgt. Pepper's Lonely Hearts Club Band* in 1967. McCartney and Eastman started dating in August 1968, and they eventually got married on 12 March, 1969. Although Linda McCartney was initially despised by many female Beatles fans, their marriage became known as one of the most stabile relationships in showbusiness, and it lasted until Linda McCartney's early death in 1998. Soon after her death, Linda's long-time friend Danny Fields published her biography, which provided a personal and accurate view of Linda's life. In 2000, CBS produced a television dramatization of Linda's life, which was titled *The Linda McCartney Story*. The CBS Sunday Night Movie was based upon Danny Fields' recollections and depicted the love story of Paul and Linda McCartney from 1966 to 1998, highlighting some of the better known episodes in the couple's life together.

The production was aimed not exclusively at a target group of Beatles fans but at a more general audience, who had followed the dramatic circumstances surrounding Linda McCartney's death in the media. The story had generated great interest, as Paul and Linda McCartney had spent most of the time from 1994 to 1998 away from public attention, except for Paul McCartney's occasional public appearances to promote The Beatles' *Anthology* (1995) and his own album *Flaming Pie* (1997).

Although Linda McCartney had not been very popular with the press and with many fans of her husband Paul, the news of her death stunned the public in April 1998. Paul and Linda McCartney's love story had become a legend, and press reports emphasized their rare love for each other. McCartney's press officer Geoff Baker intentionally misinformed the media about the location where Linda McCartney had died, in order to enable the McCartneys to mourn in private. Unfortunately, Baker's PR strategy did not work out, because it only increased the tabloids' interest in the circumstances surrounding Linda McCartney's death. For example, Reuters published the following article: "Linda McCartney's Death Probed. Mystery surrounds the death of Paul McCartney's wife Linda, with police saying that no death certificate was filed in California and reports she may have died in California instead" ("Latest News" 2005). In addition, rumors of suicide and euthanasia were distributed by the yellow press. After a private ceremony, the McCartneys issued a statement saying that Linda McCartney had died in Arizona, and that none of the rumors were true.

While the media exploited the sad event, the public felt compassion for the McCartney family. Paul McCartney himself retreated from public life for more than a year. As a tribute to his wife, he finished and released a Linda McCartney solo album called *Wide Prairie* (1998), which she had been preparing for several years. Together with his daughter Mary, Paul McCartney also produced *Wingspan*, a television documentary exploring the couple's career with their pop group Wings in the 1970s. Amidst this wave of interest surrounding Linda McCartney, CBS produced the movie *The Linda McCartney Story*, which set out to describe the life of one of the most prominent women in the rock'n'roll business.

Linda McCartney was played by Elizabeth Mitchell, while the role of Paul McCartney was embodied by Gary Bakewell, who had already portrayed the younger McCartney in Iain Softley's *Backbeat* almost a decade before. In addition, the character of John Lennon was performed by Mark McGann, who had first played Lennon in *John & Yoko: A Love Story* in 1985. While Bakewell's performance is quite credible and enables him to re-interpret some of McCartney's facets that he had not had the chance to portray in *Backbeat*, McGann looks too old for a 25-year-old Lennon and does not have the chance to develop the character. The Lennon in *The Linda McCartney Story* is characterized by aggression and violence and is not allowed to display his more sensitive side. The portrayal of George Harrison and Ringo Starr oddly parallels the way they were depicted in *John & Yoko: A Love Story*, as they are again characterized by pointless one-liners and fake moustaches.

By taking Danny Field's well-researched biography as the basis for the film, the producers avoided factual errors in their adaptation. Linda McCartney is described as a successful photographer and a strong person, who rescues her husband from depression and alcoholism after the break-up of The Beatles in 1970. Although the story of the McCartneys' 1970s pop band Wings is also included, the film does not focus on Linda's musical contributions to the band. Instead, her talents as a photographer and as a loving mother of four children are her central characteristics. Her contribution to animal activism and her very successful business career as the owner of a food company devoted to the production of vegetarian meals are also not explored in detail. However, the main focus is on her tremendous optimism and courage during her battle with cancer.

The Linda McCartney Story works in the tradition of tele-dramatizations of 'real-life stories', combining elements of melodrama, biography, and soap opera. In order to achieve the desired effect of emotional appeal, the dramatic chapters in Linda McCartney's life were selected and dramatized to ensure a most moving effect. However, despite the idealization of Paul and Linda McCartney's relationship and the extremely sentimental portrayal of Linda McCartney's last years, the movie contains a bulk of accurate information and completely excludes the sensationalist stories that flooded the press after her untimely death.

DOCUMENTARIES ABOUT THE BEATLES

The Authenticity of Documentaries

A documentary about the past is typically presented as an authoritative account of the subject matter it deals with, its form suggesting a higher level of objectivity and credibility than a fictionalized account of the past. This air of authenticity is usually established by the inclusion of historical footage, interviews with witnesses and experts, and a factual over-narration voice. In general, documentary films are regarded as educational and informative, although their degree of factuality, objectivity and authenticity actually depends exclusively on the integrity and journalistic ability of the filmmakers. Just as a dramatization of history is created within the restrictions of the fictional genre it is part of, a documentary about the past is usually also scripted, and the way it is constructed follows a dramatic pattern which is designed to convey what Stuart Hall calls an 'intended meaning' (vgl. Stuart Hall 1981:128-138). The filmmaker creates the intended meaning of a documentary by the choice of subject matter, the documentary's focus, the choice of material included in the film, and the relationships he or she establishes between individual scenes or segments in the editing process. Meanings are further created and affected by the quality of the research, the way the footage is filmed (camera perspective, etc.), and by the filmmaker's overall attitude toward the subject matter. While the form of a dramatization is defined by the conventions of the narrative genre it is part of, the form of a documentary is primarily defined by its intended function and purpose. Its function may be to entertain, to educate, to propagate certain values, or to make a political or social statement. The recipient then decodes and interprets the meaning of the text – the documentary – in the context of his or her own experience. Therefore, in spite of the fact that documentaries of the past claim or suggest to represent past events in an objective and authentic way, they are not necessarily more adequate or more dependable portrayals of history than dramatizations. However, their convincing appeal and their image of factuality make them a powerful influence on the historical consciousness of mass culture audiences.

In addition to constituting a relevant economic factor in the music video- and DVD market, documentaries about The Beatles fulfil two primary functions. On the one hand, the 'official' documentaries – which are also the most dominant and most widely distributed ones – propagate an often censored version of history, which the band members prefer the public to perceive because of commercial or personal reasons. On the other hand, numerous smaller-scale productions, such as *The Beatles with Tony Sheridan* or *Brian Epstein: Inside the Fifth Beatle*, deal with certain chapters in the the band's history, often emphasizing an individual's contribution to the band's development and success. While these productions may offer interesting insights to certain aspects in the band's history, they have hardly got any impact on the way the general Beatles audience perceives the band, because they lack the promotion and distribution of official Beatles products. However, both kinds of documentaries, official and unauthorized ones, contribute to an overall impression of The Beatles and their history, which is considerably distorted, as any documentary contains factual errors and contributes to the distribution and reinforcement of myths and misunderstandings.

Official Accounts

The First U.S. Visit and *The Beatles Anthology*

While there had been several television programs about The Beatles' career, the first serious attempt to capture the history of The Beatles' amazing impact on film had been initiated by Brian Epstein in 1964, when he hired Albert and David Maysles to follow and film The Beatles during their first stay in the United States. The Maysles' direct cinema documentary *What's Happening – The Beatles in the USA* was first shown on British television in February, 1964, and it was released on DVD renamed *The First U.S. Visit* forty years later. The film is quite unique, as the Maysles filmed The Beatles backstage and in their hotel rooms. Even though Albert Maysles points out that The Beatles were professionals and knew what was expected from them in front of the camera, the film contains some private scenes that Epstein and The Beatles were probably not fond of at the time the footage was first aired. While Ringo Starr and George Harrison stage quite some entertaining scenes on the train, Paul McCartney is seen in a short sequence admitting that he is not in a good mood at all. Other revealing scenes show The Beatles at a nightclub, drinking and dancing with New York DJ Murray the K and a crowd of girls. Although the image of wild rock stars would appeal only a few years later, the scene was a rather daring inclusion in the film on the Maysles' part.

In 1969, Neil Aspinall, the director of Apple until 2007, was asked to collect film material featuring the group.

"In '69, in all the chaos, the traumas – things were falling apart, but they were still making *Abbey Road* – Paul called me saying, 'You should collect as much of the material that's out there, get it together before it disappears.' So I started to do that, got in touch with all the TV stations around the world, checked what we had in our own library, like *Let It Be*, *Magical Mystery Tour*, the promo clips, what have you. Got newsreel footage in, lots and lots of stuff. We edited something together that was about one hour and three quarters long. But the Beatles had split up by then, so there was really no chance of anything happening with it. I sent them a copy of it each which they all quite liked, then I put it on the shelf from 1971 'til '89, about 20 years" (Du Noyer 1996: 78).

The Beatles *Anthology* was one of the first projects Neil Aspinall initiated after The Beatles' legal settlement. The announcement of *The Beatles Anthology* caused an unprecedented media hype, which reminded one of Beatlemania in the mid-Sixties. *Newsweek* called *The Beatles Anthology* "the most fearsome flood of product since the days of the Beatle wig" (Giles/Chang 1995: 62). In fact, The Beatles' history project was designed to generate millions of dollars with merchandise products alone. In 1995 and 1996, The Beatles earned $ 130 million with *The Beatles Anthology* (vgl. Reed/Norman 1995: 125). In an interview, Paul McCartney jokingly admits the cash-in philosophy behind the project: "Once we started to resolve all our differences – now we're chatty and all mates again – we began booking for the CD, the T-shirt and the cookbook" (Reed/Norman 1995: 125). The Beatles, however, were not the only ones making profits from their unexpected reunion. For instance, Tommy Hanley, who had worked as a photographer for Apple, sold a photograph showing Paul McCartney, George Harrison, and Ringo Starr together in London to *The Sun* for £100,000 (vgl. Badman 2001: 540).

The documentary was designed to be broadcast in several parts, the premiere date being coordinated with the release of the single "Free as a Bird" and the first *Anthology* double album. Prior to the broadcast, the UK press reported of the "biggest bidding war in TV history" (Badman 2001: 530) for the upcoming *Anthology* television series. In the United States, ABC TV paid Apple nearly $20 million for the broadcast rights in the U.S. (vgl. *Forbes* 1995: 131), while ITV paid £5 million for the series in Great Britain (vgl. Badman 2001: 535). ABC showed the six-hour series in three parts, while ITV decided to broadcast *The Beatles Anthology* in six parts. The media hype surrounding the documentary guaranteed healthy record sales as well as high television ratings. In the United States, the first episode was broadcast on 19 November, 1995, and it was watched by 48 million viewers, making it one of the top-rated programs of the year. In Great Britain, the first show was aired on 26 November, 1995, and attracted 14.3 million people. Although the show was a tremendous success, the number of viewers dropped quite significantly as the series progressed. In Great Britain, the shows dealing with The Beatles' early years attracted between 10 and 14 million viewers, while the last two episodes were watched by only three to four million people (vgl. Badman 2001: 547-548). The public was apparently more interested in the parts of The Beatles' story depicting their early careers up to the frenzy of Beatlemania than in their 'psychedelic years' and the story of their break-up.

Despite its main function as a money-generating product and its mainstream appeal, *The Beatles Anthology* is surprisingly honest in its portrayal of some of the less pleasant chapters in The Beatles' history. Instead of ignoring or minimizing, for instance, the controversy surrounding John Lennon's remark about Christianity or the business troubles with their company Apple, George Harrison, Paul McCartney, and Ringo Starr thoroughly and soberly discuss these issues. They also present themselves much less nostalgic than other Sixties icons. In fact, they even express criticisms of their own work and look back at several events with a healthy dose of humor.

While this approach increases the documentary's credibility, it is also consistent with The Beatles' rather honest and open attitude from 1965 onwards, when their manager Brian Epstein's regulations lost their significance for The Beatles. Despite their honesty and their attempt at factual accuracy, *The Anthology* contains a few simplifications and errors. For example, John Lennon's recollection of how he met Paul McCartney is inaccurate. The sound excerpt is taken from one of the last interviews John Lennon gave before his death in December 1980. In the interview, he quickly summarized the main events leading up to the birth of The Beatles and provides a rather simplified version of his first encounter with Paul McCartney: "I asked Paul to join there and then, and I think he said yes the next day" (*Anthology* 2003: DVD 1). This is simply wrong, because – as pointed out by both, McCartney and Lennon, in other interviews – Lennon asked his friend Pete Shotton to find out whether McCartney wanted to join the band days after their initial encounter, and McCartney waited for several months until he finally joined The Quarry Men.

Another error in *The Anthology* concerns Pete Best's replacement with Ringo Starr. Both, George Harrison and Ringo Starr claim that Pete Best had missed a few performances, and Ringo Starr was asked to sit in. As this particular constellation worked very well and because of George

Martin's criticisms of Pete Best's drumming abilities, Ringo Starr was asked to join The Beatles. This may sound logical, but it is not true, although it correlates to the story Ringo Starr used to tell the press in the 1960s. Pete Best had never missed a performance, and the true reasons for his dismissal have remained the source of speculations ever since.

In spite of these occasional errors, *The Anthology* solves a few mysteries concerning some individuals' involvement with the band. For example, much has been written about Allan Williams, and his tendency to exaggerate and to confuse events in interviews has diminished his credibility as to his actual contributions to The Beatles' history. Alistair Taylor, Brian Epstein's personal assistant has further fuelled the rumor that Williams is basically an impostor and had never been the group's manager. However, *The Anthology* quite clearly describes Williams' role in The Beatles' early history, and at one point Paul McCartney simply states, "We had a manager in Liverpool called Allan Williams" (*Anthology* 2003: DVD 1).

The way the new interviews with Paul McCartney, George Harrison, and Ringo Starr are filmed is also interesting in regard to their images as solo artists. While George Harrison and Ringo Starr are filmed in conventional interview situations at their lavish homes or at a studio, Paul McCartney is seen in less conventional situations: he is steering a boat while talking about George Harrison's talent as a songwriter, he is preparing a bonfire while recalling unpleasant Apple business meetings, and he is sitting in front of his giant stage of his 1993 world tour, recalling the recording of John Lennon's song "Tomorrow Never Knows". McCartney, who makes a point of wanting to appear hyper-active and multi-talented has developed a tradition of being interviewed in similarly unconventional situations. In his documentary *Wingspan*, for instance, he is driving a Land Rover while talking about Wings' first tour through Great Britain (vgl. *Wingspan* 2001).

On 7 October 1996, an expanded version of *The Beatles Anthology* was released as an eight volume video box set. In 2003, the documentary was finally released as a five volume DVD set, topping the DVD charts around the world.

The Beatles Anthology focuses on the recollections of The Beatles themselves as well as their inner circle, which in 1995 consisted of producer George Martin, publicist Derek Taylor, and Apple director Neil Aspinall. In addition, archive material of John Lennon and Brian Epstein was used to achieve an equal representation of the main protagonists in the band's history.

Imagine: John Lennon and *Wingspan*

When Albert Goldman published his Lennon biography *The Lives of Lennon* in 1987, it caused quite some controversy, because it portrayed John Lennon as a tortured soul and spoiled hypocrite, accusing him of being responsible for the deaths of two people. Goldman, whose research was inaccurate and whose interviewing methods were questionable, quite clearly exaggerated and scandalized the history of John Lennon in order to obtain international attention. His description of John Lennon's fight with Bob Wooler after Lennon's holiday with Brian Epstein serves as a good example of how Goldman intentionally twists history to defame Lennon.

"[...] Bob Wooler came up to Lennon and said, "How was the honeymoon, John?" Taking Wooler's remark as an insulting reference to the recent trip to Spain, John doubled up his fist and smashed the little disc jockey in the nose. Then, seizing a shovel that was lying in the yard, Lennon began to beat Wooler to death. Blow after blow came smashing down on the defenseless man lying on the ground" (Goldman 2001: 141).

Merseyside author Spencer Leigh showed Wooler Goldman's description of the incident. "Bob exploded when he saw this: 'This is preposterous,' he said, "Absolute nonsense. Goldman sees that the party was in the garden and rushes to the conclusion that all the garden implements are to hand. He'll have me buried in the rose bushes next'" (Leigh 2002: 183). Despite its errors and its exploitative character, the book is still one of the bestsellers among the countless Beatles biographies and has contributed to the distribution of some rather less pleasant and often completely inaccurate conceptions of John Lennon. Consequently, many fans and Beatles historians were disappointed by Goldman's depiction of Lennon and craved for a more balanced view of John Lennon as artist and as private man. In 1988, a theatrical movie called *Imagine: John Lennon* was released in the United States and soon saw a worldwide release on video. The film was a documentary by Andrew Solt, who had previously directed documentaries of other popular culture icons, such as Marilyn Monroe and Elvis Presley.

Imagine: John Lennon sets out to explore the life of John Lennon in a more objective way than, for instance, the Goldman book. Andrew Solt was allowed access to Yoko Ono's Lennon archive and chose from more than 200 hours of private recordings and footage of John Lennon. Instead of creating some sort of autobiography from the material, Solt put it in the context of new interviews and recollections of many important people in Lennon's life. The movie equally explores Lennon's time with The

Beatles as well as his solo years, featuring interviews with Yoko Ono, Cynthia Lennon, May Pang, Sean Ono Lennon, Julian Lennon, David Bowie, and many others. However, Paul McCartney, George Harrison, and Ringo Starr did not participate in the production. The main difference between *Imagine: John Lennon* and other productions endorsed by Yoko Ono is the fact that it does not exclusively focus on Lennon's time with Yoko Ono. Considering the fact that Yoko Ono usually completely ignores Lennon's relationship with May Pang from 1973 to 1975, it is quite a surprise to see her interviewed in the documentary. Pang comments that "[t]he fact that I was included, along with Cynthia and Julian, demonstrates they tried to achieve fair representation, if not a 'balance' (there were a few remarks in the narration that suggested our period together as 'incidental'). However, the absence of Paul, George and Ringo kept the movie from going as in-depth as it could have" (Pang 2003). Despite this deficiency, *Imagine: John Lennon* projects a well-researched and rather objective view of John Lennon's life.

As *The Beatles Anthology* turned out to be such a great commercial success, Paul McCartney decided to produce a similar documentary about his career with his pop group Wings in the 1970s. In 2001, the documentary called *Wingspan* was aired as a prime-time special on TV stations around the world, including ABC in the United States, and Channel 4 in Great Britain. Soon afterwards the documentary was released as a DVD, accompanied by a best-selling *Wingspan* double CD, which contained many of Wings' greatest hits.

Wingspan provides Paul McCartney's personal view of his time with Wings and includes footage spanning Wings' whole career from 1971 to 1980. As *Wingspan* was a McCartney solo project, the documentary allowed him to be more outspoken about The Beatles' break-up and about the way Yoko Ono's presence contributed to friction within the band than in *The Beatles Anthology*, which had to be approved by Yoko Ono.

"[Paul:] It was getting near the break-up of The Beatles. Yoko was coming down the studio. We didn't really want to say much to John about it, at the risk of offending him and Yoko. We didn't say, "What's she doing here?" But we did kind of imply that, which made things a bit uncomfortable. And when she moved the bed in to the middle of the recording area...
[Mary:] Are you serious...
[Paul:] I am serious. It was like, "Okay, we've got to roll with the punches here. This is a bed and she's lying down. That's okay." It was like a happening" (*Wingspan* 2001).

Not only does the way McCartney describes his view of The Beatles' dissolution differ from the band's official autobiography, but also what

McCartney has got to say about The Beatles' first long-term drummer Pete Best is quite a surprise. In the *Anthology*, McCartney only mentions that George Martin did not like Best at The Beatles' first audition at EMI (vgl. *Anthology* 2003: DVD 1). In *Wingspan*, however, he implies that Best was replaced by Ringo Starr because of personal reasons: "In The Beatles we had Pete Best, who was a really good drummer. But there was something. He wasn't quite like the rest of us. We had a sense of humor in common, and he was nearly in with it all. But it is a fine line, as to what is exactly in and what is nearly in" (*Wingspan* 2001).

Unauthorized Documentaries

When the *Anthology* was released on DVD, Passport Video released an unauthorized Beatles documentary as a 3-DVD set, in order to cash in on the revived interest in The Beatles. The documentary is called *A Long and Winding Road* – in reference to the *Anthology*'s working title – and works very well as a complementary account of The Beatles' history, as it features several contributors to the group's history, who are not represented in the *Anthology*, such as the re-formed Quarry Men, the band's first manager Allan Williams, Brian Epstein's personal assistant Alistair Taylor, and the band's chauffeur and bodyguard Alf Bicknell.

Even though the *Anthology* also features most of the facts presented in *A Long and Winding Road*, the unauthorized documentary presents the events from the point of view of various people who belonged to the group's inner circle in the past. For instance, Lennon's musical beginnings with his first group, The Quarry Men, is represented more in-depth than in the *Anthology*, simply because *A Long and Winding Road* featured interviews with some of the original Quarry Men. On the other hand, the producers of *A Long and Winding Road* rely too much on the information provided by some less reliable sources, such as the recollections of Allan Williams and Alistair Taylor. Especially Williams often confuses the sequence of events or simply re-invents what he cannot remember in a way that only partly resembles what actually happened. Although some different points of view are set against each other in the documentary, most of the information is not balanced or commented by an independent source, which leaves the audience with the impression that the documentary presents facts, when a lot of the information is actually not reliable.

The producers of *A Long and Winding Road* used some of the material filmed for the DVD set in another documentary called *Brian Epstein – Inside the Fifth Beatle*. Although Epstein's life and involvement with

The Beatles is explored quite comprehensively in the film, the documentary only features a few old interview excerpts of The Beatles and, therefore, lacks the perspective of the group members. The award-winning *Anthology*, on the other hand, explores The Beatles' history from the perspective of The Beatles and their inner circle in the 1990s. Even though the documentary offers a comprehensive and quite honest account of The Beatles' history, it is interesting that it lacks the perspective of some of the people who were actively involved in their development. While Apple claims that the idea behind the project was to have The Beatles "set the record straight", this does not explain the inclusion of interviews with Neil Aspinall, Derek Taylor, and George Martin; nor does it explain excluding their first long-term drummer Pete Best, personal assistant Alistair Taylor, and recording engineer Geoff Emerick, who were all instrumental in the group's progress. Therefore, despite the producer's attempt at a factual representation of The Beatles' story, the chance of an entirely balanced view was lost by not including some vital contributors to The Beatles' success.

While The Beatles' *Anthology* marked the first official band history since Hunter Davies' authorized biography *The Beatles* (1969), there had been a few notably successful documentaries about The Beatles before. In 1984, MGM/United Artists released a 119 minutes long video documentary called *The Compleat Beatles*, which allowed a thoroughly researched and quite balanced look on the history of the group. It featured historical footage showing The Beatles at several significant points in their career, as well as exclusive interviews with some of the more important contributors to their success, such as George Martin, Bill Harry, Tony Sheridan, and Allan Williams. In addition, the documentary, which is narrated by Malcolm McDowell (*Clockwork Orange*), also includes a rare interview with John Lennon's aunt Mimi. However, none of the surviving Beatles nor Yoko Ono participated in the production of this documentary, although Paul McCartney granted an exclusive interview to the authors and editors of a lavish songbook of the same title.

Again, The Beatles' history is told in chronological order, opening with black-and-white footage of Liverpool during the Second World War. Like The Beatles' own *Anthology* and *A Long and Winding Road*, the film recalls the evolution of skiffle and rock and roll in Great Britain, and how this musical development inspired John Lennon, Paul McCartney, George Harrison, and Ringo Starr to become musicians. The film contains archival footage similar and, partly, identical with the footage presented in The Beatles *Anthology* and *A Long and Winding Road*. *The Compleat Beatles* features quite some footage from The Beatles' company Apple's archives, such as the unreleased promotional film for the song "A Day in the Life". Therefore, the documentary must have been made with the consent of Apple. In fact, *The Compleat Beatles* may well have been the model for the *Anthology* in the way it is edited.

According to Bill Harry, *The Compleat Beatles* was one of the biggest-selling music video cassettes on both sides of the Atlantic (vgl. Harry 1985: 153).

SPOOFS

The Rutles: *All You Need Is Cash*

In the 1970s, Eric Idle, a former member of the legendary British comedy team Monty Python, featured a Beatles parody song called "It Must Be Love" on *Rutland Weekend Television*, his own television show on BBC-2. The song had been written by Neil Innes, who had previously worked with Monty Python and the Bonzo Dog Doo-Dah Band. The song was performed by 'The Rutles', a Beatles look-alike band featuring Neil Innes as the John Lennon character, and Eric Idle as the Paul McCartney character (vgl. Harry 1985: 69). In October 1976, the parody was shown on America's NBC TV's show *Saturday Night Live* as a sequel to the running gag of a Beatles reunion for $3,000. The parody went down so well that Eric Idle and Neil Innes decided to produce a feature program about The Rutles for television. Idle, who was a close friend of George Harrison, was allowed to watch Neil Aspinall's unreleased documentary about The Beatles, called *The Long and Winding Road*. Aspinall's film featured a bulk of famous footage of The Beatles, from their first televised performance at the Cavern Club in Liverpool to their last group performance on the roof of their Apple business building. Idle used *The Long and Winding Road* as a model for his fake-documentary about The Rutles and basically re-told the history of The Beatles projected upon this imaginary rock band, adding essential elements of parody and the Pythonesque sense of surreal humor.

Neil Innes provided the soundtrack for the film, re-creating the sound of The Beatles in songs that contained countless references to The Beatles' songs from each of their creative periods. Innes' songs provided the appropriate soundtrack for the footage, which was all inspired by the archival footage of The Beatles. In fact, Apple had allowed Idle to use original footage of The Beatles in the movie. Neil Innes remembers that "The Beatles were very good about it. They allowed us to use lots of their old footage – stuff that eventually became the bones of *The Anthology* series – and intercut it with newly filmed Rutles sequences to give it more authenticity" (Black 1996: 59).

The Rutles' history, as described in the movie, parallels the history of The Beatles, with Dirk McQuickly (Eric Idle, the McCartney character),

Ron Nasty (Neil Innes, the Lennon character), Stig O'Hara (Rikki Fataar, The Rutles' George Harrison), and Barry Womble (John Halsey, the Ringo character) starting out in Liverpool. Arthur Scouse, who has won The Rutles in a bet, sends them to Hamburg, where they perform at the Ratkeller. Back in Liverpool, they find a manager called Leggy Mountbatten, who improves their outfit by buying them trousers, which starts the whole Rutles craze. They get a recording contract, and 'Rutle-mania' really takes off. The Rutles go on to conquer America, make feature films (*A Hard Day's Rut* and *Ouch!*), quit touring, find a guru, produce masterful albums, and split after filming their last movie, *Let It Rut*. Among the classic Rutles albums mentioned in the film are *A Hard Day's Rut*, *Sgt. Rutters' Only Darts Club Band*, *Tragical History Tour*, and *Let It Rot*.

Eric Idle and his co-director Gary Weis re-created and re-interpreted many of the well-known scenes from The Beatles' movies and television footage, and added a more absurd dimension to it. For example, Ron Nasty – the Lennon of The Rutles – falls in love with a Nazi woman, while the equivalent of Maharishi Mahesh Yogi, The Beatles' Indian guru, looks like a bank accountant. The sequence parodying The Beatles' cartoon feature *Yellow Submarine* was created by some of the original artists involved with The Beatles' production. The Rutles' film is called *Yellow Submarine Sandwich* and features the song "Cheese and Onion". As it was apparently not possible to increase the lovely absurdity of The Beatles' original motion picture, the *Yellow Submarine Sandwich* looks more like a genuine tribute to the movie, imitating and re-creating the psychedelic style of the original.

Other scenes evoking The Beatles' famous film and television performances include their first appearance on *The Ed Sullivan Show*, the filming of *A Hard Day's Rut*, and the performance of "Love Life", the equivalent of The Beatles' "All You Need Is Love". Although basically a fictional parody of The Beatles, *All You Need Is Cash* merges fact and fiction in the way original 1960s footage is combined with Rutles footage from the 1970s as well and the way it recalls The Beatles' success story, whose mythic character Idle's film reveals and reflects. Eric Idle's friend George Harrison, who even appears in the movie as a reporter, was a great admirer of The Rutles and liked to express some of The Beatles' experiences by comparing them to The Rutles, emphasizing the surreal quality of The Beatles' overwhelming success. In his autobiography *I Me Mine* (1979), Harrison expressed his enthusiasm for The Rutles and the way The Beatles' history has been mystified ad absurdum.

"The Rutles told the story so much better than the usual boring documentary. [...] It is all so silly anyway, all the way through. Ringo's story was funny, you know. We were talking about school once, and he said that he had been in hospital so much, that when he went back to school [they] said to him: 'you never went to this school' and he said: 'yes, I did. I've just been in hospital a lot.' Then, he said, a couple of years later, they were saying, proudly, 'This was Ringo's desk. The great man sat here.' Madness" (Harrison 2002: 65).

According to Gary Weis, the co-director of *All You Need Is Cash*, George Harrison played a significant role in the production of the film: "George Harrison was involved from the beginning. He was around quite a lot, even when he didn't need to be there. [...] I think he was the only one of The Beatles who could see the irony of it all" (Black 1996: 59).

The prime-time special *All You Need Is Cash* was first shown on television in both, the United States and in Great Britain, in March 1978 and soon became a cult movie. The Rutles soundtrack album was equally successful, reaching #12 in the UK Top 40. When The Beatles reunited for their *Anthology* project in 1995, Neil Innes released another spoof album called *The Rutles Archaeology*. In 2005, Eric Idle initiated another Rutles revival when he released a sequel to *All You Need Is Cash* on DVD. The film, which was only released in the United States, was called *Can't Buy Me Lunch* and consisted of re-edited footage and outtakes from the first film, and new interviews with David Bowie, Tom Hanks, and Bonnie Raitt, talking about The Rutles' enormous impact on pop culture and society.

Further Tributes and Spoofs

The Beatles' appearance, their music, as well as their album covers have been imitated countless times for various reasons. On the one hand, critics of the band, who have considered them as a hype rather than an artistic phenomenon, have made fun of their distinctive outfits or appearance. For example, the American enfant terrible of rock music, Frank Zappa, imitated The Beatles' cover of *Sgt. Pepper* for his own album called *We're Only In It For The Money* (1968) to criticize the commercial character of The Beatles' music and image. Despite his criticisms, Zappa later collaborated with John Lennon on a live recording in 1971. Other artists have imitated The Beatles' famous album covers to show their respect for the band. For example, the Red Hot Chili Peppers' *Abbey Road* E.P (1988) features the famous zebra crossing outside the Abbey Road Studios. The cover is an imitation of The Beatles' *Abbey Road* (1969) album cover.

Similar to the way The Beatles' sounds and music have been imitated and quoted in countless popular songs, their cover artwork has become subject of humorous tributes as well as malicious ridicule. No other act's album artwork has got a similarly iconic status as The Beatles'. Although there have been occasional imitations of Elvis Presley's and The Rolling Stones' album sleeves, The Beatles are probably the only band whose artwork has achieved such fame. This supports the notion that The Beatles always strove for powerful visual images and innovative and unique designs to support and project their image not only as pop singers but as artists in a broader sense.

CONCLUSION: IMAGE, MYTH, HISTORY, AND THE BEATLES

Popular Culture and the Evolution of The Beatles' Image

Popular music, like all other forms of popular culture, is primarily a form of commercial entertainment, created with the intention of generating money. Every genre of popular culture consists of a set of specific patterns, stereotypes, and clichés, which enable the recipient to categorize each text and to regard it in the context of the genre it represents. The audience of mass culture has 'naturalized' the specific characteristics of a genre and expects a popular culture text to fulfil these qualities. Literary critic Linda Badley compares mass audiences to a preschool child "who requests the same stories over and over" (Badley 1996: 23). Therefore, the chance of commercial success is increased by fulfilling the expectations of the target audience.

On the one hand, the process of 'naturalization' has led to a formulaic way of producing pop culture texts, including TV shows, movies, comics, and songs. On the other hand, the audience has come to expect a text to work according to the conventions of the genre he or she prefers, and to fulfil certain patterns characteristic of the genre. The recipient is not necessarily aware of this process, because the genre conventions have become so natural in the recipient's perception that he or she only becomes aware of them when a convention is broken.

A mass audience does not exist as a homogenous accumulation of individuals but of a mass of people consuming pop culture texts individually, perceiving each text in the context of their own social and emotional situation and experience (vgl. Riemann). However, history and experience show that there are particular qualities in texts, which appeal to large numbers of people. These qualities become defining conventions of a genre and can be used by the producer of popular culture texts to consciously attract a certain target group. On the producer's side, this set of conventions, stereotypes, and formulas constitutes what Stuart Hall calls the 'preferred meaning' (vgl. Hall 1981: 128-138). – it is the information the audience is intended to receive.

In popular culture, a star's 'public image' constitutes an important part of defining his or her commercial potential, as it projects an artificially created persona, which is deliberately designed to convey a certain intended meaning and thereby attract a specific target group. A public image consists of a star's appearance, attitude, behavior, and the world-views and opinions he or she expresses in the media. In the sphere of pop music, a star's public image is significantly shaped by the conventions of the musical genre the star is part of. The genre may not only determine the sound but also the appearance and the ideology expressed by the star's image.

The Beatles considered themselves as artists and were very aware of their appearance and the importance of their image. With their art-college background, John Lennon and Stuart Sutcliffe designed an artificial image for the band, which was inspired by the appearance of Teddy Boys (which none of The Beatles was). Their friendship with German art students Astrid Kirchherr and Jürgen Vollmer inspired them to change their look and to adapt a combination of 1950s rocker outfits, consisting of leather jackets and trousers, boots, and a feminine hairstyle fashionable among European art students at the time. Kirchherr and Vollmer were also responsible for the first professional photos taken of the group, which became iconic representations of the group's period in Hamburg and were a considerable influence on The Beatles' official press photos and album covers in the early 1960s. Their unusual clothes and hairstyle became The Beatles' distinctive trademark, adding to their unique appearance on stage, which was further characterized by the way The Beatles held their guitars and their careless attitude.

When Brian Epstein took over The Beatles' management, he modernized their look by persuading them to change into more fashionable suits, which made them more acceptable in the world of showbusiness. Initially, Epstein made The Beatles also cut their hair, but they soon adopted their previous 'Exi'-hairstyle again, when they found out that this particular hairstyle (as well as their unique vocal style) got attention in the press. From 1962 to 1966, The Beatles always wore the most stylish suits and boots, and their look was imitated by other pop groups, such as The Byrds, as well as by their leagues of fans.

Like Elvis Presley, The Beatles were among the pioneers of using a variety of media channels to distribute their image to the public. For example, The Beatles' movies were important means of establishing and perpetuating their powerful visual image to the world. Their first movie *A Hard Day's Night* was one of the most influential factors in defining and distributing the band's collective image as well as each band member's individual public image. The movie was released at the height of their success as entertainers and had a lasting impact on the way the public has perceived the group ever since. Television was an equally important means of distributing the band's image to the world. Steven D. Stark argues that "[w]ith television finally beginning to penetrate the vast majority of English homes, the Beatles were among the nation's first TV phenomena – which was hardly surprising, since their appeal was always visual as well as musical" (Stark 2005: 143). Between 1962 and 1965 The Beatles appeared on more than thirty TV shows in Great Britain, a number unparalleled by any other artist (vgl. Stark 2005: 143). When The Beatles and their management realized that they would be able to increase their presence on worldwide television by sending out promotional videos for their songs instead of appearing live on selected TV shows, they contributed to the evolution of contemporary music videos, which are now an extremely important factor in promoting popular music releases.

Despite their continuing – and even increasing – success as recording artists in the second half of the Sixties, the way they encountered the public in the years 1963 to 1965, including their outfits, their instruments, as well as their choreography on stage, has become an iconic image of the early Sixties, and one of the most lasting visual representations of the band in the last forty years. Their unusual haircuts, their fashionable suits, their instruments, and the way they held their guitars higher than most guitarists became an image imitated by countless pop groups evolving in The Beatles' shadow. However, the fact that Paul McCartney played his guitar left-handed and John Lennon and George Harrison played right-handed created a unique appearance on stage. As described by Steven D. Stark, "when two approached the microphone together, it tended to created a choreographed symmetrical picture with the guitars gracefully to either side rather than poking one another" (vgl. Stark 2005: 143).

The perception of The Beatles and of each individual member is still shaped by the image they established and projected to the world at the time of their initial, overwhelming commercial success. Although The Beatles kept changing their outfits as well as their manners and opinions constantly until the group's break-up in 1970, the way they dressed and behaved at the time of 'Beatlemania' has lingered most persistently in the public's collective memory. It seems as though the public – the media and their audiences – has chosen to remember The Beatles in the idealized way they projected themselves in the early Sixties. As long as they behaved according to the patterns they had successfully developed with their management, their popularity exceeded every previous phenomenon in the entertainment business. Around 1965 and 1966, The Beatles were getting weary of their artificial public image, and it became increasingly difficult for them to embody this particular image, as they had experienced many personal developments, which contradicted their image as pop singers. Their expanding musical horizon, their increasing interest in art, literature, and spiritual enlightenment, as well as the consumption of psychedelic drugs, i.e. LSD, influenced their perception of themselves and led to an astonishing development away from teen idols to pop artists. The Beatles gradually removed their Mop-Top personae and began to express their views on politics and society – an absolute first in the world of pop music. Consequently, they did not fulfil the public's expectations anymore. The public, in turn, was shocked by The Beatles' change. The scandal concerning John Lennon's remark about Christianity is probably the most drastic example of what can happen when the audience does not get what they want.

The public was stunned by The Beatles' new outspokenness and by their unexpected behavior. The media began to criticize The Beatles, and the group's estranged audience turned to other, less controversial pop acts. It is hardly ever mentioned today, but The Beatles' popularity diminished significantly in 1966. They did not sell out their second performance at Shea Stadium, where they had celebrated their most spectacular concert in front of 55,600 people the year before (vgl. Lewisohn 2000: 229). In addition, the group lost out to The Beach Boys in *N.M.E.*'s annual reader's poll.

It is quite ironic that The Beatles' popularity decreased the year the group transformed into more serious artists. In 1966, they recorded their most valued album *Revolver* and practically invented contemporary music video with their promotional films for "Paperback Writer" and "Rain". The band also stopped touring and decided that they would exist only as a recording band in the future.

A Hard Day's Night, Merchandise, and the Creation of History

In 1964, *A Hard Day's Night* was the most effective means of reinforcing The Beatles' official image in the public consciousness, as it captured the attention of a world-wide audience and has since been used as an 'authentic' representation of the band's most exciting period. However, the semi-documentary style of *A Hard Day's Night* is symptomatic for the constant confusion of reality and myth in The Beatles' history. Devin McKinney points out the movie's apparent function: "*A Hard Day's Night* seeks to place the Beatles, pretty much as they are, at the center of a portrait approximating their real lives and true selves. The film will soften a harsh truth but not polish an ideal: it seeks, essentially, to quash Beatle myth before any can be born" (Kinney 2003: 64). While this may appear true on the surface, the movie does actually establish a considerable set of myths about the band, which have been responsible for the stereotyped view of the group and its members even long after the group's break-up. The movie's air of authenticity conceals the fact that it was a cleverly designed piece of merchandise that deceived the public into thinking that what is presented in the movie reflects the lives of the real Beatles in an accurate way.

Similar to the way The Beatles' movies paved the way for a certain kind of rock movie, distributing the image of its stars, The Beatles phenomenon practically led to the invention of contemporary rock and pop merchandise production, which nowadays contributes significantly to the amount of money generated in the music business. Geoffrey Ellis, who worked in The Beatles' management agency and was later instrumental in creating the hype surrounding Elton John, points out that "[p]rior to the Beatles, merchandising was a gimmick, a novelty, something – usually little more than a programme, poster or badge – produced so that the fans would have a keepsake or memento of a concert or public appearance" (Ellis 2004: 99). The immense popularity of The Beatles, however, changed this particular paradigm and led to the recognition of the market potential in teenage entertainment.

"By 1963 it had become apparent that the Beatles presented a merchandising phenomenon that no-one – the band, their management, the merchandising companies or even the fans – could fully comprehend. Such was the fever for the group that fans would have bought virtually anything that had the band's name on it. [...] Most notable in the plethora of Beatles-related knick-knacks was the Beatles wig. In the early 1960s their collar-length hair was fashionably 'long' [...] and was virtually the Beatles' trademark" (Ellis 2004: 100).

Their image was used to sell all kinds of products, including hats, flags, candy, cups, toys, T-shirts, sweaters, buttons, notebooks, pencil cases, pens, bags, instruments, 'Beatles bread' (!), biscuit tins, comic books, ice cream, record players, record carrying cases, jigsaw puzzles, bathroom rugs, diaries, hair pomade, lampshades, shoes, glasses, plates, crockery, headphones, watches, alarm clocks, costumes, and toothpaste.[1] The Beatles' omnipresence in the media, as well as the fact that their image

---

1   For a detailed overview of Beatles-related merchandise see Richard Buskin. *Beatle Crazy! Memories and Memorabilia*. London: Salamander, 1994.

of 1964 was displayed on all products imaginable, made sure that the group's appearance entered the public consciousness of the Western hemisphere. In the United States, where the commercialization of The Beatles was much more developed than in Great Britain, their impact was unprecedented, and is still remembered and appreciated today. In 2003, *Time* magazine recalled the advent of Beatlemania as one of the 80 defining moments in the 20th century. Christopher Porterfield emphasizes the point that The Beatles were perceived as a visual phenomenon rather than a musical one. "You could hardly hear the music, but what did that matter? The Beatles' sheer presence was the point – their air of wholesome charm and cheeky wit, their instinctive connection with their audience. (It would be another couple of years before albums like *Revolver* and *Sgt. Pepper* showed that they were a musical phenomenon too)" (Porterfield 2003: 47).

Not only were The Beatles the first pop group to cash in on the new market of pop merchandise, but they also introduced a new dimension of tie-in merchandise with their television cartoon show and – to an even greater extent – with their cartoon feature film *Yellow Submarine*. Their immense commercial appeal in terms of memorabilia and merchandise is unparalleled in the field of pop music, because no other act has had the ability to appeal to such a diverse audience. On the one hand, The Beatles have always appealed to children, not only because they occasionally wrote songs for children, such as "Yellow Submarine" (1966) and "All Together Now", but also because their image easily translated into a cartoon version of the band. The Beatles' cartoon representations exist independent from the real Beatles. In turn, The Beatles themselves, as a group phenomenon, have existed for more than 35 years without its members. The Ex-Beatles themselves often refer to the group in third person. George Harrison explained the way he separated his own image from his Beatle-image in an interview with *Q* in 1995.

"The Beatles will go on and on – on those records and films and videos and books and whatever, and in people's memories and minds. It's become its own thing now. And The Beatles, I think, exist without us. [W]e can carry on being individuals. For me, Beatle George was a suit or a shirt that I once wore, and the only problem is for the rest of my life, people are going to look at that shirt and mistake it for me" (Du Noyer 1995: 124).

The way The Beatles' image was introduced at the height of their success had such a powerful impact on the public's conception of the band that the group's members have since been perceived only in connection with their past image.

Similar to the way the public chooses to behold a certain positive image of the star, the public's historical consciousness also beholds a simplified and idealized version of the past. Therefore, the less pleasant chapters in The Beatles' history are usually not of great interest to the larger segment of the public, because they are not compatible with what the fans want to believe. In films, the most accurate portrayal of history is not necessarily accepted by the public as authentic, if it fails to fulfil the expectations of the audience. On the other hand, a simplified or distorted representation of history may find acceptance if it meets the conventions of a popular genre and the viewing audience's preconceptions of the past. The past becomes what the public chooses to remember.

The Beatles' history has become a mythtified contemporary legend, which continues to be re-told in all kinds of modern mass media. While The Beatles' story has previously been told from various points of views, The Beatles themselves set out to present their own view of their history with *The Beatles Anthology* in 1995. In one of his rare interviews, George Harrison expresses his view of history after working on Anthology.

"[Q:] Is it possible, with *Anthology*, to paint a complete picture?
[George Harrison:] Well, there's a way of twisting history – because if you find a roll of film on a cupboard, that's going in the documentary. I may have been doing something far more important on the same day, but because I didn't film it, it's no longer important. I think in the end it's shown me that all history must be total rubbish – because if we can't even tell our story, and we're still alive, then God help all those stories about the Romans or Alexander the Great or ... anyone" (Du Noyer 1995: 124).

Although Harrison exaggerates by calling all history 'rubbish,' he quite effectively points out the selective character of what the majority perceives as history and the power of the media in simplifying and (re-) creating history. On a larger scale this means that the rather arbitrary and selective way history is presented on film will shape all future conceptions of the past.

WORKS CITED

Books, Essays & Articles

Axelrod, Mitchell (1999): BeatleToons. The Real Story Behind the Cartoon Beatles, Pickens.

Badley, Linda (1996): Writing Horror and the Body. The Fiction of Stephen King, Clive Barker, and Anne Rice, Westport.

Badman, Keith (2001): The Beatles Diary. Volume 2: After the Break-Up. 1970-2001, London.

Baird, Julia/Giuliano, Geoffrey (1988): John Lennon, My Brother. Foreword by Paul McCartney, New York.

Barrow, Tony (1999): The Making of The Beatles' *Magical Mystery Tour*, London.

Barta, Tony (Hg.) (1998): Screening the Past. Film and the Representation of History, Westport.

Barta, Tony (1998a): "Screening the Past: History Since the Cinema". In: Screening the Past. Film and the Representation of History, hg. v. Tony Barta, Westport, S. 1-17.

Barta, Tony (1998b): "Introduction". In: Screening the Past. Film and the Representation of History, hg. v. Tony Barta, Westport, S. ix-xi.

Barthes, Roland (1977). "Change of the Object Itself. Mythology Today". In: Image-Music-Text., hg. v. Stephen Heath, London, S. 160-172.

Baxter, Lew (2003): Allan Williams is...The Fool On The Hill...how the beat went on after his BIG BEATLES blunder, Wirral.

Beatles, The (2000): The Beatles Anthology, München.

Benson, Ross (1992). Paul McCartney. Die Biographie, München.

Best, Pete/Doncaster, Patrick (2001): Beatle! The Pete Best Story, London.

Biguell, Jonathan (1997): Media Semiotics, Manchester.

Black, Johnny (1996): "The Making of The Rutles-All You Need Is Cash". In: Q 113, S. 58-59.

Bordwell, David/Thompson, Kristin (1979): Film Art, London.

Brodax, Al (2004): Up Periscope Yellow. The Making of The Beatles *Yellow Submarine*, New York.

Brown, Peter/Gaines, Steven (2002): The Love You Make. An Insider's Story of The Beatles, New York.

Buskin, Richard (1994): Beatle Crazy! Memories and Memorabilia, London.

Campbell, Joseph/Moyers, Bill (1994): Die Kraft der Mythen. Bilder der Seele im Leben des Menschen, Zürich.

Carnes, Mark C. (Hg.) (1996): Past Imperfect. History According to the Movies, New York.

Carr, Roy (1996): Beatles at the Movies, New York.

Chatman, Seymour (1980): Story and Discourse. Narrative Structure in Fiction and Film, London.

Clayson, Alan (1997): Hamburg. The Cradle of British Rock, London.

Clayson, Alan. Ringo Starr (1996): Straight Man or Joker?, London.

Coleman, Ray (1992): Lennon. The Definitive Biography, New York.

Davies, Hunter (1969): The Beatles. The Authorised Biography, London.

Davies, Hunter (2001): The Quarrymen, London.

Davis, Rod (2001): "A personal addendum from Rod Davis about John's guitar". In: Davies, Hunter (2001): The Quarrymen, London, S. 260-262.

Dening, Greg (1998): "'Captain Bligh' as Mythic Cliché: The Films". In: Screening the Past. Film and the Representation of History, hg. v. Tony Barta, Westport, S. 19-44.

Dewe, Mike (1998): The Skiffle Craze, Wales.

Du Noyer, Paul (1995): "They were the most brilliant, powerful, lovable popular group on the planet ... but now they're really important!". In: Q 111, S. 118-128.

Du Noyer, Paul (1996): "Just Out of Shot. Interview with Neil Aspinall". In: Mojo 35, S. 74-79.

Du Noyer, Paul (2002a): "Across the Universe". In: 1000 Days of Beatlemania. The Early Years – April 1, 1962 to December 31, 1964, Mojo Special Limited Edition, S. 64-67.

Du Noyer, Paul (2002b): "Action!". In: Mojo 108, S. 70-82.

Du Noyer, Paul (2004): Liverpool. Wonderous Place. Music from the Cavern to the Coral, London.

Dyer, Richard (1995): The Matter of Images. Essays on Representations, London.

Ellis, Geoffrey (2004): I Should Have Known Better. A Life in Pop Management. The Beatles, Brian Epstein and Elton John, London.

Epstein, Brian [ghost. Derek Taylor] (1998). A Cellarful of Noise. The Autobiography of the Man Who Made the Beatles. With a New Companion Narrative by Martin Lewis, New York.

Everett, Walter (2001): The Beatles as Musicians. The Quarry Men through *Rubber Soul*, New York.

Everett, Walter (1999): The Beatles as Musicians. *Revolver* through the *Anthology*, New York.

Frith, Simon (2005): "Zur Ästhetik der Populären Musik", http://www2.hu-berlin.de/fpm/texte/frith.htm, 05.03.2005.

Garry, Len (1997): John, Paul & Me. Before the Beatles, London.

Geller, Debbie (Hg.) (2002): In My Life. The Brian Epstein Story. Anthony Wall, New York.

Gentle, Johnny/Forsyth, Ian (1998): Johnny Gentle & The Beatles. First Ever Tour. Scotland 1960, Runcorn.

Giles, Jeff/Chang, Yahlin (1995): "Come Together". In: Newsweek. Vol. 126. Issue 17, S. 60-68.

Giuliano, Geoffrey (1991): Dark Horse. The Private Life of George Harrison, New York.

Giuliano, Geoffrey/Devi, Vrnda (1999): Glass Onion. The Beatles in Their Own Words, New York.

Goldman, Albert (2001): The Lives of John Lennon, Chicago.

Goldsmith, Martin (2004). The Beatles Come to America, New Jersey.

Gross, Edward (1990). Fab Films of the Beatles, Las Vegas.

Hall, Stuart (Hg.) (1981): Culture, Media, Language, London.

Hall, Stuart (1981): "Encoding and Decoding in the TV Discourse". In: Culture, Media, Language, hg. v. Stuart Hall u. a., London, S. 128-138.

Harris, John (1996): "1966. Band On The Run". In: Q 115, S. 85-91.

Harrison, George (2002): I Me Mine, London.

Harry, Bill (1985): The Beatles. Volume 4. Beatlemania. The History of The Beatles on Film. An Illustrated Filmography, New York.

Harry, Bill (2000): The Beatles Encyclopedia. Revised and Updated, London.

Harry, Bill (2003b): "The Birth of Mersey Beat 5", http://triumphpc.com/mersey-beat/birth/birth5.shtml, 09.07.2003.

Hebdige, Dick (1983): "Subculture – Die Bedeutung von Stil". In: Schocker – Stile und Moden der Subkultur, hg. v. Diedrich Diederichsen, Dick Hebdige und Olaph Dank-Marx, Hamburg, 1983, S. 8-120.

Hebdige, Dick (1999): "The Function of Subculture". In: The Cultural Studies Reader, hg. v. Simon   Durin, New York, S. 441-450.

Hieronimus, Robert R. (2002): Inside the *Yellow Submarine*. The Making of the Beatles' Animated Classic, Iola.

Hunt, Chris (Hg.) (2002): 1000 Days of Beatlemania. The Early Years – April 1, 1962 to December 31, 1964. Mojo. Special Limited Edition.

Inglis, Ian (Hg.) (2000): The Beatles, Popular Music and Society. A Thousand Voices, London.

Kolloge, René (1999): The Times They Are A-Changin'. The Evolution of Rock Music and Youth Cultures, Frankfurt.

Leach, Sam (1999): The Rocking City. The Explosive Birth of the Beatles, Gwynedd.

Leigh, Spencer (1998): Drummed Out! The Sacking of Pete Best, Hants.

Leigh, Spencer (2002): The Best of Fellas. The Story of Bob Wooler. Liverpool's First D.J, Liverpool.

Lennon, John (1997): In His Own Write & A Spaniard in the Works, London.

Lewis, Martin (1998): "With a little help from their friend... An Appreciation of Beatles Manager Brian Epstein". In: Epstein, Brian (1998): A Cellarful of Noise. The Autobiography of the Man Who Made the Beatles. With a New Companion Narrative by Martin Lewis, New York, S. 1-45.

Lewisohn, Mark (2000): The Complete Beatles Chronicle, London.

Lewisohn, Mark (Hg.) (2002): Wingspan. Paul McCartney's Band On The Run, London.

MacDonald, Ian (1994): Revolution In The Head. The Beatles' Records and the Sixties, London.

Male, Andrew (2002): "The Night Before? Interview with Albert Maysles". In: Mojo 108, S. 80.

Martin, George and Jeremy Hornsby (1994): All You Need Is Ears, New York.

McCartney, Paul (1994): "Introduction". In: Yule, Andrew (1994): The Man Who "Framed" The Beatles. A Biography of Richard Lester, New York, S. i-xiii.

McDevitt, Chas (1997): Skiffle. The Definitive Inside Story, London.

McKinney, Devin (2003): Magic Circles. The Beatles In Dream And History, Cambridge.

Miles, Barry (Hg.) (1978): Beatles. In Their Own Words, London.

Miles, Barry (1997): Paul McCartney. Many Years from Now, London.

Miles, Barry (2001): The Beatles Diary. Volume 1: The Beatles Years, London.

Murray, Andy/Rolston, Lorraine (2001): The Ultimate Film Guides. *A Hard Day's Night*, London.

Murray, Charles Shaar (2002): "Four on Film". In: 1000 Days of Beatlemania. The Early Years – April 1, 1962 to December 31, 1964. Mojo Special Limited Edition, S. 116.

Neaverson, Bob (1997): The Beatles Movies, London.

Neaverson, Bob (2000): "Tell Me What You See: the Influence and Impact of the Beatles' Movies". In: The Beatles, Popular Music and Society. A Thousand Voices, hg. v. Ian Inglis, London, S. 150-162.

Neaverson, Bob/O'Dell, Denis (2002): At the Apple's Core. The Beatles from the Inside, London.

Norman, Philip (1981): Shout! The Beatles in Their Generation, New York.

O'Connor, John E. (Hg.) (1983): American History/American Television. Interpreting the Video Past, New York.

O'Connor, John E (1983): "Introduction: Television and the Historian". In: American History/American Television. Interpreting the Video Past, hg. v. John E. O'Connor, New York, S. viii-xliii.

Pang, May/Edwards, Henry (1992): John Lennon: "The Lost Weekend", New York.

Patterson, R. Gary (1998): The Walrus Was Paul. The Great Beatle Death Clues, New York.

Porterfield, Christopher (2003): "80 Days That Changed The World. 'Yeah, Yeah, Yeah!". In: Time, 31.03.2003, S. 47.

Reed, Susan/Norman, Pete Norman (1995): "Reunion Man". In: People. Vol. 44. Issue 17, S. 124-125.

Reeve, Andrew J (2004): Turn Me On, Dead Man. The Beatles And The "Paul-Is-Dead" Hoax, Bloomington.

Reising, Russell (Hg.) (2002): "Every Sound There Is." The Beatles' Revolver and the Transformation of Rock 'n' Roll, Hants.

Riemann, Silke (2005): Die Inszenierung von Popmusikern als Popstars in Videoclips. Eine Untersuchung anhand der Videoclip-Kompilationen US – Peter Gabriel (1993), HIStory – Michael Jackson (1995) und Greatest Flix II – Queen. 1991, http://www2.hu-berlin.de/fpm/works/Riemann.htm, 03.03.2005.

Robnik, Drehli (2000): "I Bet You're Sorry You Won!". In: Viennale Katalog 2000, Wien, S. 187-191.

Saltzman, Paul (2000): The Beatles In Rishikesh, New York..

Seger, Linda (1992): The Art of Adaption: Turning Fact and Fiction into Film, New York.

Sellers, Robert (2003): Always Look on the Bright Side of Life. The Inside Story of Handmade Films. Foreword by Michael Palin, London.

Soderbergh, Steven (2005). Richard Lester interviewed by Steven Soderbergh, http://film.guardian.co.uk/Guardian_NFT/interview, 06.03.2005.

Spizer, Bruce (2003): The Beatles Are Coming! The Birth of Beatlemania In America, New Orleans.

Stark, Steven D. Meet The Beatles. A Cultural History of the Band that Shook Youth, Gender, and the World. New York: Harper, 2005.

Sulpy, Doug/Schweighardt, Ray (1997): Get Back. The Unauthorized Chronicle of The Beatles' *Let It Be* Disaster, New York.

Sutcliffe, Pauline/Thompson, Douglas (2002): The Beatles' Shadow. Stuart Sutcliffe & his lonely hearts club, London.

Sutherland, Steve (Hg.): NME Originals. The Beatles. Ed. Steve Sutherland. Volume 1. Issue 1, London.

Taylor, Alistair (2003): With the Beatles, London.

Voormann, Klaus (2003): "Warum spielst du Imagine nicht auf dem weißen Klavier, John." Erinnerungen an die Beatles und viele andere Freunde, München.

Walkowitz, Daniel J. (1998): "Re-screening the Past: Subversion Narratives and the Politics of History". In: Screening the Past. Film and the Representation of History, hg. v. Tony Barta, Westport, S. 45-61.

Wenner, Jann S (2000): Lennon Remembers, London.

Wicke, Peter. "Rockmusik. Zur Ästhetik und Soziologie eines Massenmediums",
http://www2hu-berlin.de/fpm/texte/medium5.htm, 05.03.2005.

Wicke, Peter. "Video Killed the Radio Star. Glanz und Elend des Musikvideos",
http://www2.hu-berlin.de/fpm/texte/wicke3.htm, 05.03.2005.

Wiener, Jon (1993): Come Together. John Lennon In His Time, London.

Williams, Allan/Marshall, William (1977): The Man Who Gave The Beatles Away, New York.

Yule, Andrew (1994): The Man Who "Framed" The Beatles. A Biography of Richard Lester, New York.

"A Conversation beween Eric Foner and John Sayles". In: Past Imperfect. History According to the Movies, hg. v. Mark C. Carnes, New York.

"All You Need Is Love…and Royalties" (1995). In: Forbes. Vol. 157. Issue 7, S. 130-135.

"Film of Beatles 'Fantastic Lives'!" In: NME Originals. The Beatles, hg. v. Steve Sutherland, S. 21.

"Films" (2005): http://www.beatlemoney.com/films.htm, 02.05.2005.

"Hard Day's Anniversary for Beatles" (2005):
http://www.cbsnews.com/stories/2004/07/07/entertainment/main627 899.shtml, 24.02.2005.

"Here then, is how to animate the Fab Four" (1996): In: Mojo 35, S. 19.

"Latest News" (2005):
http://www.geocities.com/SunsetStrip/Towers/1019/latest8.html, 12.06.2005.

"Music Video" (2005): http://en.wikipedia.org/wiki/Music_video, 09.05.2005.

"The Beatles" (2005): http://www.thebeatleshk.com/Cartoons/Background.html, 09.05.2005.

"The Beatles: Unreleased Videos" (2005): http://abbeyrd.best.vwh.net/unrvid.htm, 24.02.2005.

"The Vocal Group Hall of Fame" (2005): http://www.vocalhalloffame.com/Inductees/beach_boys.htm, 10.08.2005.

"Unsung. The Beatles" (1995): In: Q 111, S. 64-70.

Films

Anthology (2003, 1995): Dir. Geoff Wonfor, 5 DVDs, Apple.

A Hard Day's Night (2002, 1964): Dir. Richard Lester, 2 DVDs, Buena Vista Home Entertainment.

A Long and Winding Road. (2003): 3 DVDs. Black Hill Pictures.

Backbeat (2003, 1993): Dir. Iain Softley, DVD, Universal.

Birth of The Beatles (1979): Dir. Richard Marquand, Dick Clark Productions.

Brian Epstein. Inside the Fifth Beatle (2004): DVD, Passport Video.

The First U.S. Visit (2003, 1964): Dir. Maysles. DVD. Apple.

Help! (2000, 1965): Dir. Richard Lester, DVD. MPI Home Video.

The Hours and Times (2002, 1991): Dir. & Writ. Christopher Münch, DVD, Choices Select.

In His Life: The John Lennon Story (2000): Dir. David Carson, DVD. NBC, 2000.

I Wanna Hold Your Hand (1989, 1978): Dir. Robert Zemeckis, VHS, Warner Home Video Inc.

John & Yoko: A Love Story (1985): Dir. Sandor Stern, VHS, SVS.

Let It Be (1970). Dir. Michael Lindsey-Hogg. Apple.

Magical Mystery Tour (2000, 1967): DVD. MPI Home Video.

The Beatles with Tony Sheridan (2003): DVD. Universal Music Group.

Two of Us (2000): Dir. Michael Lindsay-Hogg, DVD, Paramount Home Entertainment.

Wingspan (2001): Dir. Alistair Donald, DVD, Capitol.

Yellow Submarine (1999, 1968): Dir. George Dunning, DVD, MGM Home Entertainment.

You Can't Do That! The Making of A Hard Day's Night (2000, 1994): DVD, MPI Home Video.

Interviews, Interview-CDs and Tapes

Beatles, The (1964a): Interview. Capitol, Capitol Compact 33 PRO 2548/49.

Beatles, The (1964b): The Beatles' Story. Capitol, STBO 2222.

Fascher, Horst (2003). Interview with the author. 30.06.2003.

Griffiths, Eric (2003). Live Performance. Scheibbs. 5.07.2003.

Kirchherr, Astrid (2003). Interview with the author. 3.05.2003.

McCartney, Paul (1991). Press Conferences 89/91. Discussion, Broads 3 CD.

Williams, Allan (2003a). Talk with Spencer Leigh and Lew Baxter. 19.07.2003.

Williams, Allan (2003b). Interview with the author. 24.08.2003.

Interviews via E-mail

Brown, Ken (2003): "Re: Some Other Guy. Feedback Form". E-mail an Roland Reiter. 03.08.2003.

Davis, Rod (2003): "Re: Quarrymen". E-mail an Roland Reiter. 09.07.2003.

Harry, Bill (2003): "Bill Harry". E-mail an Roland Reiter. 23.04.2003. April 2003.

Lowe, John (2003): "Re: Open for Engagement/Question". E-mail an Roland Reiter. 05.08. 2003.

Pang, May (2003): "Interview". E-mail an Roland Reiter. 19.03.2003.

Voormann, Klaus (2003): "Re: Questions". E-mail an Roland Reiter. 24.05.2003.

THE AUTHOR

Roland Reiter works at the Center for the Study of the Americas at the University of Graz, Austria. His research interests include various social and aesthetic aspects of popular culture.

ACKNOWLEDGMENTS

I would like to thank everybody who has been involved in the process of researching and publishing this book.
Many thanks go to Roberta Maierhofer, Walter Hölbling, Walter Bernhart, the C.SAS team & the transcript team.

Most of all, I would like to thank my parents & Verena – for their invaluable love and support.